The Essential House Book

The Essential

Getting Back to Basics

Terence Conran

General Editor: Elizabeth Wilhide
Contributors: Elizabeth Wilhide, Dinah Hall, Deborah Morant, and Gareth Parry
Americanization: Emily Van Ness and Peter Slatin

Crown Trade Paperbacks
New York

House Book

First published in the United Kingdom
in 1994 by Conran Octopus Limited
2-4 Heron Quays, London E14 4JP

Copyright © 1994 by
Conran Octopus Limited

Published by Crown Publishers, Inc.
201 East 50th Street,
New York, New York 10022.
Member of the Crown Publishing Group.

Random House, Inc. New York, Toronto,
London, Sydney, Auckland.

CROWN TRADE PAPERBACKS
and colophon are trademarks of
Crown Publishers, Inc.

Manufactured in China.

Library of Congress
Cataloging-in-Publication Data
Conran, Terence.
The essential house book : getting back
to basics/Terence Conran. — 1st
American ed.
Includes index.
1. Interior decoration—Handbooks,
manuals, etc. I. Title.
NK2115.C769 1994
747—dc20   94-8955
CIP
ISBN 0-517-88231-0

10 9 8 7 6 5

Project Editor
Simon Willis
Art Editor
Helen Lewis
Production Manager
Sonya Sibbons

Editor
Charyn Jones
Editorial Assistant
Charlotte Coleman-Smith
Proofreader
Gareth Jones
Indexer
Karin Woodruff

Designers
Karen Bowen, Alistair Plumb,
Robin Whitecross
Design Assistant
Louise Hillier
Visualizer
Jean Morley
Illustrators
Paul Bryant, Angus Shepherd,
Brian Ma Siy
Production Controller
Jill Macy

Picture Editor
Nadine Bazar
Picture Researcher
Emily Hedges
Picture Research Assistant
Ann Hallwood

The publisher would like to thank
the following for their invaluable
assistance with this book:
Anderson-Schwartz Architects;
Amanda Baker; Antoine Bootz;
Ted Muehling; John Newman;
Jasper Morrison; Craig Allen,
Bridget Bodoano, Chris Vercoe and the
staff at The Conran Shop, London;
Dr. Jonathan Fisk; Disabled Living
Foundation; Rick Mather;
Amanda Robinson; Michael and Jo
Peters; Ron Smith; Deborah Weintraub;
Richard Lavenstein; Laszlo Kiss;
Peter Cook; Paul Ryan; Steve Marshall
and Alfred Munkenbeck;
Ben Richardson; Kate Fontana and
Tony Niblock; Nico Rensch;
Sabine Léon-Dufour; Alison Cathie;
Nancy Christensen of GE Lighting;
Paul Fuge of Plaza Hardwood, Inc.;
Marcy Graham of FSC Wallcoverings;
George Heidekat of the Hardwood
Manufacturers Association;
Robert J. Kleinhans of the Tile Council
of America; and Marion H. Zukas of
MHZ Designs, Inc.

Contributors
Terence Conran (Part 1)
Elizabeth Wilhide (Part 2)
Dinah Hall (Part 3)
Deborah Morant (Part 4)
Gareth Parry (Part 5)

Consultants
John McGowan (Parts 2 and 5)
Robin Hillier (Part 2)
Rupert Thomas (Part 4)

CONTENTS

The Essential House Book was originally going to be called *Back to Basics*. In America, we've kept this as the book's subtitle, but in Britain – where certain politicians adopted the phrase and managed to turn it into something very different from what I had in mind for this book – we had to give it up altogether! Never the less, both versions of the title indicate that the book is intended to be much more than a simple guide to interior decoration. Rather, it is a serious attempt to explain how your house works in a fundamental way, much as a doctor might explain to you how your body functions and how its various systems interrelate.

Style isn't irrelevant – far from it – and our lives would be much less fun without it. But no style works well unless you pay some attention to what's underneath – the bare bones of structure, design and fixtures. For this reason, this book concentrates largely on design and architecture rather than decorating. While the visual appearance of the space you occupy is also of vital importance, you are unlikely to enjoy the decorative aspects if your home does not function efficiently, or provide you with the right framework to enjoy life to the full.

The mission of this book is to help you to understand the myriad options that are open to you in the design and fitting out of the space in which you live. It will, I hope, pose questions that will enable you to analyze what you really want and need from your surroundings, and offers a wide range of alternative solutions for you to consider and put into practice.

Working on this book has given me enormous pleasure. I would like to thank the homeowners from all around the world who have allowed us and our photographers to investigate the workings of their homes. Without them, the book would not have been possible.

Terence Conran.

A SENSE OF PLACE

Home is the heart of life. Unlike an office, a workshop or a school, typically defined by a limited range of functions, the place you live in has to accommodate a broad range of activities, from sleeping to cooking, washing to relaxing. For the daily routine to be comfortable and enjoyable, your home must function well in each of these spheres. As well as an arena of activity, the home is where all kinds of different equipment, provisions and personal possessions are kept – a storehouse of belongings all under one roof competing for space and accessibility. There will be private places for individuals to retreat to and public areas where family and friends can gather. As the years pass and needs alter, there will be changes of use and emphasis. To meet these far-reaching requirements demands careful planning and sensible, flexible organization.

But a home is greater than the sum of its parts and getting the practicalities right is only half of the story. For most people, the special significance of 'home' lies at a deeper level. Home is where we feel at ease, where we belong, where we can create surroundings which reflect our tastes and pleasures. Creating a home has a lot to do with discovering those elements that convey a sense of place.

Investigating these basic ideas relegates 'style' to something of a side issue. Fashions in decorating fluctuate like hemlines, whereas notions of comfort and intimacy date back hundreds of years. This is not to say that style isn't fun or even useful. But it is ultimately more important to find out what you really like, the unique combination of space, light, color and materials which will continue to refresh your spirits long after the latest 'look' has had its day.

The impression a room creates is a blend of many different elements – color, pattern, texture, light and space – which combine to give a sense of place. In this kitchen corner, blue-gray painted woodwork, white-washed walls, and a simple collection of earthenware jars create a mood of tranquillity.

Past and present

1

2

2 The easy sweep of a cantilevered stone staircase leads the eye upward in the entrance hall of an old farmhouse. The raftered ceiling, brick paved floor and terra cotta urns provide a reassuring sense of continuity in both tone and texture.

3

There are no objective standards in design and decoration. What is airy and uplifting to one person is spartan and brutal to another; one person's cozy clutter may be someone else's visual indigestion. What we do share, despite all our differences, is a vocabulary of proportion, arrangement and decorative practice. These familiar traditions, developed over the centuries, shape the way we look at our surroundings and affect our expectations, however unconsciously; they aren't easy to ignore. Although it may be tempting to write off popular revivals of 'period' styles as exercises in nostalgia, beneath it all there lurks a desire to remain in touch with the architectural and decorative conventions and ideals that have stood the test of time.

Social historians trace the beginning of the domestic interior, as we understand it today, to the bourgeois households of seventeenth-century Holland. It is almost unimaginable, despite the best efforts of Hollywood, to conceive of life in a Norman castle, or to relate the way we live today to a ceremonial progression through the grand suites of a Baroque stately home. But the quiet interiors and intimate scenes painted by Vermeer, de Witte or de Hooch are instantly and recognizably homelike, human in scale and disposition.

In his book *Home*, the writer and architect Witold Rybczynski argues that the Dutch were the first to think of the house as a separate, special place and, owing to the preeminence of the Netherlands in trade and finance, this was an ideal that spread throughout the rest of northern Europe and eventually to the colonies of North America. Rybczynski lists many qualities of the Dutch interior which still seem familiar. An awareness of space and a delight in the play of light and shade, a taste for simple, practical furnishings, the serviceable beauty of black-and-white marble floors, polished brass, pewter, china and white linen are all features which recur in Dutch genre paintings of the period. Dutch houses were impeccably clean and shipshape; the kitchen was an important room and the garden a lovingly tended private domain.

Each age has made a contribution to our concept of the interior. From late seventeenth-century France comes the idea of decorative unity, using furnishings, particularly fabric, to make an harmonious composition. Window drapery, fabric-hung walls and upholstery were coordinated for the first time. The salons at the court of Louis XV saw the first attempts to make furniture truly comfortable for relaxation and leisure in the way we understand it today.

4

3 Simple American country furniture in a Long Island house lends character to a space arranged for modern convenience. Soft, neutral shades make a soothing background for a successful blend of old and new.
4 Bright blue paintwork frames a view through the living areas of a French house on the Isle de Ré. The freshness of the simple color scheme enhances architectural detail without stooping to period pastiche.

The classically inspired architects and designers of Georgian England transformed the ordinary townhouse into a model of order, symmetry and elegance. The proportions, scale and detailing of eighteenth-century rooms – derived from the classical orders of the ancient world – still look comfortable and appropriate to the modern eye. For these designers 'beauty' and 'usefulness' were inseparable notions.

By the beginning of the nineteenth century different rooms were becoming associated with distinct functions. The 'dining room' became a fixed feature in the late eighteenth century; by the nineteenth, bedrooms were always private, drawing rooms the most prestigiously decorated. More importantly, with working life taking place in factories and offices, the house became the bastion of the family, a sanctuary expressing personal tastes and aspirations.

From the Aesthetic Movement of the late nineteenth century came the idea that decoration, particularly color, could express ambience, a notion that promoters of modern paint ranges take for granted. The same period saw William Morris and his followers in the Arts and Crafts Movement challenge the mediocrity of mass production, championing traditional forms and reviving handcraft skills, the genesis of what we now call 'country style'. By promoting an 'honest' use of materials and rejecting derivative ornament, Morris anticipated many principles of modern design.

In the last 100 years, the advances in domestic technology – electric light and power for labor-saving appliances, central heating and modern plumbing – have made entirely new uses and arrangements of interior space possible. The radical designers of the Modern Movement expressed these changes by rationalizing the home, applying principles of industrial production to make 'machines for living in'. The fact that Modernism in its purest form remains a minority enthusiasm has not lessened its impact on our ideas of how a home should actually function.

The extent to which technology has transformed daily life can partly be measured by how much we take it for granted. In the mid-1890s making fires accounted for an estimated ten hours' housework a week, time freed by the arrival of central heating. The advent of electricity meant houses became cleaner, fresher, brighter and easier to run.

1

2

3

4

1 Intense and vibrant primary colors articulate bold planes in this modern room, achieving depth and sophistication despite the relative simplicity of both the detailing and finishes.

When we select soft, light colors for a bedroom, we are echoing a style that began with Madame de Pompadour. When we place a chair rail one third of the way up the wall, we are preserving a basic eighteenth-century proportion. But when we organize the kitchen to make an efficient workspace, we are inescapably modern. The expectation that the home should be comfortable and convenient on a more profound level than ever before is the single most important contribution of this century. Few devotees of period decoration would wish to revive eighteenth-century sanitary arrangements or nineteenth-century heating systems, though they may go to some lengths to conceal radiators, telephones and televisions in otherwise historically accurate rooms.

On the other hand, a recent American survey discovered that over 90 per cent of those questioned wanted a fireplace in their home, even those who lived in areas which were warm all year round. The reasons can hardly be practical. The fireplace, as our ancestors knew too well, is an inefficient source of heat; it creates dirt and waste, and in many areas of the world the types of fuel which may be burned are now subject to strict environmental controls. But the association of hearth and home is ancient and has proved to be a tie which even technology cannot break.

You do not have to be a social historian to have absorbed a host of preconceptions about how rooms should look and how they should work. Today, design books, lifestyle manuals, glossy magazines, film and television provide a deluge of images, presenting every conceivable variation on the theme of the interior, from beach houses to city lofts, suburban villas to rustic retreats. Thanks to a burgeoning industry in home-improvement products, today's consumers are offered a wide variety of affordable colors, patterns, materials and furnishings, enabling them to turn their ideas into reality.

2 A room in the Hancock Shaker Village, Pittsfield, Massachusetts is a powerful demonstration of the beauty of ordinary things. The high pegboard, use of plain textiles and meticulous woodwork are characteristic of the work of this nineteenth-century sect.

3 Matchboarded walls and floorboards painted chalky white create a luminous, light-filled interior. Displays of twigs and leaves in weathered metal containers add a natural vitality.

4 There is nothing hesitant about this creative clutter of color and pattern. Calligraphic squiggles and bold shapes create both a dynamic sense of movement and an irrepressible warmth and cheerfulness.

From a house to a home

The sheer range of decorating and furnishing options available can confuse as much as inspire; understandably many people still approach the process of creating a home in piecemeal fashion, acquiring a sofa here, a lampshade there, without any coherent idea of how it's all going to fit together. The aim of this book is to simplify and direct your decision-making by analysing spatial, organizational and structural issues relating to the whole house; by looking at the common activities that take place under the same roof and different ways of accommodating them; and by supplying a comprehensive and up-to-date directory to make selection easier.

There is one thing no book can do, and that is tell you how you want to live. Before you start to consider floor plans, storage requirements, tables and chairs, it is vital to discover your own tastes and preferences. Once you have an idea about where you are going, it's relatively straightforward to get there.

Making a home is a form of creativity open to everyone. Fear of ridicule, lack of confidence, or simply a sense of being overwhelmed by too many alternatives can still be inhibiting. We expect to be able to 'read' rooms and assess a person's character – and much else – from the way they choose to live; this level of exposure can force the self-conscious into conventional, predictable solutions that won't worry the neighbors but do little to enhance their own lives.

The idea that a home can be a vehicle for self-expression is relatively new, the means to make it so, newer still. When you consider how much time you spend at home and how much money you invest on improvements, it's only natural to fashion your home in a way that means something to you. Successful interiors have a definite flavor, an unmistakable vitality that allows personality to come through. 'Anonymous' rooms are depressing precisely because they lack individuality, or any sense of being inhabited by real people.

1

1 Inspired recycling contrives a 'pop' montage from urban debris in a New York loft. Packing crates and old wood create a partition between kitchen and living space, a witty low-tech framework to house modern apparatus.
2 The uncompromising natural look of this kitchen combines the bleached-out tones of driftwood and stone with basic furniture simply constructed from weathered planks and boards.

2

3

3 Direct and unpretentious, decoration that responds to climate creates a powerful sense of place. The cool ceramic tiled floor, whitewashed ceiling and uncluttered furnishings in this Corsican house are the visual equivalent of a breath of fresh air.

Many people only fully appreciate their surroundings during vacations, when, relaxed and away from a familiar environment, they pay closer attention to colors, textures, form and light. Other impressions can be equally valuable. Vacation houses reacquaint us with the virtues of the simple life, a time when we find it surprisingly easy to make do with the minimum of equipment and technology, where furnishings are robust and economical and the emphasis is on enjoyment and basic everyday pleasures. Beyond acquiring the odd souvenir and preserving memories on film, however, few think to apply these inspirations in the context of their own home. Yet here is an ideal opportunity to assess what you can and cannot live without. If, by the end of the vacation, the whole family is climbing the walls for want of the television, so be it; but if you hardly missed it, you might consider moving the TV somewhere less prominent when you get home.

A good starting place for discovering what you really like is to make a list of some of the houses, rooms, stores or even restaurants that have appealed to you in the past, no matter how vague or amorphous the reason. Dredge up your memories, indulge in a little creative day-dreaming and try to recall not just how such places looked, but how they sounded, smelled and felt. A house from your childhood, a place by the sea or in the country where you once stayed, a wonderful hotel, a room in a friend's home that you admire. Although its relevance may not appear immediately obvious, by analyzing precisely why such places are evocative and meaningful, you can begin to distill the elements that might be put to work to enrich your own home.

I can personally relate the experience of being in a warm greenhouse, with its earthy musty smells, to my enjoyment of spaces which act as a transition between interiors and the world outside,

where nature can be brought closer and appreciated in relative comfort. Seashore houses, too, have an elemental quality, a 'look' which can be suggested in bright colors and natural textures even if the traffic noise and police sirens are the unwelcome urban equivalents to the restful sound of waves lapping or crashing against the seashore.

4

4 The simple pleasure of strong, bright colors in vibrant sunlight is universal.
5 Getting away from it all was never more appealing. This slatted summerhouse on stilts makes an irresistible retreat, lookout and hideaway.

5

1

I enjoy the luxury of space – my ideal would be a great open room which could be subdivided whenever I wanted, in the flexible manner of Japanese houses with their sliding partition screens. In the same spirit, I like interiors which merge with their settings, where there are no hard boundaries between inside and outside, where there are views and vistas that emphasize the sense of expansiveness. I like objects to be solid and well-made, not flimsy, and made of materials that mature well, aging gracefully and acquiring their own beauty with use and time. It doesn't worry me when the edges of a stair carpet show signs of wear and tear, when curtains bleach in the light or ceilings darken and mellow. At the same time, cheerfulness and optimism are important to me, the freshness of a room after a really good spring cleaning, the vitality of flowers, the way a room can change its dynamics through subtle rearrangement to reflect the seasons. Finally, I enjoy comforting, hospitable houses which are well-stocked with provisions.

When it comes to creating your own home, you can derive personal inspiration from a wide variety of sources. As well as houses you have visited or seen, theater sets, films, books, exhibitions and magazines can all generate ideas for

1 As elemental as its setting, Tigre del Mar by Mexican designer Gian Franco Brignone and architect Jean-Claude Galibert blurs the distinction between outdoors and indoors. Natural pigments rubbed into the exterior dissolve the walls into the horizon.

2

2 Warm ochre walls and wood strip flooring create an atmosphere of tranquillity that makes the most of natural light. The simple lines of the furniture complement the angles and planes of walls and ceiling.

doors and walls, bathrooms in view of the front door, visible plumbing and poor maintenance are bad. Remedies for awkward or oppressive features include mirrors to increase light and openness, growing plants indoors, wind chimes and shades. It may be difficult to accept the interpretations – evil spirits rushing around a house are thwarted by a well-placed mirror – but *feng shui* encapsulates a universal response to fresh air, light and harmony in the interior.

What I've called 'a sense of place' is a barely definable, abstract quality, a combination of many factors that generates a specific atmosphere. The remainder of this chapter is an exploration of some of these elements. In practice, they aren't experienced in isolation and although it is useful to consider each individually, keeping the whole picture in mind will help bring them together in an harmonious whole.

3 A small London studio apartment overcomes the restriction of size with minimal furnishings and a fastidious attention to architectural detail. The base of the walls are finished with inset metal beading which provides a clean, graphic edge.

the use of colors, patterns, textures and materials to be adapted in your surroundings: some of the most original and satisfying interior schemes have arisen from cross-fertilizing ideas from different disciplines. Keep a scrapbook of tear sheets from magazines, postcards, scraps of fabric – anything which serves to jog your memory and foster your creativity. It's all part of the same process of discovering what you like.

It is instinctive to identify with the place in which you live. In dream analysis the house is usually interpreted as a symbol for the human body. Artists and writers have made extensive use of this psychological insight to portray and describe interiors that evoke states of mind or aspects of character. The artist Leonora Carrington believes there is a 'psychic shape' to a house, its form molded like a container to its occupants over a period of time.

Less profoundly, it can be entertaining to extend the metaphor. Like the body, the house has its own mechanical systems of ventilation, energy and plumbing! Equally, it can be dressed up and decorated, cosmetically improved and fashionably turned out. The way that furnishing styles mimic changes in dress has been remarked upon by many

historians of the interior – high-waisted Empire dresses echoed in filmy window drapery, Victorian layers of upholstery and trimming corresponding to the intricately detailed layers of fashionable nineteenth-century clothing.

The ancient Chinese discipline *feng shui* – 'the science of wind and water' – also relates the house to the body, the house possessing its own metabolism which channels *ch'i* (the life force) to determine the health, prosperity and luck of its occupants. Even the most sceptical cannot disagree that human beings function better in favorable locations, or fail to appreciate the enlightened common sense of many *feng shui* rules, based on centuries of close observation of the way people react to their surroundings. Some *feng shui* practices have to do with preserving the vitality of a house by paying attention to light, the movement of air, orientation, shape and scale – elements which play upon the senses, not just sight.

In Chinese society, *feng shui* experts are consulted on everything from the placing of a chair to the siting of a new restaurant. Generous, light entrances, graceful curving stairs, windows that open wide and uncluttered living rooms are good *feng shui*; low beams, slanting

3

Space and light

Space is the greatest luxury of the twentieth century. With most of us crowded into towns and cities, battling through traffic jams or jostling for elbowroom in packed commuter trains, there is an acute need for our personal surroundings to allow us room to relax in comfort and relative privacy.

Space – as in square feet – is expensive. For many people there comes a point when moving to gain another bedroom or a bigger kitchen becomes financially impossible. The answer is to find other ways of increasing the sense of space. 'Room for Change' (pages 30–113) addresses the structural, technical and organizational ways in which space can be maximized – physical changes that can enable you to make better use of the space you have at your disposal or to extend your house relatively economically.

But there is another side to the issue which has to do with the *quality* of the space at your disposal and how this affects your perception of it. There are many small apartments and houses which give an appearance of being wonderfully spacious simply by virtue of being well-organized and appropriately used, or because sympathetic and sensitive decorative choices work to dispel any feeling of the rooms being cramped or enclosed. On the other hand, there are plenty of large houses in which generous space is wasted by poor planning and arrangement. Big rooms can be just so much 'dead' space if they are badly designed and shoddily detailed.

One important element is unity. Rooms look awkward when there is a mishmash of conflicting styles and tastes clamoring for attention. Using the same sorts of colors and textures in connecting areas such as hallways and stairs, employing the same family of basic materials for surfaces and finishes and avoiding abrupt aesthetic leaps from style to style bring a sense of coherence to a sequence of rooms and help to define the essence of a home.

Another vital issue to address is the question of proportion. A common response to the problem of small rooms is to knock down partition walls and open up the spaces into one large area. In many cases the result is an immediate improvement, particularly if the new room serves two complementary functions such as cooking and eating. But imposing an open-plan layout on a conventionally arranged house isn't always successful. Proportions which look right when the rooms are separate can look distinctly odd when you take away the walls. Doors, windows, fireplaces and other architectural details may suddenly seem out of scale. One solution is to retain a hint of separation by making distinct areas for different activities within the new space; another is to scale up fixtures to provide definition and visual weight.

If you decide to accept the spatial limitations of a small room and work with them, you can bring out the special benefits of an enclosed space – coziness and intimacy, the comfortable feeling of having everything within reach – without suffering the drawbacks. Study other small spaces, such as ships' cabins and mobile homes, places that are appealing because they are so intensely workable and well-considered. A small space with little in it will always remind you of its limited size, but one that is elegantly laid out and thoughtfully furnished to an appropriate scale has its own atmosphere and character.

Quality of space has relatively little to do with room size. Thinking about the house as a whole, how each room relates to the other and to the world outside and, crucially, considering the needs of everyone who lives there, is the basic message of this book. Space is dynamic rather than static. It is appreciated through movement, use, sound and light – all fundamental aspects which cannot simply be reduced to the empirical facts of the habitable floor area within four walls.

There will always be the need for a balance between privacy and openness in any home – large communal areas for people to gather in and small private rooms to retreat to. It may seem an obvious point, but in houses where every space runs into the other, life can become tiring: sound is amplified, intimate conversations are virtually impossible and different activities set up competing areas of attention. Whereas if your rooms are uniformly small, there is nowhere to celebrate and entertain without feeling claustrophobic.

As well as variations in room size and scale, there should also be places which delight and surprise. Alcoves, window seats or generous hallways with reading corners may appear superfluous in a strictly functional sense but these are all features which people enjoy precisely because they add a different and often unexpected dimension to the way in which the space is used.

1

2

1 A tiny studio apartment converted from a small garage presents a particular challenge: how to accommodate different areas of activity within the same proscribed space without sacrificing light and openness. A compact kitchen wall is screened from the sleeping area with a large hardwood panel.
2 A room with a view is inherently spacious. The tongue-and-groove paneled walls, low bed and sympathetic furnishings do not detract from the expansive outlook beyond the window.

3 Internal windows bring light into the heart of the house. A large window provides an appetizing view of the kitchen in this Italian house and maintains a valuable connection with the outdoors. The pattern of panes unifies the different-sized openings and makes the effect look considered.

4 A pleasing play on light and space is achieved by the careful positioning and detail of internal walls. The gentle curve of the wall that divides the living from dining areas is accentuated by the suspended ceiling, leading the eye along the main axis of the house. Openings in the flanking walls provide views through, as well as frames for display.

1 Dappled light filtered through leaves has a magical vitality. Houses which preserve the link with the outdoors are instinctively appealing.

Another key consideration has to do with the relationship between the interior and the outside. What you see beyond, through windows, doorways and adjoining areas is just as important as what the room itself contains. In *A Pattern Language* by Christopher Alexander and others there is a short passage on what the authors call a 'Zen' view, those tantalizing glimpses of the outside world offered by 'places of transition' – at entrances, on stairs, along hallways. These views remain fascinating because they are only experienced briefly as you move from place to place.

I have often referred to the work of Sir John Soane in this context and make no apologies for doing so again! His interiors, particularly at the London museum he created to house his collection of antiquities, show a mastery of interior space. At Lincoln's Inn Fields in the center of London, the modest proportions of a Regency townhouse are transformed by a series of ingenious visual devices. The eye is not so much deceived as delighted by hidden vistas, sudden changes of scale and intriguing reflections. Soane fitted window frames with thin mirror panels to reflect light and views; there are lowered ceilings and small entrances giving way to large open rooms and everywhere there is a sense of contrast. 'Hazard and surprise', the guiding principle of Soane's approach to design, is a recipe for vitality that does not depend on grand surroundings.

3

4

4 A sunroom forms a link between kitchen and living room, thus making a core of light in this waterside house. Eating under a glass roof with open views to both sides provides the best of both worlds. The wooden structure and shingled walls are naturally complementary in the woodland setting.

A lot of what makes a particular space enjoyable has to do with light: the two issues of space and light are really inseparable. Natural light enhances the spatial character of a room, throwing detail into relief, drawing the eye to warm sunny spots, shrouding corners in cool shadows, making dappled patterns where it is diffused and filtered. Uniformly bright artificial lighting, on the other hand, gives any room the subtlety of a hospital corridor. Many people view artificial lighting as a practical means of illumination without giving thought to its aesthetic impact; the results are surroundings which resist any attempt to bring them to life.

Natural light is always changing; at different times of the day and in different seasons there are variations of tone, intensity, color. Part of the pleasure everyone experiences sitting outdoors on a summer's day comes from these infinitesimal changes. Artificial light is no substitute for daylight, but with modern lighting systems, sources and fixtures it is still possible to filter, direct and modulate light to provide essential contrast and variety.

A positive enjoyment of natural light, views and spatial diversity are all part of the same picture. It isn't merely a case of trying to get closer to nature, but a question of making the home a more natural place, in tune with the instinctive ways in which people feel comfortable, healthy and happy.

5

5 Lighting is one of the most effective means of creating a sense of architectural drama and surprise. Two flights of narrow, enclosed steps are picked out with small lights inset in the treads and top lit by a skylight to make an exciting transition between levels.

Color

Color, pattern and texture are the decorative elements which express a sense of place, cosmetic in one sense, but more than skin deep in another. How you decorate your house, what you apply over the bare bones of the structure, can be as easy and economical to change as paint, or as integral as a floorcovering. The initial approach should be holistic, related to material use and mix, rather than a series of isolated decisions where the whole effect is never considered.

Decorating should be fun, a chance to give your creativity free rein. But a lot of people get bogged down in the fraught process of selection and end up retreating to predictable choices on the false assumption that these will prove practical or easy to live with. In fact, it's far easier to live with something you enjoy, rather than merely tolerate.

Before you confront a color chart or sample book of fabric swatches, think in general terms about the kinds of room you enjoy. Do you like places that are bright and airy, cozy and cluttered, rich with color and pattern, soothing and neutral?

Build up a picture in your mind of the kind of materials that might work together to create the effect you want. A wood floor has pattern in its grain, texture in its finish and color; a granite countertop is cool, hard, smooth and flecked. In practice, we don't dissociate these qualities, they all work together. In the past, there was a natural association of material with color: woodwork was often painted and grained brown to enhance its 'woodiness'. It's worth going back to these basic associations to investigate why we respond to certain colors, patterns and textures and not to others. You could translate an affection for seaside places, for example, into a palette of gray-blue, aquamarine, buff and white, and chalky, sandy textures; into enlivening accents of sharp color against misty neutral backgrounds; into nautical stripes, or into materials like bleached or painted wood, sisal and coir.

Color is one of the most subjective areas in decoration and no amount of analysis is going to predict how two people will respond to the same shade. At the same time, almost any generalization you can make about a particular color can be overturned in practice. Nevertheless, you have to start somewhere. Even if you don't have a 'favorite' color, there will inevitably be a family of colors to which you are instinctively drawn, colors which keep cropping up in your choice of clothes, in treasured pictures or possessions; and there will be other colors you absolutely abhor.

Use these clues to guide your choice when it comes to decorating and don't be put off by the stock decrees that blue must be chilly, yellow is sunny and so on. Quite subtle differences in tone can make all the difference. If you love red, you don't have to paint your living

room walls crimson, you can derive just as much pleasure from details such as sofa upholstery or a tartan throw. And, of course, colors take on quite a different dynamic in combination, in electric partnerships of opposites or complementaries, in soft modulated tonal families, paired with crisp, refreshing white or graphically contrasted with black.

It takes time to gain a sense of how color behaves; like everything else, it's a question of widening your visual horizons. If you decide to play safe, start with a neutral background, such as

1 Nature offers many examples of colorful harmony: a bougainvillaea in bloom provides a sharp accent against the distressed paint of an old shed door and the rustic charm of the wall and fence.
2 Simple, utilitarian objects can marry function with decoration. Powdered paints in ordinary glass jars gain much of their effect from their ad hoc arrangement.

5

3 Flowers are a simple means of ringing decorative changes. This bowl of yellow daisies forms a vibrant focal point against the turquoise paintwork.
4 A large window floods this room with light, giving breathing space to the colorful collection of objects.

8

6

7

white walls, plain floors, and experiment with color in objects and furnishings which can be easily changed. How you decorate large surface areas will have a determining effect on the room, so give yourself time to live in the space and get used to its particular characteristics. Ask yourself how you intend to use the room, what it looks like in the morning, or at night, which features are worth emphasizing and which you want to play down. It's easy enough to paint the walls at a later date, or add rugs, curtains or blinds as your decorative sense develops.

9

5 Bold planes of color arrest the attention, delineating the space of a building.
6 As simple a device as picking out the chair rail in a contrasting color can enliven the pace of a room.
7 Duck-egg green is elegant and simple.
8 Time and nature are the inspiration behind this still-life.
9 A mirror increases the dramatic intensity of the orange walls.

Pattern and texture

Neutral backgrounds leave you free to concentrate on another important dimension to the interior of a room – texture. The pleasing combinations of textures which arise from matching different materials and finishes gives any room depth and interest, which is why uniformly bland, artificial materials can seem so lifeless. Chalky matte paintwork, stripped, scrubbed and waxed floorboards, robust canvas and nubbly linen may all be tonally very similar but they are inherently lively in combination simply by virtue of their textural differences.

What is evocative and stimulating about this approach is the way textures reinforce a link with nature, which has been a source of decorative inspiration through many centuries. There is no better way of going back to basics than reveling in the simplicity of wood, stone and natural fibers such as unbleached cotton – materials with a raw elemental beauty and an effortless way of working well together. Natural materials do not date and they transcend conventional distinctions between styles; more importantly, they age well, wearing attractively with use and time. Synthetic finishes singularly lack this ability; any change to their original condition is a change for the worse. This is not to dismiss the undoubted practicality and benefits of using artificial materials in many situations, merely a reminder that natural materials repay your initial investment by improving with the years, mellowing and acquiring the patina of use, which, more than any other factor, contributes to a sense of place.

Pattern is inherent in decoration. As subtle as the self-colored design of a damask cloth or as bold as a sofa layered in Oriental textiles, pattern transforms our appreciation of color and texture, adding rhythm and movement, intrinsically suggestive of order and repose. A well-balanced print is a good way of living with the intensity of strong color and an excellent mediating influence between strong shapes and plain surfaces. Pattern breaks up the expanse of large areas, giving depth and

1

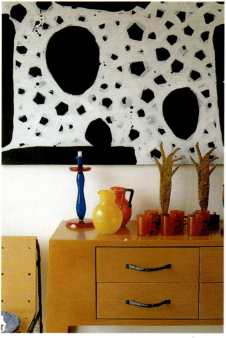

2

3

1 The pale tints of the plain rendered walls and stairs provide a subtle differentiation of tone and emphasize the chalky finish.
2 Pattern arises naturally in the way objects are arranged. A display of brightly colored glass set off against a graphic abstract picture brings together different elements in a lively, companionable way.
3 Textural variety gives depth and physical presence to understated neutral backgrounds. In the absence of strong color, metal, stone, carpet and paintwork provide essential contrast in the ways they reflect light.

character: the success of broken-color paint techniques demonstrates the effectiveness of tone-on-tone prints, which reveal the marks of brush, sponge or rag, at leading the eye beyond the flatness of a two-dimensional surface.

Pattern and texture do not, of course, arise solely in the context of textiles, carpets and wall finishes. A collection of glassware, a shelf full of books, a group of family photographs – all of these create a special dynamic of their own and add to the texture of the room. Although, to an extent, they can be seen as finishing touches, you shouldn't underestimate the effect such displays will have. If you have a special item of furniture, a painting or a piece of sculpture that you know you want to keep in a particular room, this can provide a useful starting-point in establishing a decorative scheme.

During the nineteenth century there was an exceptional tolerance for rich, busy patterns, a level of visual distraction most people find uncongenial today. As with any other decorative element, the way in which pattern is used matters almost as much as what it looks like in isolation.

Pattern can be used to define – as in a border of checkered tile work – or to provide an accent and focus – as in a wonderfully rich kilim in a modern space, an effective contrast of mood and style. Although we are not attuned to the enveloping quality of nineteenth-century decoration – where surfaces were layered in intricately detailed fabrics, printed papers and floorcoverings – mixing patterns that share some basic affinity can give a room a warm, embracing quality which feels both very comfortable and easy on the eye.

Arrangement and detail

1

People seem to fall into two distinct camps – either they like clutter, or they don't. In some mismatched households, you can sense a kind of open warfare between the person who is always straightening up and putting things away and the accumulator who leaves a trail of possessions in their wake.

I must admit to preferring less rather than more, the sparse and simple rather than rooms where the basic qualities of light and space are overwhelmed by objects and furnishings. Even so, I'm not a minimalist and there are some who adopt a much more rigorous approach, comfortable only in nearly empty spaces where few of the accouterments of daily life remain on view.

Whichever side of the divide you find yourself on, what counts is the courage of your convictions. Many people end up sharing their lives with unwanted and useless things because they can't work out what to do with them, or haven't the nerve to give them away – clutter by default. Over a hundred years ago William Morris formulated his 'golden rule': 'Have nothing in your houses which you do not know to be useful or believe to be beautiful', a message which retains its relevance today.

Teach yourself to evaluate what you see. Ask yourself what you think about everything you own: do you positively like it? If you do, why? What does it contribute – practicality, a memory of a happy event or a special place? Plenty of people have experienced the shock of returning home after an absence and suddenly seeing familiar surroundings in a new, critical light. Make use of this feeling to change things for the better.

Exercise the same critical faculty when it comes to new possessions. It is better to wait until you find what works in a positive sense rather than to put up with second best. If this means postponing a purchase until you have saved up enough money, or spending more effort to find the right materials, it is well worth it. A sense of place grows with time, as different elements are juggled and refined until everything feels right.

Few really successful or interesting rooms are created overnight. Yet homes are never really 'finished': new stages in your life make their own demands, forcing you to adapt and reappraise the way you live. Your tastes may alter, perhaps radically. Instead of being frustrated or dismayed by this, you should welcome and even initiate change, since this is precisely what keeps houses alive.

2

2 A luminous Chinese porcelain dish balanced on a narrow ledge sings out against white walls in a near-empty room. This composition has the tension and precision of a technical drawing.
3 Everyday things in the corner of the small kitchen make a practical and pleasing display. The comfort and reassurance of familiar objects is part of what makes a home.

Room size and shape often dictate an optimum arrangement of fittings, services and at least the larger pieces of furniture. But there is usually a way to vary the positioning of some elements, even if it is only rearranging a display of objects, or putting some pieces away for the time being and bringing others out. Maintaining a room in the way it was first furnished and decorated, leaving furniture rooted to the same places from year to year, dusting objects and putting them back in exactly the same position means there will come a time when you hardly see them any more.

Even small changes can be refreshing. Use a good spring-cleaning or the coming of a new season to play with emphasis and arrangement. A century ago, the advent of summer in many households meant rugs were taken up, slip covers placed over heavy upholstery, thick draperies replaced with lightweight cotton versions – a general lightening of rooms to suit the warmer weather. There are many good reasons for reviving this practice, but perhaps the most persuasive is the fact that it fosters a new awareness of your surroundings.

Arrangement has much to do with detail – such apparently small things as fresh flowers, or the witty or personal touches that make a disproportionately large impact on the way you view a room. At the same time, the importance of detail often lies in what you don't see. It means adopting a thorough approach from the start so there aren't trailing wires and overloaded electric outlets, clumsy junctions between ceiling and walls, unattractive baseboards or cheap handles that strike a jarring note. Detail is the narrow focus, the necessary complement to the wider picture.

Creating a home is a complex process, but it isn't the least bit mysterious. Getting it right isn't a question of adhering to a set of rules or toeing a fashionable line – it means finding out what you like and incorporating this into the way you want to live.

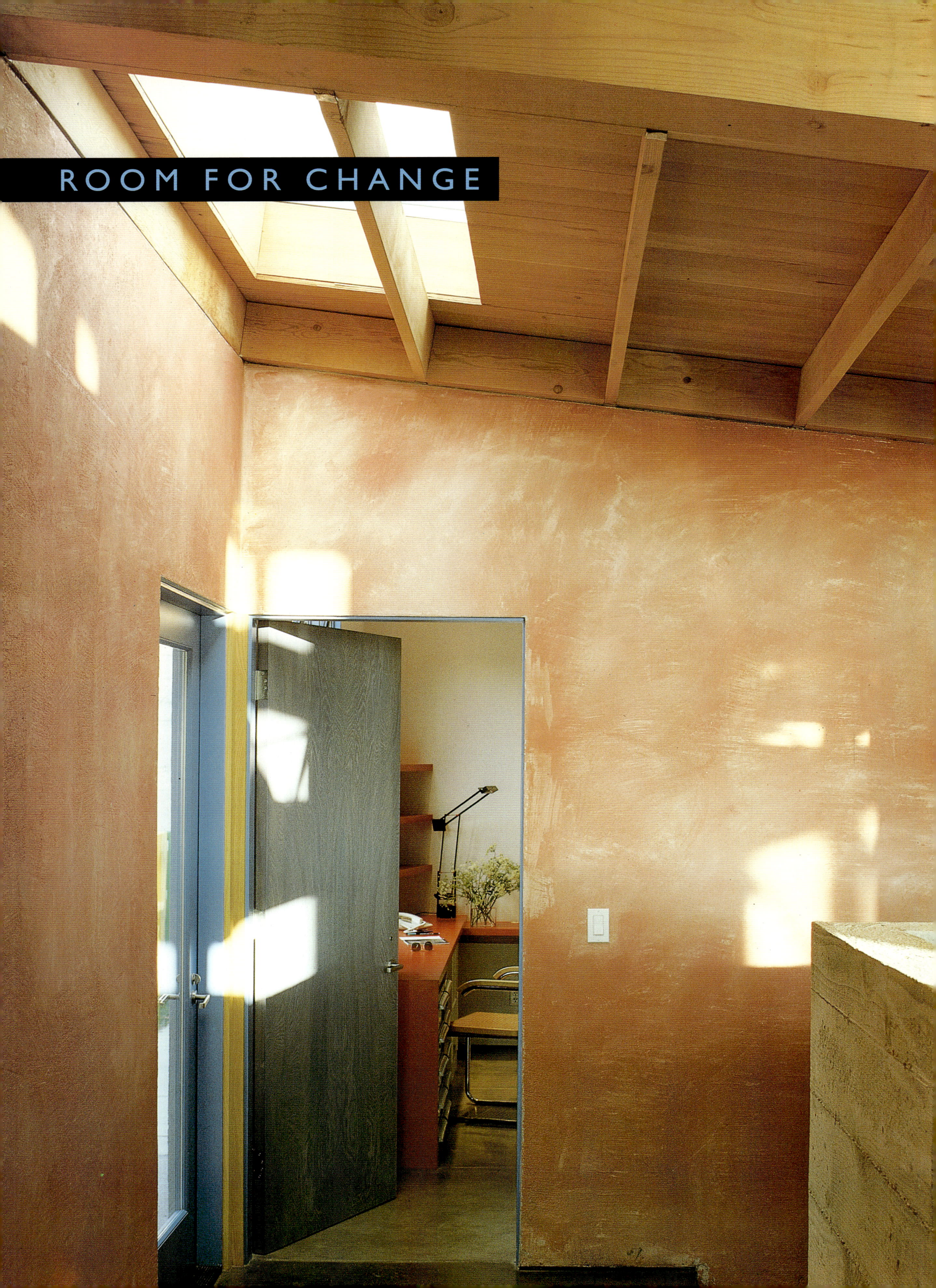

Our lives don't stand still. Work patterns, family circumstances and how we occupy our spare time may alter considerably from year to year. A new baby is guaranteed to turn most households upside down; the arrival of children instigates a sequence of changes as one stage of development quickly succeeds the next. With or without children, possessions accumulate, tastes are redefined. The surroundings which once suited our needs no longer fulfill our most basic requirements.

At certain critical points, the best solution may be to move to a new place. But it is neither possible nor practical to move each time your home fails to match up to a change in circumstances. In any case, it is more than likely that even a new home will meet only some of your needs, and that adjustments will be required to provide a perfect fit.

This section should enable you to envisage the scope and potential of spatial change. In this context, it is important to view your home as a complete entity, rather than a collection of disparate parts. Simple alterations to the fabric of your home can have a knock-on effect, bringing benefits which go beyond the obvious.

Major spatial changes always involve professional help. If you are thoroughly briefed on the range of possibilities, aware of potential hazards and familiar with common procedures, working with professionals becomes more of a partnership and less of a leap in the dark.

Even if you haven't reached an obvious turning point, there may be ways of improving your surroundings which will add to the pleasure and effectiveness of daily life. The following pages will show you how to take a fresh look at your home, challenge your preconceptions and discover room for change within your own four walls.

The main living areas of this house are at the back, down from the entrance level. A self-contained home office adjacent to the front door provides a means of separating work from social life. Roughwashed walls and painted trim give a warm feel to this modern building.

LOOKING FOR POTENTIAL

One of the most abused terms in the real-agent's vocabulary, or the most useful, depending on your point of view, 'potential' generally denotes a property not so much alive with possibilities as neglected beyond belief. But 'room for change' does not necessarily mean you are confronting the daunting prospect of total renovation and renewal. Each and every home has potential – you just have to know where to look for it. If you are among the fortunate few who are fairly satisfied with things as they are, there may still be ways of making improvements that you have overlooked. Or you may have the vague sense that you aren't making the best use of the space at your disposal, but find yourself unable to put a finger on exactly how it is you could improve the existing layout of your house or apartment.

People tend to be buzzing with plans and schemes when they move to a new house, but often find it difficult to decide which course of action would give the greatest long-term benefit or represent the best investment of time and money. Then, having settled in and spent a while in the same place, it's all too easy to become accustomed to the way things are and learn to tolerate imperfections and minor inconvenience. Even after the first flush of enthusiasm has died down there may be some problems, of course, that are too glaring to ignore. The solutions, however, may not be so obvious. Spatial, structural and organizational changes can be complex, disruptive and expensive, so it is understandable that many people only tinker around the edges without ever coming to grips with the underlying problems.

This section aims to provide you with the means to undertake a thorough analysis of your home: from identifying what you like and what you want to change, through to explanations of the various options available to you; from simple redecoration to more ambitious schemes that involve structural alteration. If you can look at your home in a fresh light, analyzing its use in terms of how you live your life and the way in which different rooms do or do not respond to the demands you make, all manner of possibilities may suggest themselves to you. Provided you budget sensibly and schedule the work carefully, you can make changes that will improve the quality of your life and, quite possibly, increase the resale value of your house.

1 The views through a house – from room to room, level to level, inside to out – make an important contribution to spatial quality. Color underscores the sense of transition.
2 Contrast of materials defines different areas in a minimally furnished interior. In near-empty rooms, the focus falls on such telling details as switches, baseboards and the junction between finishes and floor coverings.

3 Entrances set the scene. An open stairwell creates a soaring sense of space and provides views in every direction. Hardwood flooring throughout the first floor emphasizes the expansive effect.

4 Dividing up the space need not entail loss of light. A kitchen is neatly contained within an area formed by two half-height partitions, providing a demarcation of activities within a large open room.

5 Open-plan living, where there are few divisions between rooms or even levels, dramatically alters the perception of interior space. It is important to incorporate private areas to maintain balance and flexibility.

4

5

Assessing your home

1 The kitchen is the hardest-working area in the home. Integrating all of the elements to provide an efficient use of space requires thorough planning; the necessary improvements may amount to a substantial proportion of your budget, but the positive effects are far reaching.

Making a list of the positive and negative qualities of your home takes a degree of objectivity, a critical eye not dulled by overfamiliarity. To put yourself in the right frame of mind, imagine showing your home to a real-estate agent or a prospective buyer, or if that scenario is too grim to contemplate, imagine you're showing it off to a friend on their first visit, some-one with an open mind, but who doesn't necessarily share your affection for the place or isn't used to turning a blind eye to the state of the baseboards or the worn stair carpet.

Start at the front door and work your way through each area. How would you present what you see? There may be rooms that you would hurry through, mumbling excuses; there may be outstanding features, fine details, or good views you would emphasize. Think about all the questions a buyer might ask

concerning services, technicalities or the basic structure. Are there deficiencies in the way the physical systems work? Which intrinsic spatial qualities would you take pains to point out, elements that perhaps aren't immediately obvious but ones you have come to appreciate through living there?

The next step is to identify exactly what needs changing. Think carefully about how you live, about the everyday experience of using your home. Ask everyone in the household to contribute their views, so that you have a well-rounded picture that takes everyone's perspective into account:

• What delights you most about your house or apartment?
• What annoys you most?
• Are there bottlenecks where people always seem to be running into one another?
• How do you move around the house? Are there redundant doors or entrances that you never use?
• Do you have to travel too far between key areas, or are any of the main routes tortuous and awkward?
• Where does clutter accumulate despite all your best efforts at organization?
• What is each room used for? Are there conflicts of interest and activities?
• Which room do you feel most comfortable in, and why?
• In which rooms do family and friends naturally congregate?
• Can you entertain guests comfortably? How many?
• Is there a room that is under-used, or one that people tend to avoid or just ignore?
• Which areas are too small – or too big – for your present needs?
• Is there enough natural light? Does the existing arrangement of artificial lighting serve your needs?
• Do you ever feel overwhelmed by noise?
• Do any of the main services, such as heating or plumbing, require constant and costly repair? Do you find your home expensive to run?

• Is your home physically comfortable – is it warm in winter, cool in summer?
• Do you have enough power outlets?
• How secure is your home and neighborhood? Have you been burglarized?
• Is your home safe for children, the elderly or for a family member with special needs?
• Are surfaces and finishes practical where they need to be – in the kitchen, the bathroom or children's areas?

If you intend to stay in your home for any length of time, try to imagine what your answers would be like in two, five or ten years' time. What changes to your lifestyle can you anticipate?

This general exercise in consultation and analysis is an essential prelude to undertaking any major change on the home front. It is important to keep an open mind and identify any potential areas for change. Don't worry too much

3

4

2 A bedroom adjoining a living area in a French house is furnished with the simplest elements. The bare metal frame of the bed creates the sense of a room within a room.

3 The central hearth is open on two sides, providing a visual connection between the bedroom and living area, and a dramatic double view of the fire.

4 Bedrooms which are dominated by clothes storage generally fail to function well as peaceful retreats. In this small bedroom, the dressing area is just beyond the glass doors – a logical and practical use of limited space.

at this stage how such changes are to be implemented. And do not rule out alterations because you imagine they will be too expensive or difficult to accomplish – they may not be after all. Simply set yourself the task of visualizing the best possible surroundings for you and your family and enumerate every obstacle that currently stands in the way of you achieving this goal.

Listen to what others in your household have to say. You may be pleasantly surprised to discover that everybody shares your reservations about the condition of the bathroom, or chagrined to find that someone else has plans for the spare room which don't match your own. Compromise can come later; now is the time to look at your home as dispassionately as possible – as an entity, with both strengths that should be maximized and weaknesses that you need to overcome.

5 Services – heat, light, power, water – constitute the infrastructure of your home. Making spatial changes often involves alterations behind the scenes to ensure the new layout functions as it should.

5

A profile for change

1 An internal window offers a view into the kitchen area and counteracts any feeling of enclosure. Color articulates the architectural elements.
2 In a Paris apartment, great attention has been paid to the materials used: white stucco walls and large oak floorboards open up the space. Steel beams enclose an open raised hearth that runs the full length of a wall, transforming the fireplace into a piece of modern sculpture.

Once you have made an initial assessment of your home, you can begin to analyze what you have discovered and determine the type and level of change required. Your preliminary list may include both specific observations – 'new bathroom flooring needed'; 'overloaded electrical outlets in living room'; poor paint job in hallway' – as well as the less tangible – 'kitchen feels claustrophobic'; 'breathtaking view from living room'; 'no quiet office space'. The following stages will help you to translate these impressions into a blueprint for action.

First take a look at your answers and try to determine whether there is a particular pattern to the responses. If many of your concerns have to do with storage, accessibility and the ease with which various functions can be carried out, the solutions may involve replanning or reorganization. If you are basically just short of space, conversion or an addition may be the answer. If spatial quality is lacking, you can consider the possibility of architectural alteration. If there is a fundamental lack of efficiency in how any or all of your home's systems function, you may need to replace or upgrade them. Or, as is often the case, if problems are scattered across the board, you will need to think hard about where your real priorities lie.

The types of changes that are open to you fall into distinct categories, broadly determined by the extent of their impact on your home, your lifestyle and your budget. In practice, many improvements involve changes at different levels – if a wall needs replastering, it will also need redecorating, and so on – but it is important to be aware of what each type of change can offer.

REDECORATION

Technically the most superficial level of change, redecoration isn't necessarily the least important. You won't make your home structurally sound by giving it a new coat of paint, but you can make it more cheerful and allow its positive

3

qualities to shine through. Decorating is about enhancing what you have, bringing good features into focus, making the most of natural light and views, creating a sense of harmony and comfort. It also means choosing finishes and materials which are appropriate for the job they have to do and which will withstand the wear and tear they will receive.

If there are no outstanding problems with the basic structure or layout of rooms, but you still feel dissatisfied with your home, the solution probably lies in its presentation. In this sense, the term presentation encompasses all the main surface treatments for walls, ceilings and floors, as well as the way your home is furnished and lit. Good, sensitive lighting is a vital element in creating sympathetic, safe and workable surroundings and should never be underestimated.

Many of the options that fall within this category are relatively inexpensive and painless to carry out, involving far less disruption than building work or major repair. Particularly if you live in a rented space, are restricted financially, or expect to stay in your home for only a

short period, redecoration may be the most sensible action; the furnishings you acquire can easily be transplanted to a new location. But if the real problems lie deeper and it is within your power to rectify them, redecoration is largely irrelevant until they are sorted out, and it may even be a waste of time and money.

REPAIRWORK

The physical condition of your home is of prime importance. If you own your property, its structural health is inextricably tied to your financial fortunes. Making repairs isn't the most creative option, but doing so will prevent unwelcome and expensive changes being forced upon you and halt deterioration before it becomes disastrous.

Major structural faults will require immediate action and you may need to consult a number of experts to determine the precise nature of the problem and to help you to put it right. Buildings are attacked by a range of adverse factors, from land settling, earthquakes and erosions to dry rot and pest infestation. The symptoms may not always be obvious,

but unexplained cracking, patches of damp, persistent musty smells, sudden leaks, uneven floors and bulging plasterwork are all signs that something is going wrong somewhere. While every homeowner dreads the discovery of a major defect, delay will usually make matters worse – not to mention more expensive to fix. Large-scale repairs are generally disruptive and expensive, but you can make the best of a bad situation by taking the opportunity to extend the work and incorporate changes which actually improve your home, rather than merely restore it to decent condition.

You should also allow money in your budget and time in your schedule for minor repairs and upkeep. Poor surfaces aren't always symptomatic of underlying decay, but they effectively counteract any improvements you make elsewhere; painting cracked or veined plasterwork will give it a superficial freshness but won't disguise the basic problem and may end up looking even worse. Keeping on top of small problems as they crop up dramatically lessens the risk of a major calamity at a later date.

3 Partition walls that fall just short of the ceiling create a box room that separates the kitchen from the living area in this architect-designed house in San Francisco. The open fire, with its warmth and vitality, makes a natural focal point, an established tradition that retains a powerful appeal in period and contemporary interiors alike.

REORGANIZATION

Some of the most immediate and far-reaching changes you can make to your home have to do with its organization. A new layout can conjure space from thin air and transform confused, irritating daily routines into models of clock-like efficiency. Many of the solutions are, in fact, startlingly simple.

Many people are surprisingly conventional when it comes to assigning uses to rooms. Yet in many houses and apartments there is scope for choice, and breaking away from an unthinking acceptance of traditional arrangements can liberate much useful space. There's no reason, for example, why the biggest upstairs room should be the parents' bedroom when it is the children who would really benefit from the extra floor area. Provided relocation doesn't involve moving services around, this is one of the simplest changes you can make. Only marginally more complex are the types of alterations which reorganize 'circulation', or the way you travel from room to room. Blocking up doorways or creating new entrances can simplify room use dramatically and greatly add to the convenience of daily life.

Home organization naturally has a great deal to do with how and where things are kept. As your possessions accumulate, storage facilities often lag behind until confusion threatens to take over. Well-planned storage that is easily accessible is vital for a smooth-running household and represents a great space-saver in itself.

CHANGING SYSTEMS

The physical systems that serve your home – its heating, cooling, electricity, sewage and ventilation – are elementary for health, comfort and general well-being. Deficient or faulty systems are at best inconvenient and uneconomical; at worst, they may pose a real physical danger to yourself or to the fabric of your home. Replanning these systems to suit new spatial arrangements varies in

complexity and expense, but it is fair to say that the majority of this type of work requires professional assistance and is best carried out as early as possible in your program of alterations.

The environmentally aware hold to a wider definition of health and efficiency, which encompasses the longterm effects on the community and the planet. This has particular implications for energy consumption and waste disposal in the home and, as altruism is increasingly reinforced by public legislation (e.g., in mandated recycling programs), this dimension of home design and planning assumes greater importance.

ALTERING SPACE

For a real improvement in spatial quality, a fundamental change in light, volume and scale, you will need to alter the basic framework of your home: move walls, erect partitions, create openings, change levels or convert redundant space. The prospect of major restructuring fills most people with dread – understandably given the horror stories that survivors of this type of home improvement like to tell. If the risks are greater, then so are the benefits: if you prepare yourself properly ahead of time and are thoroughly acquainted with the pitfalls, you are less likely to drop into them.

A good deal of the complexity and, therefore, expense of such work hinges on whether the alterations are structural or not. Knocking a hole in an internal wall may not be; whereas breaking through an external wall certainly will be. You may need an architect, engineer or surveyor to tell you which is which. Some alterations require the approval of local agencies, such as the municipal building department; for most you will need the services of a qualified builder.

CREATING SPACE

In order to provide a real increase in overall area, the only option short of moving is to extend your home by adding on a new room or rooms, adding a

1

1 Roughly white-washed plywood partitions divide up a New York loft. A low platform covered in coir defines the sleeping area; a roll of thick industrial sheet-plastic serves as a shade to screen the space. Cork tiling inset in painted floorboards defines the sitting area.
2 In an Italian warehouse converted into a fashion designer's studio, large pieces of freestanding furniture provide practical storage and a means of visually anchoring and demarcating the space.

2

3 Stairs that double as drawers and cubby-holes make ingenious use of the space and provide storage for household necessities.
4 A thorough-going architectural approach to storage is evident in this imposing full-height library wall bisected by a mezzanine.

3

new story, or by making existing rooms bigger. The direct benefits of gaining more space are easy to imagine, but the implications go much farther than a simple increase in floor area. An addition such as a new wing or extra floors could affect your neighbors, and must be permissible under local building codes or zoning regulations; it will also affect the structure and stability of your home (which is why you need professional guidance); it will affect the external appearance of your home and possibly decrease usable yard or garden area; and it will affect the value of your property.

The decision to add on to your home must ultimately rest on whether you would be better staying put or moving. But if you're prepared to evaluate all the options objectively, and employ professional help when necessary, the results will easily repay your time and trouble.

4

Building from scratch

The ultimate challenge on the domestic front is to build your own home. The advantages are obvious, considerable and very real. No other option allows you to express yourself. If your wallet permits, you can specify every element of the design, materials and finishes, from the shape of the windows to the type of doorknobs, and take advantage of the latest technical knowhow, construction and materials. In areas where land is readily available and relatively cheap, building your own home can be very cost effective, provided you don't get too carried away.

In many parts of the world, building a new house rather than moving into an old one, is far from unusual. In Scandinavia, for example, it has been common practice for people to build their own homes for many years and standards are high, thanks to considerable official encouragement. In the U.S., while general patterns of real-estate development around the country make buying a newly built – but not custom-designed – house more likely for most, it is still quite possible to start from scratch. Land prices, zoning laws and other forms of regulation vary widely, as do regional styles, materials and even construction quality, so it's advisable to begin with thorough research of practices in your locality.

The idea of 'building it yourself' conjures up an image of log cabins in forest clearings. But in any house you build yourself, from a simple bungalow to a modernist masterpiece, the services of an an architect, surveyor and builder are usually required. Designing a private house is a commission architects love. If you and your architect are well matched, both sides will benefit from the work.

Finding a site can be somewhat tortuous. Desirable single lots on the edge of suburban sprawl can be hard to find. It is sometimes possible to buy an abandoned or derelict property, demolish it and replace it with your dream house. But pay careful attention to local size

1

requirements; you may have to rebuild within the 'footprint' of the original structure, which effectively rules out replacing a tiny cottage with a rambling family home. In the city, you may be required to relate the façade of your new house with existing properties in the street, which will not only affect its external appearance but may also determine its internal layout.

Unless you want to run the risk of buying land you are then forbidden to build on, the safest route is to approach a real-estate agent and buy a plot which has already received planning permission for domestic use. Depending on your area, planners may have plenty to say about the materials you can and cannot use in construction, as well as the appearance, size and style of your new house.

If you can surmount these obstacles, you are limited only by your imagination and budget. Building your own home allows you to create an environment which suits you in every respect.

2 Creating a new building in an urban setting entails sensitivity to architectural context. The A-line structure of this modern design in Paris reflects the proximity of a church, the shape echoing the view of the spire from the glazed end wall. A mezzanine level with a glass floor retains the sense of openness internally.

2

3

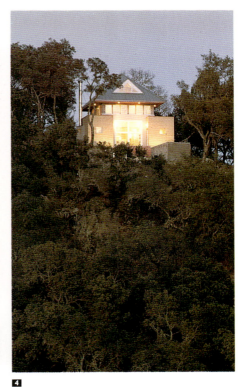

4

1 With all the appeal of an outsize tree-house, this Australian home makes brilliantly imaginative use of simple materials. The sail-like corrugated-iron roof follows the lines of the landscape and the path of the sun. The basic wood construction and expansive panels of glass form a three-story tower of single rooms – a powerful design which makes the most of the wilderness setting.

3 Perched on the rim of California's Napa Valley, a small family house commands great views of the country-side. The loft space forms a large bedroom, with big dormers that punctuate the roof and open up vistas through the surrounding trees.
4 Nestling among a wood of oak and pine trees, the south face of the house is almost a complete wall of windows on the ground floor, with a thin band of windows above, sheltered by the broad pyramidal roof.

Smith House, New York

Situated in the Catskill Mountains, New York, this new house is a small structure with a large voice. Its rigorous simplicity consists of three basic elements that converge to form the house: an L-shaped concrete wall, poured in place and forming a wall to the garden and the house; a two-story, wood-framed barreled vault which incorporates all the service functions (entrance hall, utility room, staircase, bathrooms and kitchen); and a perforated, wood-framed L-shaped wall sheathed in corrugated metal.

Perched on top of a small mountain, the house is approached up an inclined drive, the top of which becomes a circular parking court which sets up a formal and geometric relationship between house and garden. This is the public face of the building. On the northern side, the long concrete wall is punctuated first by a 'picture' window framing a view of the back of the house and thereafter by the sparse rhythm of tall, thin windows to the interior. The barrel-vaulted 'barn' intersects this wall at a slight angle.

The rear, which faces south, enjoys spectacular views of the mountains, a ski slope and a small village in the valley below. This private façade opens up to the light, and is mostly windows.

The interior design is predetermined largely by the formal clarity of the architecture. Although the house is small, its open-plan layout treats the interior as a complementary extension of the exterior, using a simple palette of materials. The kitchen cabinetry, for example, is built flush along one wall of the barreled

1

1 An impression of the perspectives afforded by the house and its site: from the back, windows open out onto the valley and surrounding mountains; the end of the concrete wall affords a view through the 'picture' window; the public façade at the front of the building.
2 The corrugated metal wall at the rear of the house is punctuated by tall windows, some of which, in fact, are doors. The living area is simply furnished and decorated so as not to distract from the simplicity of the structure.

2

3

vault using the same marine mahogany plywood as the exterior. This creates one continuous surface, inside and out, the kitchen disappearing into the wall when not in use. In the ground-floor bedroom, large sliding doors play up to the scale set by the expanse of wood, concrete and glass. When closed, the doors offer privacy; when open, they slide across to become a part of the wall, enclosing the entrance to the bathroom. Throughout, lighting is integrated to highlight the architecture and finishes. Color is used as a mediator of the architecture, rather than as decorative punctuation, blending interior with exterior, house with environment.

4

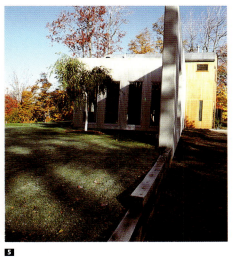

5

3 An exploded view of the house shows the location of the main rooms and services.
4 The large window in the poured-concrete wall affords spectacular views through to the open countryside.
5 The three basic elements of the house create a juxtaposition of form and materials that is at once both bold and harmonious.

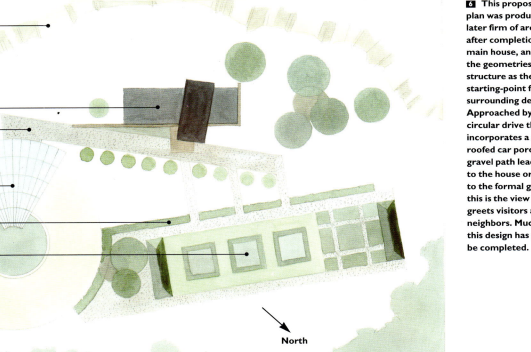

Cliff edge

House

Gravel path

Car porch

Hedge

Formal garden

Drive

North

6

6 This proposed site plan was produced by a later firm of architects after completion of the main house, and takes the geometries of the structure as the starting-point for the surrounding design. Approached by a circular drive that incorporates a clear-roofed car porch, a gravel path leads either to the house or across to the formal garden; this is the view that greets visitors and neighbors. Much of this design has yet to be completed.

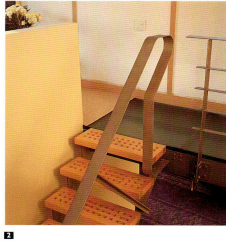

1 Brazilian walnut flooring runs through the main living area, which enjoys abundant natural light. The wood-burning stove supplements the forced-air heating and natural solar heat gain.
2 At the top of the staircase, a glass landing bridges the master bedroom and bathroom. The wooden stair treads, metal rail and glass floor unite three materials used in the main construction.

3 From the first-floor bedroom, doors open onto the white marble entrance foyer, which in turn leads to the main living area. The view also looks up behind the staircase to the glass landing above.
4 Apart from the island-unit sink, all the major kitchen utilities are housed in the barreled vault. When not in use, they are seamlessly integrated with the wall behind marine mahogany doors.

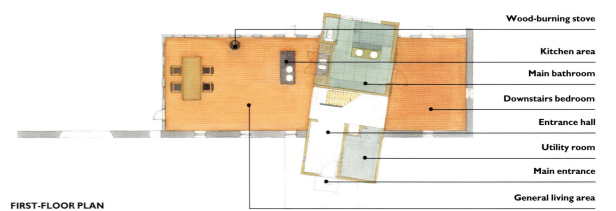

Wood-burning stove

Kitchen area

Main bathroom

Downstairs bedroom

Entrance hall

Utility room

Main entrance

General living area

FIRST-FLOOR PLAN

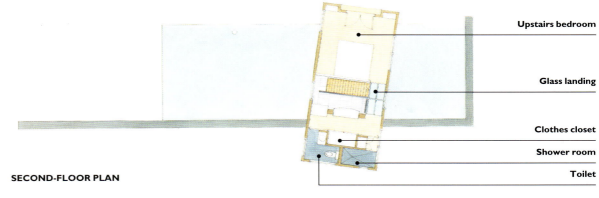

Upstairs bedroom

Glass landing

Clothes closet

Shower room

Toilet

SECOND-FLOOR PLAN

5

5 The shower in the main bathroom is in a step-down area behind the sinks. The wall of sandblasted glass blocks floods the room with natural light at the same time as retaining a sense of privacy.

6 Vermont slate tiles on the floor and walls complement the two cast-bronze sinks. The mirrored wall enhances the sense of space and light in the room. The sliding Japanese-screen doors lead to the toilet.

7

7 The upstairs bedroom makes a feature of the barreled roof. As is the case downstairs, the closet doors slide along the full width of the room and have a dual function. As shown here they form doors to the clothes closet; when pushed aside they cover the entrances to the toilet and shower room beyond.

Architects: Deborah Weintraub, A.I.A. and Scott Lane; additional interior detailing by Richard Lavenstein; subsequent site plan and proposed landscaping by Kiss + Zwigard.
See 'Useful Addresses' (pages 258-65) for full details.

6

KNOW YOUR HOME

A precondition for change is knowing what you've got in the first place. You may think you know your home, and if you've lived there for a while, you'll certainly be familiar with it, but do you really understand how it works, how each room relates to the others in terms of scale, shape and orientation? Do you know the dimensions of the rooms, the ceiling heights and sizes of the windows? Do you know the date it was built, or the structural and cladding materials? If you're sensitive to the age, layout and environment of your home, you'll be far more likely to arrive at a scheme for change that fulfills as many of your criteria as possible than if you embark on an ill-thought-through plan to knock down as many internal walls as possible, just because you're fed up with the cramped dimensions of the existing kitchen. Similarly, if your budget will only allow you to undertake essential work at the moment, it's still worth drawing up a list of long-term plans rather than embarking on alterations in a piecemeal fashion as the funds become available.

Part of the process of assessment is providing yourself with a concrete framework in which you can test your ideas. You may already have determined where improvements could be made, but before you rush out to commission the work, it is important to establish how your ideas jibe with and complement existing conditions. This may take the form of taking measurements, making floor plans and scale models, seeking advice or engaging in local research. This preliminary work should also enable you to make a realistic assessment of the extent to which you can carry out some or all of the work yourself. Many people are unduly suspicious of architects, designers and contractors – qualified professionals who should be there to make life easier for you. If you undertake an overambitious task yourself you are on a certain road to ruin. Undoing the damage will be costly and involve even further disruption; it is far better to ask around for personal recommendations of people in the construction trade, to inspect examples of their work, and to let someone better qualified take on the task of seeing through your plans. If you have a good understanding of the cost, scale and potential pitfalls of the job, you won't be taken for a ride.

1 Part of the process of assessment is to identify those details and features of your home which are intrinsically appealing. This shallow flight of curved steps calls for no improvement.
2 A pristine conversion of an old farm building in Portugal allows the form of the original structure to shine through without compromising comfort or intimacy.

3 An American townhouse has undergone a bold conversion in which the back is opened up to form a wall of glass. In the living area, a modern fireplace dramatically inset in the glass wall takes center stage.

4 Thoughtful allocation of space is essential for the smooth functioning of a multi-purpose layout. A dining area forms the buffer between living space and the kitchen built in along the end wall.

4

5 The sheer delight of this flight of stairs, fanned like a deck of cards, makes a strong architectural statement. Assessing your home is as much to do with identifying what you like as it is what you want to change.

5

Making a floor plan

A conventional kitchen layout – the L-shape – is turned inside out in an unusual plan that takes advantage of the view of an internal courtyard in this Parisian home.

Making a floor plan is time-consuming but otherwise presents few problems. Begin by making a rough plan of the room in question, then measure and fill in all the dimensions; from this you can draw up a scale plan on graph paper. Elevations – wall plans – are produced in exactly the same way: first make a rough sketch onto which you should transfer dimensions; then make a scale plan on graph paper.

Anyone can make a plan of their home. Getting it all down on paper will give you a much clearer picture of your home's space and proportions. It is very easy to misjudge the size and shape of rooms when you're relying exclusively on visual evidence and comparisons; there's no arguing with accurate measurements.

Making floor plans is an exercise in objectivity, enabling you to observe your home realistically. Plans are also an invaluable means of communicating your wishes to those you employ, and thus can prevent misunderstanding in instructing contractors, architects or suppliers. They are essential for testing the feasibility of your schemes and proposals.

Begin by sketching a rough diagram of each floor or room, showing the approximate shape and size, together with any connecting hallways, and the position of doors, windows and fixed features such as alcoves, fireplaces, radiators and built-in storage. If you aren't used to thinking diagrammatically, you may find this difficult at first, but keep at it until you have a fairly clear representation of the existing layout.

Now you should take measurements. Work as accurately as possible, using a tape measure or folding wooden rule. Don't rely on pacing – the figures need to be precise. Make sure you write down your findings. Measure the length and

width of each room, including the dimensions of features such as chimney breasts and alcoves. Measure the thickness of walls or partitions, the width of doorways and windows and the dimensions of built-in fixtures such as kitchen units. Transfer each measurement to the appropriate position on your sketch.

The dimensions you have taken may already indicate some inaccuracies in your sketch plan. The next step is to use your measurements to convert the sketch plan into a true scale drawing. This task is easier than it sounds, as long as you're prepared to work methodically. Before you start, equip yourself with a good ruler, a T-square, graph paper and a calculator.

A scale drawing is made using a fixed ratio that translates the actual dimensions of the room into ones of manageable proportions. In other words, you decide on a scale of conversion – say $\frac{1}{4}$in to 1ft – and use this as the basis for converting all the dimensions you took into the dimensions of your drawing. Professional designers and architects work at different scales, depending on the level of detail required on the plan. You may wish to double the scale suggested above for representing intensely planned areas such as a kitchen or a bathroom, but do not combine different scales on the same copy of your plans.

With a sharp, hard pencil, draw in the walls, using a T-square to form right angles at the corners (provided they exist). Mark on all the features in their correct positions. There are a number of

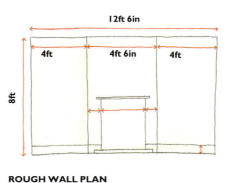

ROUGH FLOOR PLAN

SCALE FLOOR PLAN

ROUGH WALL PLAN

SCALE WALL PLAN

conventional symbols that you may wish to adopt to show details such as the direction in which doors open, or the position of switches, radiators and power outlets. Include all relevant detail, maintaining the same degree of accuracy throughout. You might also include other factors, such as a note of ceiling heights, the principal orientation of each room and the times of day it receives direct sunlight.

Once you are reasonably satisfied with your floor plans, make several photocopies of each one so you can begin to try out your ideas for making changes. If you want, draw in a furniture layout on one set – remember to work to the same scale, and measure each item accurately. Alternatively, you can cut out the shapes of your furniture and move the pieces

2 This kitchen alcove has been rigorously planned to make the most of the available space. Shelves suspended from the ceiling provide storage overhead; a high counter serves as a breakfast bar and space divider. Accurate measuring is essential to integrate built-in units with appliances.

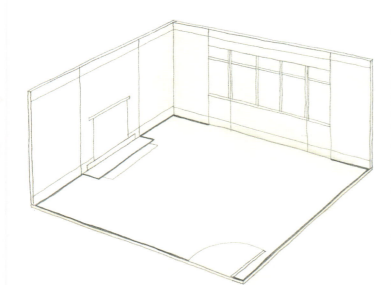

Using the scale floor plan and scale wall plans you can make a model of any room you are planning to change.

around on the plan to experiment with different arrangements. Again, work to the same scale, label each piece and color them in if it helps you to visualize what the effect might be. You can try out different spatial layouts by placing a sheet of tracing paper over your original drawing and sketching out the alternatives. Reserve one set to mark with the details of defects and essential repairs.

OTHER VISUAL AIDS

You can use the same basic technique that is involved in drawing up a floor plan to construct a more three-dimensional representation of any rooms in your home that you are planning to change. For this, you need to consider the vertical elements of the structure, as opposed to the horizontal features shown on a plan. What an architect terms the 'elevation' shows walls (interior or exterior) represented diagrammatically and exactly to scale.

Use the method already described to make sketches and then scale drawings of each wall in the area you are considering, showing the positions of windows, doors and other openings, as well as built-in features such as fireplaces or kitchen appliances. Stick the drawings, along with the appropriate floor plan, on sheets of cardboard or foam-core and carefully cut each piece out. By taping these pieces together, you can then assemble a scale model of a particular room or sequence of spaces.

Models are much easier for a lot of people to read and understand than drawings because they give a clearer

impression of volume and proportion. However, if you still find it difficult to visualize the effect that different alterations or arrangements may have, you can try working life-size. For this, you will need to buy a few rolls of wrapping paper and draw out the features you wish to add or change, such as a new door, window or opening between rooms and tape the paper up on the wall in the appropriate position. As with scale plans, the more accurate you can be about dimensions the more useful the exercise. Conversely, you could use the paper to mask out any openings you plan to block up. Rearrange the furniture to take account of the proposed changes and live with the new layout for a while to assess its impact on your home.

You could also make life-size cut-outs of existing furniture or of various pieces of furniture you plan to buy and then move these around on the floor. This will obviously save you a great deal of physical effort, while it will also help you to discover whether entrances are big enough to accommodate moving large items such as sofas, beds and dining tables in and out of various rooms.

Understanding structure

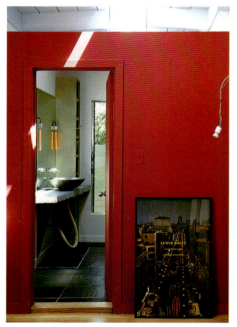

1

1 A strong earthy red
delineates the partition
wall enclosing a
bathroom. The wall is
taken high enough to
provide privacy but
stops short of the ceil-
ing, allowing light to
spill down from the
roof windows.

Until faced with the prospect of making
major alterations, few people give much
thought to the way their home is constructed. Most of us have some sketchy
notions about how buildings manage to
stand up, and even vaguer ideas about
the implications of moving walls around
or of changing windows and doors.
Understanding a little more about the
main structural elements will help you to
assess the cost and feasibility of a whole
range of spatial solutions.

Houses come in all shapes and sizes,
but they all hold together in roughly the
same way. You don't need a degree in
physics or structural engineering to
appreciate the principles of construction
– if you've ever built a house of cards or a
sandcastle on the beach, you'll realize
instinctively that the main issue is how
the weight of the building is supported.
If you overload the structure or weaken
it past a certain limit, the cards fall down
and the castle caves in.

All houses have foundations, external
and internal walls pierced by a number
of openings, one or more floors and a roof
covering it all. Starting at the top, the
weight of the roof – slates, tiles (natural
or synthetic), wood, perhaps glass – is
largely carried by the outside walls of the
house. These walls also support the floors
that span across them, with some of the
inside walls helping to carry the load. All
of this great weight rests on the foundations. The roof and the upper floors are
not merely passive loads to be supported,
but also act to brace the entire structure
and to give it rigidity and stability.

There are a number of variations in
how the support systems of different
buildings work. In large buildings, where
the outside walls are widely spaced apart
and the roof spans a great distance, there
may be internal columns that provide
additional support for the roof or there
may be substantial tie beams or trusses
between the walls to hold it all together.
On a domestic scale, the main variables
have to do with which internal walls play
a supporting role and which do not.

Many of the walls inside your home are
partitions – they divide up space but
play no part in holding anything up.
Others are structurally integral because
they help to carry the weight of the
floors above. Some walls may be semi-
structural if they are positioned directly
beneath walls on an upper level and
therefore act as a support for this weight.
If your house has wooden floors, you can
determine which internal walls are structural by looking at the direction of the
floorboards. The 'joists' or beams which
support the floor run at right angles to
the floorboards on the level above, which
are generally laid across the width of the
house. Any wall which carries the joists
will be structural: these are likely to be
the walls which also run side to side
across the house.

If there is an element of doubt about
the status of internal walls, there's no
uncertainty about the external walls. It
is likely that any substantial change to
an outside wall will affect the entire
structural system of the house. The same
goes for major changes to the upper
floors, roof and, of course, foundations.

2 Part of the appeal
of loft and warehouse
conversions is the
visibility of the main
structural components.
In domestic buildings,
identifying which
elements support the
house and which do not
may not be quite so
straightforward.

If you took away one of the outside walls, your house would fall down. In the same way, if you remove a portion of one of the exterior walls – to make a doorway or a new window, for example – you adversely affect the ability of the wall to perform its essential supporting job. Thus such alterations need to include a strengthening element, such as a beam or RSJ (rolled-steel joist) above the new opening to compensate for the weakness that the alteration introduces to the overall structure.

This also helps to show how certain defects can pose such a threat to stability. Dry rot, which attacks wood beams and joists, and settling, which undermines foundations, are among the factors that can cause severe and dangerous weakening to the structural elements of a house (see page 248).

3 Supported by steel beams, a new mezzanine level housing a bedroom and play space for two small children is slotted within a double-height space converted from a redundant warehouse. The toughened plate-glass window looks down on to the living space and kitchen area.

SUSPENDED TIMBER FLOOR CONSTRUCTION

Damp-proof course

Joist

Wall plate

Sleeper wall

SOLID FLOOR CONSTRUCTION

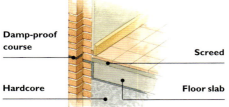

Damp-proof course

Hardcore

Screed

Floor slab

IDENTIFYING NON LOAD-BEARING WALLS

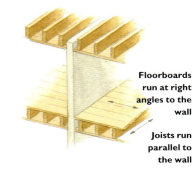

Floorboards run at right angles to the wall

Joists run parallel to the wall

IDENTIFYING LOAD-BEARING WALLS

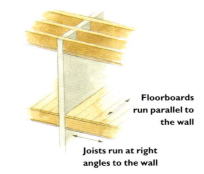

Floorboards run parallel to the wall

Joists run at right angles to the wall

3

■

■ An internal box-bedroom formed within a New York loft is crisply defined with color. Enclosing space with partition walls does not affect the structure of a building. ■ The kitchen, a step down from the living area, gains definition from the change in floor level. The same flooring throughout unifies the space.

This general picture should help you to assess some of the implications of spatial changes. All structural work should be properly appraised at the planning stage by an architect or engineer to establish the precise change in loads and to advise you on effective substitutes and safeguards to the structure.

As a summary, alterations to layout and new building work may have structural implications if it involves:

- Making a new opening in an outside wall, such as a window, door or French windows. This also applies if the opening forms a link with a new addition, such as a sunroom.
- Enlarging an existing opening in an outside wall, especially if the opening is widened, for example, by turning a single doorway into French windows. (However, making an existing opening bigger by extending it downward – for example, if you removed a lower section of wall under an existing window to turn the window into a doorway – may not have very great structural implications.)
- Removing all or part of internal load-bearing walls, for example, by turning two rooms into one or by creating an open-plan layout across one floor.
- Removing a chimney breast.
- Removing a portion of an upper-story floor to create a double-height space through the house.
- Altering the position of a staircase or adding a new one.
- Excavating a basement below the existing foundations so that it can be made into living space.
- Converting a loft into a habitable room, particularly if the ceiling joists have to be strengthened.
- Cutting away part of a roof to form a dormer window.
- Adding a new story at roof level or on top of an existing addition.
- Renovating a roof, and thereby increasing the weight of the roofing material, such as replacing slates with concrete tiles.

STRUCTURAL SURVEYS

If you are buying a new property or about to embark on a major program of renovation, it is a good idea to commission a full structural survey to determine the basic condition of your house. If there are any underlying problems of a serious nature, these must be corrected before you go on to spend money on improvements. Even if your house has a clean bill of health, an inspection can indicate precisely which elements are structural and help you to refine your plans. An inspector should also be able to advise you on the condition of various services – heating, plumbing and wiring.

Make sure any engineer – mechanical or structural – or other inspector is licensed in your area, and insist on a detailed written report. If you feel your inspector has been either too cavalier or too picky, get another opinion to ensure you have been given a realistic picture of the situation. If there do turn out to be serious structural defects, an inspector may suggest you go on to seek the advice of a structural engineer who will be able to tell you exactly what's involved in putting it right.

DATING YOUR HOUSE

The more you know about your house the better, and the older it is, the more sense there is in learning its history. Most of us are insatiably curious about previous occupants and their way of life, and older houses have fascinating stories to tell about evolving styles and uses. The whole issue becomes one of more than idle curiosity if you intend to renovate a period house or you plan to restore special features and characteristics lost through unsympathetic conversion.

Documentary evidence in the form of maps, deeds and census rolls may provide information on houses built since your county, city or town was incorporated and began keeping records, paticularly in urban areas that have been systematically developed. The local municipal or county archives or histori-

cal society should help you hunt down facts such as date of construction, details of ownership and possibly even original plans of the house. From these and other sources of written information or even historical photographs it may be possible to build up a surprisingly detailed picture of furnishings, size and use of rooms.

Where documents are sketchy, contradictory or missing altogether, you will have to look for clues in the architectural style of the house and any others like it that may be in the vicinity. Dating houses that have a long history can be problematic, since many will have been substantially altered and rebuilt over the decades. Old farmhouses, cottages or even urban brownstones may have had false fronts added at some point in their more recent life, or the core of the structure may have been almost completely obliterated beneath layers of subsequent additions. In some extreme cases, the true date of such houses only becomes apparent when repair or alteration brings evidence of much earlier period of construction to light.

Construction methods and architectural styles are not an infallible guide, however, since in rural or farming areas away from the fast-moving fashions of the town, innovations were slower to be adopted and older methods of building lingered on. Pay close attention to regional styles as well as adaptations of distinct European influences in areas with large concentrations of immigrants from a particular country. The most important thing to bear in mind is that renovation and redecoration should be sympathetic to the period, scale and character of the property.

2

3

4

3 The mellow quality of worn flagstone floor and battered wall finishes are pleasing indications of age and use. Natural materials wear attractively, acquiring character with the years.
4 Good architectural bones require little in the way of cosmetic dressing. Plain white walls and linen leave well enough alone.

Planning for change

The best-laid plans may often backfire, but setting out to change your home without any preparation is just begging for trouble. Planning is a state of mind that comes naturally to some people; others find it frustrating to curb their impulsiveness. If you're one of the latter, console yourself with the thought that by keeping your cool and imposing a little order and method on your approach, you will save yourself from almost certain disaster later on. Astronomical bills, months of dust, upheaval and inconvenience, and eventually a botched job are practically givens if you try to move forward without working your way carefully through all the variables, making contingencies for unexpected problems, and scheduling the work to cause as little disruption and frustration as possible.

Planning is the art of the possible. It involves reconciling ideals with reality and working out the best route to an end result. You shouldn't expect to sit down and immediately come up with a detailed plan of action straight away; the process should be gradual, as needs are refined, information gathered and options weighed, until you know you are ready to begin, and what it is precisely that you want to achieve.

At the beginning, the kinds of changes you wish to make may amount to a coherent, comprehensive program or simply a list of seemingly unrelated items, some of which conflict. But whatever shape your ideas are in, they are your starting place and represent one half of the planning equation. The other half comprises a number of vital issues which will determine how you proceed. Sooner or later you'll come up against a fixed point – it may be the amount of money you can spend, the time at your disposal, what is legally or technically feasible. These parameters give a plan shape and direction and suggest the best way of going forward. Without limits, plans remain vague and unfocused, with no real starting point or goal.

WORKING OUT A BUDGET

Money is probably the biggest determining factor in any home-improvement scheme. No one likes nasty financial surprises and since many types of alteration carry the risk of unforeseen expense, your financial planning should be detailed, cautious and conservative.

The advice given here assumes that you are a home owner; if you rent, different considerations come into play. As a tenant, you may be able to claim money for repairs and essential improvements from your landlord, depending on the terms of the lease. Anything else that you intend to do must be strictly affordable within your present budget, and achievable well within the timescale of the period you propose to stay in your home. You will need to consult your landlord for approval. Unless you have the security of a long lease, it is better to put your money into economical forms of decorating and furnishings you can take with you when you leave.

3

1 Big open rooms are exhilarating and versatile. In the heart of Paris, a couple in the fashion business bought a disused garage mechanic's workshop and set about transforming the space, opening it up to the light and enlivening it with furniture and fixtures from flea markets and building sites. **2** A shower alcove, tiled in ice blue, occupies a corner of a bedroom, a small loss in floor space for a large practical gain. **3** White appliances and kitchen units, neatly installed under a chunky wooden countertop, make a discreet, sympathetic addition to an old house.

The first step is to figure out what you can afford. Most people accept the need to budget for large-scale projects, such as a renovation or addition, yet resist forward planning for ongoing schemes of decoration and furnishing. However, even if your plans merely consist of a rolling program of relatively small-scale improvements, unless you set aside specific amounts for the expenses you will incur, you may find yourself deep in the hole in no time at all.

Consult your accountant, stockbroker, or financial planner to work out the safest and most sensible way of funding your proposals. Planners will help you to compare costs and can advise whether or not you will be able to deduct any of your expenses (including interest on a home-equity loan) or even if you are eligible for any tax credits.

Options for financing include:
• Utilizing a lump sum, such as all or part of your savings, an inheritance, or the balance on the sale of a property.

Borrowing part of the money, even if you have ready cash, may be cheaper in the long run; you may have other uses for your capital which have to be weighed against the benefits of paying for the entire scheme up front.
• Credit, such as short-term loans, overdrafts, credit-card borrowing. This is often an expensive solution and is best restricted to funding small-scale decorating and furnishing projects.
• Home-improvement or home-equity loans. You will need to work out how much you can afford to repay per month and whether your income will support this additional expenditure for the duration of the loan period.
• A second mortgage. If your current mortgage is much lower than the resale value of your home, the remainder – the 'equity' – can provide a basis for extra borrowing. The risk with this approach is that property values can, and do, fluctuate; being mortgaged up to the hilt is an uncomfortable position

in a declining market. You need to be sure that the improvements you are planning will add real value to your home, so you stand some chance of recouping your investment when you decide to sell.
• Grants. Houses in designated historic districts or those registered or landmarked as historic buildings themselves are sometimes eligible for local, state or federal government grants or assistance from private preservation organizations. Grants – not to mention historic homes – come with strings attached, however, meaning there are often stringent requirements about the standard and type of work that can be carried out.
• Making sacrifices. To raise small amounts of money you may be able to cut back in other areas – forgo the annual vacation or new car, perhaps.

Once you have arrived at a realistic figure which represents both what you can afford and what you are willing to spend, the next step is to cost out your proposals and see how it all adds up. Here lies trouble – reject vague optimism in favor of cold, hard fact. Some unscrupulous contractors and suppliers are all too happy to encourage the optimist, knowing that once work is under way you will be most vulnerable to extra demands for cash and least likely to resist digging deeper into your pocket.

To arrive at a reliable total estimate, first do your homework. Research the market. If you are buying materials or furniture yourself, compare different suppliers with a ruthless eye for variations in quality. If you are planning any kind of building work, find out what the work should cost. Ask neighbors or friends who have had similar work done what they paid for it. Get at least two or three detailed estimates in writing from recommended contractors or professionals. Always make sure that estimates cover both labor *and* materials, up to and including all those little extras, such as handles, catches and fixtures.

■

■ **Dividing up space offers the opportunity for imaginative constructions, such as this plywood-faced structure containing a mezzanine level used as a sleeping area.**

Remember to add in the cost of finishing the work. The true cost of rewiring, for example, includes replastering and redecoration as well as the electrician's fee and the cost of new fixtures.

These are the direct costs of your proposals. But there will also be hidden costs. These may include:
• The cost of financing, such as interest on loans or fixed repayments. You should also consider how your improvements will affect the investment potential of your home – will you be adding to its value in real terms? Some alterations may make your home harder to sell. Also, there's no guarantee that you will recoup the entire cost of your renovation or addition.
• Fees for advice, from accountants, architects, engineers or any other professionals whom you consult before commissioning the work.
• The cost of your time, if you plan to carry out some or all of the work yourself. Even if you delegate the entire job to a contractor, you should allow time for supervision or administration.

• An allowance for potential disruption or inconvenience. You can't put a price on sheer aggravation, but you can allow for the cost of eating out while a kitchen is out of commission, or for the price of having carpets and furnishings cleaned professionally if dust and debris prove excessive.
• Additional running costs. Will your home cost more to heat, light or insure once the work is complete? Will your property tax be higher?

Life is nothing if not full of surprises and some forms of building work seem guaranteed to come up with the unexpected. If there is the chance that you may uncover more than you bargained for, you should also set aside a percentage of the total cost as a hedge against disaster. This 'contingency allowance', as it is generally known, is roughly ten per cent for large jobs, but each case should be considered individually, depending on the scope of the job. Decorating, furnishing, applying new surfaces and finishes are largely predictable procedures if well planned, but

the more invasive operations, including any form of remodeling, major repair or new building work, may expose hidden difficulties along with the underlying structure. When the contractor brings you the bad news about the patch of mold or dry rot that has just been uncovered, knowing your budget can take the strain will help soften the blow. Overestimating how much you need to spend also allows you some flexibility as work progresses, if, for example, a chosen material proves to be impossible to get and the alternative is more expensive. Don't give yourself too much leeway, however, or you may be tempted to respecify and upgrade the work as you go along – there are few more certain short cuts to financial ruin!

ECONOMIES: TRUE AND FALSE

By now you should have some idea of how much you want to spend and how much your plan is going to cost. Unless you have either surplus cash or relatively modest ambitions, the two figures are bound not to match and you will have to

2

2 Sleek minimal interiors demand superb detailing and rigorous planning. Only the shelves of cook-books betray the presence of a kitchen area, installed behind a waist-high counter in an open-plan space.
3 Thorough planning is essential to achieve the best possible organization of fittings in a bathroom. In a small space, a matter of a few inches in either direction may make the difference between a layout that works and one that does not.

badly as well, repainting will be more frequent. If you cost out the greater quantity of paint needed and extra time spent, what little you appeared to save at the beginning will have evaporated. This kind of analysis is called 'value engineering', and your architect can probably help you with it.

Another temptation is to reduce the costs of labor by doing it yourself. Only you know your level of skill, but beware the new-found confidence that follows a high estimate. If you originally planned to hire a contractor or other professional to do a particular job, you should trust this original assessment of your abilities and look for other ways of economizing. Your time has value, too, and doing-it-yourself is not doing-it-for-free. Basic materials will cost more, since you will not be eligible for the contractor's 'trade discount'. You may also need to rent or

look at ways of bringing the cost down in line with your budget. The simplest and perhaps most sensible course is to tackle the really essential work first and postpone the rest of your plans until you can afford them. This enables you to complete the work in phases to the required standard of finish, which is ultimately more satisfactory than making do with second best on a larger scale; it will also give you some experience. It's important to see each stage through to completion; half-finished projects have a tendency to stay that way indefinitely.

Excessive cost may indicate that your plans could bear simplification. Run through your ideas with an architect, designer or contractor to look at other ways of getting the same result for less money. Standard components and building techniques are always cheaper than custom features: a straight partition wall costs less to build than a curved wall, for example. If the design is based on the dimensions of standard units – such as stair flights, kitchen units, windows and doors – it will be much simpler and hence

more economical to realize. This type of economy can be creative and you may even end up with a neater and more elegant solution.

Tantalizing shortcuts can turn out to be more costly; if it sounds too good to be true, it probably is. Cheapening up by downgrading materials, doing without specialist help and taking on more of the work than you are qualified to do can create a domino effect of disaster and spiralling costs.

The price of materials usually forms a substantial part of the cost of any alteration, and there is a temptation to cut corners in this department. If you've specified a luxury finish, there may be an affordable option which will do the job just as well for a fraction of the outlay, or a cheaper lateral solution of the same quality. But there is a line below which you should not go. Substandard products perform badly right from the start and you may have to redo the entire job. Cheap paint, for example, has such poor coverage that more coats will be needed to achieve a decent finish. Since it wears

3

A two-story house has been opened up to bring daylight from the roof windows down into the ground-floor rooms such as the kitchen and significantly increases the perception of volume. Running above the kitchen, a high-level walkway made of perforated steel makes a dramatic connection between different areas of the home, bridging rooms on the second floor and offering dynamic views through the space that offer multiple readings of the house and make it feel considerably larger than it is. The exhaust fan above the cooktop sits in an air-conditioning duct made from galvanized sheet steel and hangs from the ceiling way above, again emphasizing the height and maximizing the potential of the opened-up space.

buy tools. If you're inexperienced, you run the risk of ruining materials, causing damage to your house or even yourself, not to mention taking twice the time to complete the work. Is it really worth it?

Yet another common false economy is to do without professional advice. Obviously, there are plenty of home improvements that do not require outside assistance, but for large, complex projects that affect services and basic structure, some form of informed guidance is essential. Only politicians and lawyers are viewed with less esteem than building professionals. A lot of people fear exorbitant fees, or being bulldozed into solutions that they don't want, or being confused by terminology and unable to convey their wishes. These can be persuasive arguments for doing without advice when a little financial belt-tightening is in order.

Such objections largely spring from a misconception of what design professionals actually do. The right architect, engineer or designer should save you time, trouble and money by rationalizing plans, anticipating possible areas of difficulty and negotiating building permits.

A properly accredited professional with experience in the type of work you require is worth every cent of the fee (which may not be that high, especially for simple consultation). A signed contract and a written scope of work will give you legal authority and some personal leverage over the professionals working for you. If you are unhappy with the work, seek your lawyer's advice, contact the local building department and local oversight agencies. By the same token, anyone you employ to work on your home should come from a reputable firm.

ASSESSING PRIORITIES

A glance at the price tag may be enough to decide which changes are essential and which you could happily live without. If money is tight, repairs should take precedence over cosmetic improvements.

It is more difficult to assess priorities in cases where there are competing demands for the same space. If you're both clamoring for a study at a time when the children need separate bedrooms, you will probably have to accept that someone is going to lose out. Here it is best to opt for the changes which will benefit the whole household over the longest period, spreading out the value. A study may not be essential for the person who already has an outside office, whereas it may dramatically increase the efficiency of someone who exclusively works at home; separate bedrooms for growing children can cut down on sibling squabbles and give everyone a more peaceful life. Tricky as such negotiations can be, coming up against irreconcilable desires can force you to re-examine how you already make use of your entire home, and in the process you may find a better way of organizing space.

TIMING

Time is money; and in building terms, time also equals disruption. The cost of changing your home may be nothing compared to the emotional price of living on a building site for weeks on end. Before you put your plans into action, you should be aware how long it will take to complete the work and decide whether this is acceptable to you and the other members of your household.

Just as your budget should include contingency allowances, you should be generous in your allocation of the time needed to realize any project. Building work initiates a complex sequence of events which has the potential to break down at any point. Thorough planning can minimize delays, but there are always unpredictable factors.

Ensuring that work proceeds in the correct order is vital for avoiding costly and frustrating delays. This is the most difficult aspect to organize and varies widely depending on the complexity of the work. There are some procedures which can be grouped; others which

can't. There may be work which needs to pass inspection by local officials before the next stage can take place.

You should also plan to undertake the work at a time which fits in with your other commitments. Don't turn your home upside down and inside out when you're already overstretched at work, or you'll be battling on two fronts. The same applies if you've just had a baby, if you've just changed jobs, if someone in the household is studying for exams or getting over an illness. There may not be a perfect time, but some are definitely better than others.

Scheduling should also take account of the seasons. If you are building an addition or making structural alterations that involve working outdoors, choose a period of the year when the weather is on your side; except in areas of the South and West, winter is no time to replace a roof or cut a hole in the back wall. On the other hand, winters can be unseasonably mild or summers stormy, and there may be no real advantage in postponing work until the spring. Contractors are usually less busy off-season and may therefore price the job more competitively and finish it faster than during the peak building period.

FEASIBILITY

The remaining constraints concern the practicalities of achieving what you hope to do and whether or not your plans are legal. It shouldn't be too difficult to discover if what you envisage is physically possible or not. Get advice early on and be prepared to modify your plans accordingly. You may find that the work is more complex and more expensive than you'd imagined because of unforeseen structural problems, or that it's virtually ruled out for technical reasons, from complying with local building ordinances to your home's physical systems. More often, if you seek advice along the way, you'll discover that what you want is broadly feasible but there are a few complications you hadn't considered.

2 Three-quarter height partitioning encloses the entrance hall to this house without blocking out natural light.

Large-scale alterations and new building work generally have to comply with a number of legal requirements designed to ensure that what you do is safe and acceptable to the community. Planning or zoning laws may determine the size and scale of an addition, the materials out of which it can be constructed and its relationship with adjacent properties. If you live in a designated historic landmark, the rules about what you can and can't do vary. Check with your local building department and historic preservation office about size, scale and extent of what you can build onto your home.

Remember, building and zoning laws vary widely, not only from state to state but city to city and even among suburban townships, as well as neighborhood to neighborhood in large urban areas.

- Positioning. Building onto walls shared with neighbors (party walls) is sometimes subject to consent. Ask your lawyer to review your deed. You may also have to ensure that your plans don't block light or views from other houses.
- Density. If you increase the amount of accommodation in your home, the new density level (in residential districts, the number of units per dwelling) must conform to local zoning rules.
- Structure. Some alterations must be approved by local building inspectors to ensure that your home will still stand up after you've made changes to the basic structure. Building materials are especially open to scrutiny.
- Health. New rooms or a new layout of space must also conform to local building codes, which may require standards for size, height or ventilation.
- Fire risk. Fire codes also vary among the states, but protection from fire and means of escape in case of fire are paramount standards everywhere that must be met.
- Specific approvals and some assistance may be needed from gas, electric or water utilities, or from environmental or building inspectors.

Getting it done

■

■ **Basement areas are notoriously dark and enclosed. This glazed addition, half a level down from the garden, introduces light to a basement bedroom and provides a welcome sense of connection with the world outside.**

There's an obvious difference between planning to paint the back bedroom on the next rainy afternoon and planning to extend the kitchen by constructing a new sunroom or creating an extra bedroom in your roof. In the first case, you can afford to act on impulse, drop your brush when you've had enough and pick it up again when you feel like it; whereas the second type of plan demands careful forethought and discipline if you're not going to make a complete wreck of what you've already got.

Things get much more complicated when a job requires outside assistance. Even before a single tool has been lifted, you will need to have devoted considerable time and effort to making sure that everything has been properly organized. Hiring people to do the work for you is the only safe and sensible course of action for tasks that demand specialist knowledge, skills and equipment, but finding the right professional help is more than a matter of dialing the first number you find in the Yellow Pages. Researching the market, thorough briefing and consultation and efficient scheduling won't guarantee a successful result, but should tip the balance in your favor.

WHO DOES WHAT

Before you can employ anyone, you have to know what services you require. The more complicated the job, the more advice and assistance you'll need. Most jobs can be broken down into three stages: planning and design; supervision and administration; and the actual building work. You may need help in all or some of these spheres to see your plans through to completion.

PLANNING AND DESIGN

Architects, designers, engineers and inspectors can help make a job run smoothly; more importantly, they can play a critical role in formulating what needs to be done. The architectural profession regularly attracts controversy, the mystique of the design process accounting for at least some of the bad press that it receives. But for every high-profile designer of contentious landmark buildings, there are hundreds of others who work happily on the domestic scale, carrying out sensitive and appropriate alterations to ordinary homes. On this level, if you choose the right person, you won't need to worry about sky-high fees, avant-garde solutions (unless that's what you want) or professional arrogance. What an architect should offer is a new way of solving a spatial problem; a special knowledge of building materials and techniques; legal requirements; and structural constraints. The work may range from an hour's consultation to a more ongoing involvement producing a detailed specification for a contractor to work to, or a set of drawings to submit for a building permit. An architect may also be able to put you in touch with the right contractor or subcontractors for the job. Fees are scaled according to the level of involvement.

You may also need the services of a surveyor or structural engineer at this initial stage if you require a detailed assessment of structural defects to your house or apartment or a report on the condition of existing services.

SUPERVISION

A full architectural service includes 'on site' supervision of the job. As such, the architect acts as your representative and ensures that all the contractors work to plan, schedule, budget and agreed standard. If the work involves legal consents or official inspections, the architect should handle these matters as well. When the contractor announces that the job is complete, the architect will perform a punchlist inspection to ensure the work is truly satisfactory, an invaluable service if your eye isn't trained to spot oversights, shortcuts and imperfections. The architect is fully capable of demanding that shoddy work be redone at no cost to you. It is difficult to overestimate the importance of this function.

On a large job, organizing and scheduling the work is a major headache and it may be well worth the extra money to have someone else do this for you, whether either the architect or the main contractor. For an uncomplicated alteration, there's no real reason why you can't manage this role yourself, provided you understand what's involved, and it may well be difficult to find an architect who's prepared to oversee a small job in any case. A comprehensive architectural service is usually billed as a percentage of the overall cost of the work.

BUILDING WORK

There is a vast range of trades and crafts associated with home building, repair and restoration. Some firms are expert in only one or two related fields; others are multi-discipline; most employ a core of staff which is supplemented by subcontractors for the more specialized work. You need to be sure that the range of skills implicated in the proposed work is adequately covered by the firm you eventually engage to carry it out.

The alternative, especially for work such as rewiring, changes to your plumbing arrangements, new plasterwork, and so on, is to employ craftspeople on a direct basis, without using a general contractor as an intermediary. If the job demands only one or two disciplines, it may be more effective to hire a different person for each stage – say, an electrician to do the rewiring and a designer to make good surfaces afterwards. This is only feasible if there aren't too many separate stages to go through, unless you really want to go to the trouble of finding a whole number of different craftspeople, briefing each one and obtaining a series of estimates for each job. It is also essential to identify the correct sequence of procedures; and remember, if you decide to go it alone, you may also have to organize the deliveries of materials and fixtures.

On the other hand, you may discover that it's hard to track down anyone prepared to tackle a really small job. Small jobs simply aren't cost-effective, even for many small firms; and, together with the aggravation factor, this may mean that you either get an unreasonably large estimate for the work or an open-ended commitment to fit the job in as larger, more profitable projects permit. Either you can pay up, sit out the wait (which may be considerable), or you can revise your plans and group a number of related jobs together to make a more attractive package for pricing and scheduling.

The advantages of using a general contractor, especially for a large, complex job, are obvious. You will pay more for the service, but there are hidden savings to be made. When work is extensive, in part because there are inevitably areas of overlap, the role of the contractor is to coordinate everyone's efforts so that each job proceeds in the most efficient way. Without anyone on site acting in this supervisory role, it is all too easy to waste time, money and effort. If, for example, an electrician lifts some floorboards to lay a new length of cable, replacing the boards afterwards, and then a plumber comes along the next day and needs to take up the same section of floor to install pipework, you can see how, by failing to anticipate each

procedure, you might end up effectively paying to have work duplicated, not to mention suffer the consequent delays and irritation for everybody, as well as increased potential for mistakes or poor workmanship. Subcontractors – such as electricians, plumbers and mechanical engineers – like to target their efforts and hate being kept waiting. They expect the building to be ready for them when they arrive so they can get on with the job and proceed to the next as fast as possible.

Some general contractors also offer what is called a 'design/build' service, which can be an attractive alternative to using an architect if the proposed plans are straightforward. In this case, the contractor will commission drawings of the changes, which can form the basis of a planning submission if one is required. At its best, this approach can be faster and cheaper. But if you're after an original solution or an approach that departs from standard building practice, it's far better to employ a professional designer.

FINDING HELP
Hiring the right person or firm for the job is half the battle. It's up to you to match skills and experience to the type and scale of the work; after that, it's up to them to execute it to order. Whoever you hire should be accredited professionals in their own field, trained and equipped to carry out the work to an acceptable standard, and experienced in jobs of a similar size and nature. It's easy to imagine the kind of difficulties you could get into if you employ someone who is unqualified, unscrupulous and unreliable; easy to imagine, but not so easy to avoid: it happens all too often.

Whether you're looking for an architect, builder, plasterer or plumber, the best route is personal recommendation. Ask friends if they can recommend anyone for the type of work you're planning; you're more likely to get a frank assessment this way. You can always ask to view the work to check that your friend's definition of a good job matches your own.

2

A personal testimonial isn't enough, however; you should go on to establish whether there are proper qualifications or credentials to back it up. Most professions are controlled by national trade organizations, such as the American Institute of Architects, that seek to maintain standards of training and workmanship in a particular field. If you can't find anyone through word of mouth, you could check with one of the organizations listed at the back of this book and ask for a list of reputable firms to approach. Nonetheless, professional status is increasingly a gray area; beware vague, professional-sounding titles which are no guarantee of full training. First of all, you need to be sure the people you intend to employ can accomplish what you want; secondly, and more cynically, you need to know you have some legal redress if anything goes wrong.

Once you've drawn up a short list of possible contenders, ask for references from previous clients or details of jobs completed. Don't hesitate to follow these up; a good professional has nothing to hide and won't balk at providing you with the sort of information you need to make up your mind.

2 A single-line kitchen makes good, hard-working use of a narrow area. The same basic ergonomic principles apply to kitchen design, however much – or little – space you have at your disposal.

Commissioning the work

If you intend to commission the building work directly, without architectural help, you need to be able to compare costs. This entails coming up with a specific program for the work, called a 'scope of work' and getting a number (not less than two, and preferably three) written estimates from those on your short list. Don't cut corners here; prices can vary widely and by doing your homework and a little extra research, you may make a substantial saving. Bear in mind, however, that the lowest estimate may not always be the best bet. A really low bid for a job should arouse your suspicions as much as an astronomical one. What you're looking for is a reasonable, realistic price for the work and a good overall level of performance.

An estimate is only as accurate as the program you've provided. Be specific; if you're in doubt about what you want, get some advice and firm up decisions before any of the building work begins. Put everything in writing, preferably with annotated plans attached, and keep copies of all of your correspondence on every point, however minor, especially if you change your mind. Don't take anything for granted; if you don't specify the standard you want or the finish you require, you are more likely to be dismayed than pleasantly surprised by the result. In addition to a firm idea of the eventual cost, an estimate should also provide you with a starting date and a schedule for completion. You must make clear that any subcontracts which arise and which have not been agreed to at the outset will have to be approved by you before payment can be made.

Briefing anyone who's going to perform work on your behalf is about good lines of communication. You don't have to learn a new language to make your wishes plain, although it clearly helps if you're informed and have some passing acquaintance with common terms. When you don't understand a technicality, don't be afraid to ask for an explanation. If you find it easy to be swayed by fast

talk, delegate the briefing role to a partner or friend who will stand their ground. Finally, remember that you aren't asking for a favor, you're asking – and paying – for a service and you're entitled (within reason) to get what you want. At the same time, you may find that some of your ideas simply aren't feasible, practical or legal: in this case, listen to the advice you're given and adjust your sights accordingly.

Once you have made your decision and approved an estimate, it's a sensible idea to formalize the arrangement with the people you're employing in a written contract. An architect, for example, might be commissioned on the basis of a letter of agreement, setting out clearly the services you expect, the timetable and the fee you will pay. For contractors, there are 'minor works contracts' which stipulate the time in which a job may be finished, often including a penalty clause for late completion. It is also usual to set aside a percentage of the overall fee (about five per cent), which is retained for a period of up to six months in case of defects. The contract should also set out the terms of payment: after completion for a small job; at agreed interim stages for more complicated work. By staggering payments, you have the option of withholding the next installment if you are dissatisfied with the work to date.

THE SEQUENCE OF WORK
Coordinating the work so that everything happens in the right order is a fine art. Get it wrong, and you will have delays, work unnecessarily duplicated and extra wear and tear on your home, wallet and peace of mind. Good craftspeople tend to have full calendars and if they risk losing another job because yours is not ready for them on time, you may lose their services altogether. It's no less heartbreaking to see newly plastered walls ruined because the electrician wasn't called in early enough, or to have to dig up a freshly laid floor so that the pipes can be inspected.

As a general guide, the rough sequence of events, whether you're building an addition or doing interior renovation, is as follows:
- Obtaining planning permits and other preliminary consents.
- Clearance and demolition. Depending on the work, this may range from moving the furniture out of the way to knocking down existing structures and stripping out your old systems. Unsupported structural elements will need to be propped, and Dumpsters organized to remove rubbish.
- Preventive or curative treatments, such as dampproofing, spraying against rot or pest infestation.
- Earthworks, such as digging foundations or drainage trenches.
- Laying new sewage lines, with inspection if required.
- Installation of major external connections to other systems, such as gas and electricity mains and telephone and television cables.
- New walls built and solid floors laid.
- Roof structure built and covered as quickly as possible.
- Major mechanical system work, such as the installation of boilers, air ducts and pipework or electrical conduits.
- Major carpentry work, framing up doors and windows, studwork, floor joists.
- Plastering.
- Installation of fixtures and utilities, such as bathtubs, sinks and toilets, outlet plates, radiators, fuse boxes. Alternatively, some elements of this type may not take place until after decoration is finished.
- Second phase of carpentry work, such as hanging doors, fixing door linings, baseboards and moldings.
- Some floor finishes, depending on what other work remains.
- Built-in fixtures and fittings, such as kitchen units and appliances, bedroom wardrobes and fixed shelving.
- Decoration.
- Carpeting.
- Furnishing and arrangement.

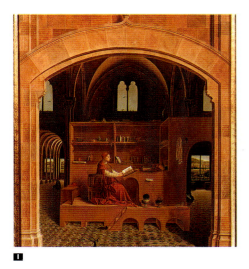

Because each job is different, this summary can only indicate the approximate order of various procedures. If you're using a general contractor or an architect to supervise and administer the work, these guidelines should help you understand what's going on. But if you're intending to supervise the job yourself, you'll have to go into greater detail. Consult suppliers and subcontractors to determine precisely how long they expect to take at each stage and the conditions they will require to do their job right. This also means getting a firm grip on delivery dates for materials and fixtures. You need to ensure that not only will the plumber turn up on the right day, but so will the sink he's coming to install. If necessary, you may have to organize a meeting of all concerned to work out a definitive schedule.

ON SITE

The big day has finally arrived and your house echoes to the sound of hammering and the clump of big boots. You may think you can sit back, fingers crossed and wait for your home to emerge, like a butterfly from a chrysalis, in its stunning new incarnation. Unfortunately, your role does not end with your signature at the bottom of the builder's contract. There's still a job to be done ensuring that work on site proceeds smoothly.

Close encounters with the building trade can fray the toughest nerves. What began as an amicable relationship can rapidly deteriorate to all-out war if you and your contractor don't establish some ground rules from the start. Before the builders put one foot on site, put your valuables in a secure place and store breakable objects: lamps, pictures, light fittings – anything easily damaged or broken. Clear the space where the work is to take place and wrap or cover as much as possible in the vicinity to keep off dust – dust can travel an amazing distance, especially if the work involves hacking off old plasterwork. Electronic equipment is particularly vulnerable.

You don't have to run a full catering service, but it is reasonable for you to provide access to the kitchen for heating up meals or making hot drinks, as well as access to the bathroom. In return, you should make it clear that you don't expect your freezer or liquor cabinet to be raided or to find a heap of your best dishes dirty in the sink.

Mess is unavoidable and some jobs are dirtier than others. Within reason, you can ask your builder to tidy up at the end of each day and allocate a place where tools and materials can be stored overnight. Obviously, thorough cleaning is a waste of time until the really messy work is complete, but you are entitled to expect a certain standard of care.

When it comes to supervision, it is important to strike the right balance. Don't hover in the background, offering what you imagine to be helpful advice – no one appreciates being told how to do their job and you'll only be in the way. On the other hand, don't disappear from the scene if there is work to inspect: you may find that by the time you come back it's too late to change anything you don't like. At the beginning of each day, ask what's likely to happen and if there are any stages that you need to approve. In the normal course of events, the end of the day is the right time to view the work and make sure everything is going according to plan. With a little luck – and you'll need that, too – it will be.

1 Inspiration can come from the most unlikely quarters. *St. Jerome in his Study* by Antonella da Mesina (1456-79) was the point of departure for the design of a home office.
2 The contemporary reworking of St. Jerome's study translates the idea of a raised, self-contained room within a room into a high-tech construction of steel and glass.

CHANGING SYSTEMS

Like the human body, the home has its own physical systems – heating and cooling to regulate temperature, electricity to power light and domestic appliances, plumbing and sewage to bring in fresh water and remove waste – and lines of communication. Equally, there are services that are supplied through largely hidden networks of cablework and wiring buried within the structure. We depend on these systems for our personal comfort and convenience as well as health and safety, but we often don't know much about them – until, that is, they suddenly break down or need replacement, when technical specifications and professional prognosis generally prove no more intelligible than medical jargon.

Technology has brought enormous changes to our standard of living in an incredibly short space of time. The physical conditions we now enjoy in the home would have astonished most people 100 years ago, and the pace of change is accelerating. Keeping up with what's available isn't always easy, especially if you start with only a sketchy notion of how the servicing of your home operates. You can't expect to acquire the expertise of a heating engineer or a qualified electrician overnight, but learning a little about the infrastructure of your home and the utilities that service it will enable you to make sensible decisions and better use of professional advice.

Changes to systems don't always arise through breakdown; they are also part and parcel of many of the spatial alterations you carry out to improve your home, such as building an addition, converting an attic or basement, installing a new kitchen or bathroom. If you are planning substantial changes to the layout and organization of your home, this will generally entail disruption of existing systems, and a rerouting of supplies or even new installation. In many cases, changing the services accounts for the greater part of the work and the expense, so it's worth taking some time to understand the options available and the processes involved. There are only a limited number of procedures that you can do yourself. Sound professional help is advisable both to plan and execute the work. Additionally, approval may be required to ensure that any changes to services meet minimum standards of health and safety.

1 High-quality materials and fixtures repay the investment in practical performance, durability and good looks.
2 Exposed ducting and pipework and a spaghetti of cables let it all hang out in the servicing arrangements of this mountain-side kitchen.

3 Heating your home can be a complex business, not least because of the increasing range of options. The polished steel flue of this modern wood-burning stove is an architectural element in its own right.

4 A wall-mounted Anglepoise lamp provides versatile and unobtrusive bedside lighting. You need to plan the position of power points and built-in light fixtures from the outset to gain the maximum benefit.

5 The conventional view is that radiators should be as discreet as possible, concealed behind grilles or painted in with the walls. Painted black, this classic radiator has a retro appeal in a New York apartment.

4

5

Heating

Central heating has quietly revolutionized the way we live, even the way our homes look. Dependably warm interiors don't need layers of heavy drapery and aren't proscribed in scale by the heat-emitting power of a single source.

Central-heating systems essentially convert fuel to heat in a boiler or furnace and then distribute it to different parts of the house. In wet systems, the heat is conducted via hot water in radiators; in dry systems, warmed air circulates in ducts, escaping via grilles (the system can be adapted for air conditioning). The alternative, for areas of the world where there are no prolonged cold spells, is to warm rooms as required with individually controlled space heaters.

Choosing a system involves taking into account a wide variety of factors, such as the cost of installation and fuel consumption, maintenance, comfort and control, flexibility and the visual appearance of heat sources. The age of your house and the degree of insulation, your pattern of room use, the region in which you live and the availability of different fuels will also influence your decision.

In general, it is better to spend more initially on a system in order to use fuel more efficiently over the life of the system. Similarly, staggering on from one year to the next with an old boiler will cost much more in the long run than installing a new appliance with all the advantages of an energy-efficient, updated design. The benefits from heating systems are maximized by good insulation; great strides have been made in this area to reduce energy consumption and minimize environmental damage.

A critical factor in any heating system is thermostatic control. A central thermostat must be sited carefully to avoid overheating the upper levels of a house and thus wasting fuel; the hallway is generally recommended as a sensible location; a better and more flexible solution is to fit individual thermostats on each radiator or else to use room thermostats which allow you to read the temperature of each area. Modern central thermostats offer digital control, allowing you to pre-set the time and temperature of both the hot water and heating, either separately or together.

ELECTRICITY

The most popular forms of electrical heating are by storage heaters or cables set into floors or ceilings. Hot water is provided by an immersion heater, which is thermostatically controlled. Storage heaters generally operate off-peak, using cheap electricity to generate heat which is then stored within the heater.

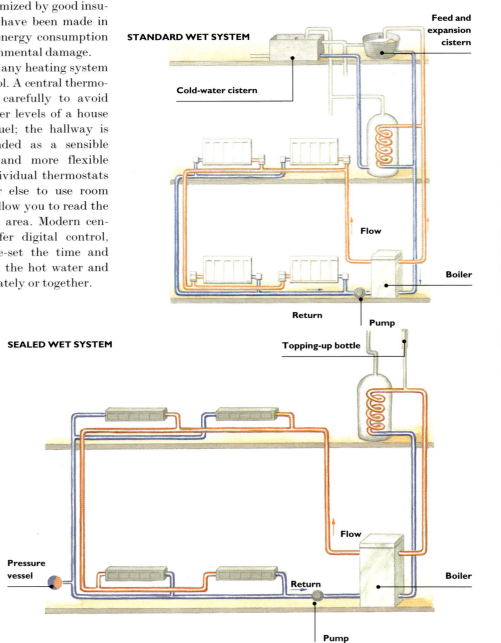

■ The cliché of fake burning logs or coals is wittily subverted by this strikingly original customized design for a gas fire. The heavy iron chain glows red as it heats up.

STANDARD WET SYSTEM

Feed and expansion cistern

Cold-water cistern

Flow

Boiler

Return

Pump

DRY SYSTEM (WARM AIR)

Outlet grille

Warm-air ducts

Return air ducts

Heater

SEALED WET SYSTEM

Topping-up bottle

Flow

Boiler

Pressure vessel

Return

Pump

The advantages of electricity include the fact that all homes already have a power supply, although this may need upgrading, while the cost of installation is low; and heaters can be individually controlled. In new homes and where insulation is good, electricity can be very efficient. In older houses, storage heaters may only be affordable as background heating. However, as insulation levels rise and the heating in a home's energy costs becomes less significant, and as electricity prices fall relative to other 'fuels', individual low-power room heaters may regain popularity.

GAS

Gas is used to power boilers in wet or warm-air systems. A new development is wet underfloor heating systems, sunk in solid floors or running in metal trays in suspended floors. Because gas is burned in the appliance, there must be a flue to vent the waste gases, either via an existing chimney or fitted in an external wall. New boiler designs are far more efficient and compact than previous generations; condensing boilers allow heat to be recovered from the flue gases; anti-cycling controls minimize the heat loss that occurs each time the boiler switches off. Increasingly, standard combination boilers heat water directly from the mains, eliminating the need for either hot-water cylinders or cold-water cisterns. Powerful enough to run a system of radiators, they may pose a problem when simultaneous demands are made.

OIL

Oil-fired central heating could decline in use if once-volatile prices return, like those following the shortage crises of the 1970s and '80s, and as awareness increases about this shrinking natural resource. A storage tank outside the house holds the supply for a boiler, which can be used with wet or warm-air systems. A check must be made on the level of oil in the tank and deliveries arranged to avoid interruption to heating.

1

1 The simple device of paneling the adjacent walls with mirror accentuates a white-painted brick fireplace, multiplying views and increasing the sense of spaciousness.

2

SOLID FUEL AND WOOD

Central heating can be powered by burning coal to heat a back boiler serving a wet system. Closed coal fires allow an attractive view of the heat source and can be installed in existing chimneys with the appropriate flue lining. However, they are messy and bothersome to light. Only certain types of coal are allowed to burn, to lessen damage to the environment; some coal-burning appliances contain a 'smoke-consuming' element to minimize the emission of waste gases. Adequate storage facilities for fuel deliveries and regular cleaning and maintenance of the flue are vital if the system is to operate efficiently.

Wood-burning stoves generate a lot of heat and far less pollution than old-fashioned coal stoves. Because the heat source is generally within living areas, stringent safety precautions for flue maintenance and installation are usually required and are certainly advisable. Wood must be properly seasoned, and some species deliver better heat than others. Your supply of firewood should be salvaged from waste piles or from sustainable, managed sources.

2 A wood-burning stove supplies additional heat and a handsome focal point. Neat and unobtrusive, low-level warm-air convectors fixed at the base of the curved exterior wall maintain a stable background temperature.
3 The radiator as space divider: the traditional chunky design of this fixture forms a low barrier at the head of the stairs.

DESIGNING A SYSTEM

It is essential that you always work with accredited professionals to design or adapt a heating system to meet your specific requirements. If you extend your system appreciably, into a new area, for example, you may need to upgrade the boiler to deal with the extra demand. Use a floor plan to work out where radiators or other heat sources are best positioned, so that they provide you with maximum flexibility when positioning furniture, and so that you will minimize heat loss and simplify any new pipe runs that are required. Seek advice as well as several opinions.

Radiators, as the name suggests, work by radiating heat and ideally should not be shielded by heavy drapery or large pieces of furniture. Proximity to a heat source can damage fine finishes and ruin musical instruments, such as pianos. There are many styles available, including standard single or double panels, which can be decorated to match wall finishes, low-level radiators, finned radiators to maximize heat surface and warm air convectors that run off wet systems. Standard cast-iron radiators are increasingly seen as attractive, although 'designed' radiator covers are available if you prefer. Don't be tempted to compromise efficiency for the sake of looks: the graphic quality of many radiant heaters can be a positive aesthetic asset, not an eyesore to be carefully concealed behind fancy covers and grilles.

INSTALLATION

Local utility companies and agencies are responsible for bringing gas, electricity and water to your property boundary; however, from there to your home, the supply is at your expense. Increasingly, there are attempts to coordinate services so that they can be routed in together, minimizing disruption to the road. Installing any main is the job of the utility company concerned.

The positioning of meters – the route, type and dimension of the pipe or wiring – is carefully controlled by local building codes, as is the positioning of gas pipes. Siting and ventilation of boilers and siting of flues is also subject to approval. Utility companies usually prefer meters to be external – siting can present something of a visual challenge!

Insulation and plumbing

1 These two houses represent the percentage of heat lost before (top) and after (below) insulation. The figures vary according to the type of building you live in – a bungalow loses an even greater proportion of heat through the roof, whilst in a ground-floor apartment there is less heat lost through the ceiling than there is through the roof of a house – but wherever you make you home it is worth ensuring it is properly insulated (see page 250).

INSULATION AND VENTILATION

Insulation keeps heat from escaping through the walls, floors, roof, windows and doors, and means you use less fuel and spend less money. It works both ways too, keeping homes cool during the summer months. Once considered merely a desirable or even optional extra, it is now increasingly viewed as one of the principal ways of maintaining even temperature levels in the home. Low-energy specialists are devising new methods of insulated construction that cut fuel needs practically to zero, although the capital costs of installation are high. However, it makes no sense to turn up the heating to cope with the results of poor insulation – you are literally throwing money out the window.

The areas to insulate include walls, under the ground floor and in lofts between ceiling joists (leaving the roof space well ventilated). Draftproofing windows and doors, laying carpet and hanging lined curtains are simple ways of keeping the heat in. In addition, hot water pipes, cylinders and storage cisterns should be lagged. Choose insulants that are HFC- (hydro-fluorocarbon) and CFC- (chloro-fluorocarbon) free.

Some forms of insulation, including secondary glazing, work by almost sealing the house hermetically, which means that no air, warm or cool, can escape. The result is often unacceptable levels of interior condensation, which builds up on windows and at 'cold bridges' or gaps between insulation. Condensation is not only uncomfortable, it also has the effect of rotting materials and finishes. The technological answer is to provide mechanical ventilation, such as extractor fans, to supplement other external openings; specific mechanical ventilation requirements are very often stipulated by law for kitchens and bathrooms. Environmentalists have shown that the sequence of insulation-condensation-ventilation still results in warm air being needlessly expelled from the home, and they offer alternative solutions.

PLUMBING AND SEWAGE

Alterations to kitchens and bathrooms can affect the supply and route of water around your home. Simple jobs, like plumbing in a new washing machine or dishwasher, involve very little effort or expense; but any work which entails alteration to drains is going to be both costly and disruptive.

Installing a connection to a water or sewer main is the job of the utility; laying drains must be done professionally and meet building regulations. Strict compliance with local rules governing the installation of waste lines is required. In most jurisdictions these rules mandate separate waste lines for sink water and for sewage.

Fresh water coming into the house is usually metered. Cold water is fed directly into the building's system, with a subsidiary line running to a hot-water heater attached to the boiler.

Drains take waste water from sinks and bathtubs and sewage from toilets away for connection to main sewer drains or to a septic tank, which is periodically pumped. Waste water reaches the drains via a trapped gully which has a water seal to prevent smells coming back into the house. The waste pipe from downstairs toilets is connected directly to the drain; at upper levels, waste pipes feed into a vertical soil line (which provides ventilation and prevents air blockages) and from there to the main sewer drains.

In general, the simpler the layout of your plumbing the fewer the problems. Pipes that weave all over the place, with frequent changes of direction, much branching and many different gradients greatly increase the potential for blockage and breakdown. There should be easy access at a number of different points for clearing blockages if these should occur. There should also be a valve for cutting off all water supply within the house, and the local water department can cut off water from the street to the house using an outside valve.

2

2 Clad in ribbed terra cotta tile, this bathroom designed by architect François Roche features sculptural stainless steel sinks and a low sunken tub.
3 A kitchen sink with a difference, by San Fancisco architects John Randolph and Bruce Tomb, wittily evokes the form of an ironing board. The waste pipe is plumbed through an opaque glass panel to connect with the bathroom services. The sink is portable and can be moved further into the room when in use.

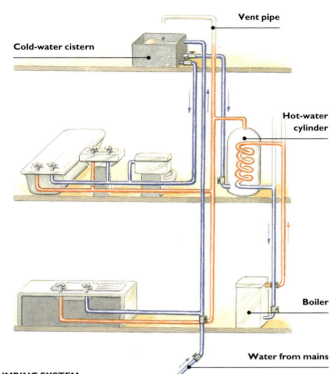

PLUMBING SYSTEM

Vent pipe

Cold-water cistern

Hot-water cylinder

Boiler

Water from mains

Drains are usually stacked one above each other in a vertical format for multistory houses, or alternatively, they can feed into a central core. This means that adding a new bathroom on a level directly above an existing one is considerably easier than installing a bathroom on the other side of the house where more complicated alterations may have to be carried out. Depending on the structure and layout of your home, you may find out that it proves impossible to achieve an adequate fall for waste pipes sited in a new location. In this context, it is also worth taking into consideration that, for reasons of health and hygiene, it is far preferable for a toilet not to be directly accessible from an area where food is prepared. If the kitchen and the toilet are adjacent it makes good sense to include provision for a sink, to cut down on the risks of infection and contamination.

If you are planning to install a new shower in your bathroom, it may be necessary to fit a pump in order to supply water of sufficient pressure and/or an additional heater to cope with the increased demand for hot water. In a windowless room, ventilation may also need upgrading.

3

4

4 A striking ladder-like arrangement of jointed hot-water pipes forms a heated towel rail in a bathroom.

Electricity

With electricity, flicking a switch is the instinctive command that summons light, power and, sometimes, heat. Its effectiveness is entirely dependent on convenience, which means ensuring there are enough power outlets to serve your needs and enough flexibility to accommodate change.

You need professional help to ensure that the existing electrical systems are safe, up to date and able to support the demands you place on them. You will also need help to change, extend or install new systems while, of course, hooking up to the power grid is always the job of the utility. Anything of any

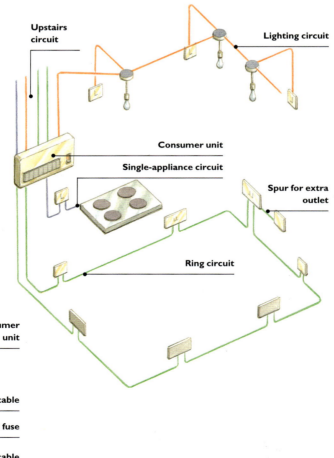

2

complexity – i.e., outside the changing of a lightbulb – should be handled by a licensed electrician. Electricity is potentially extremely dangerous so you must be sure you know what you are doing before embarking on the simplest task.

Wiring systems vary, and you may find yourself with a fuse box, a panel of circuit breakers, or both. Power will be fed from various areas of the house through different circuits, which will accommodate power outlets, lighting and appliances from stoves and refrigerators to air conditioners, fax machines and personal computers and printers. Installing new appliances which make heavy demands on electricity may warrant extra circuitry.

To plan your needs, consider:
- The age of the wiring. Systems over 20 years old will probably need replacing. You should have wiring checked every five years by a qualified electrician.
- Special appliances make new demands on the circuit, especially where these increase loads.
- Alterations to lighting.
- The number and position of power outlets. Ideally, except in bathrooms, there should be a double power outlet on each wall to allow flexibility. Converting a single outlet to a double one is not difficult.

1

ELECTRICITY AROUND THE HOME

Upstairs circuit

Lighting circuit

Consumer unit

Single-appliance circuit

Spur for extra outlet

Ring circuit

DOMESTIC FUSEBOX

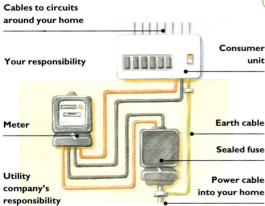

Cables to circuits around your home

Your responsibility

Consumer unit

Meter

Earth cable

Sealed fuse

Utility company's responsibility

Power cable into your home

3

The great boon of electricity is its invisibility. But this discretion is won at the cost of routing cable and wire through walls, ceilings and under floors. Naturally, this involves forethought, and subsequent alteration, if a major overhaul is needed, can be disruptive. If you need to rewire your entire home, you might take advantage of the upheaval to do some other work while you're at it.

SAFETY

- There should be more than enough outlets in a room to prevent loose or dangling wires, which can lead to serious accidents, and dangerously overloaded power outlets.
- Water and electricity are dangerous companions. Local codes may stipulate the number and spacing of outlets in the bathrooms, for example, and may also regulate the installation of appliances such as washing machines or air conditioners.
- Layout of kitchen appliances must be planned in conjunction with their power supply.
- Outdoor power supplies should ideally be routed underground in special cables. Electrical wiring in outbuildings is safest if encased in steel or plastic conduits.

- Outlets for outdoor appliances should be protected by individual circuit breakers and have some covering to shield them from the elements.

LINES OF COMMUNICATION

Telephone and tv cable lines supplying television, telephones and other communication systems are often approached as an afterthought, resulting in a spaghetti of wiring that disfigures the façade of your house. There is no reason why such wiring cannot be planned in advance; separate ducting can improve the overall appearance and maintain accessibility.

THE CUTTING EDGE

People have widely different attitudes to technology in the home. For some, each new development is irresistible and within a short space of time, indispensable; others are fundamentally uneasy. Most of us have a love-hate relationship, enjoying the convenience and comfort, but unsure about the long-term effects. On the most basic level, everyone is familiar with the tempting gadget that promises much, but frequently delivers extra maintenance, takes up too much storage space and then breaks down when you most need it. Environmental awareness has also revealed the dark side of technological change.

1 Electrical servicing in the kitchen demands careful thought to ensure that there are adequate outlets for appliances where they are needed, as well as flexible provision for lighting. Major appliances require their own circuits.
2 A music system is inconspicuously integrated within an alcove separating two areas of the living room.
3 Power outlets on landings and in hallways provide the opportunity to colonize the space for work or study.

Any predictions of how the home of the future will work is guaranteed to sound ridiculous ten years from now. But based on what currently exists in other fields and applications, it's possible to show the impact technology could have – if we want it to.

With the Information Superhighway heading for our front doors, domestic services, appliances and media equipment should soon be fully integrated, programable and interactive.

Microchip technology also means that it is conceivable that appliances could be self-diagnostic and even self-servicing. Infrared sensors have been developed that can activate showers, pre-set for intensity, duration and temperature, as soon as you step within a designated area. CD-ROMs bring sound, images and text together in a single package for interactive reference and educational use. Remote controls or voice-activated electronics could replace manual switches and many other routine functions. Virtual reality could revolutionize home planning and design, just as computer programs already are ubiquitous in architects' offices and also enable sophisticated calculations of energy use.

Whether the average home boasts such features in ten years' time will depend on attitude. Changes that are backed up by low running costs and real gains in energy use may ultimately prove preferable to those that simply promise convenience. Technology smoothes your path, but it also distances. The sacrifice is physical presence, the sheer hands-on quality of daily life, which is often missed most after it has gone. Remote-controlled door locking may be a security boon and time-saver; but doors that swing open on a voice command may be too alienating for comfort. Once cocooned in a pre-set, fully adjustable environment, will we long for the good old days when we could simply grasp a door handle, throw open a window or run our own bath? We may, but our children – already deep in their computers – may not.

Lighting

The huge seductive range of modern lighting fixtures now available encourages selection from a pure design standpoint. For many, lighting is often an afterthought, with choices and decisions made too far down the line. You can afford to wait until the basic framework is right before tracking down the perfect sofa, but you must consider lighting from the beginning.

Artificial lighting is a supplement and substitute for natural light. It enables you to function practically, safely and comfortably when it's dark or dull outside; it enhances architectural detail, and decorative features; it accentuates color and reveals texture. Literally, it generates 'atmosphere'. The most exciting space on earth will still look like a laundromat if it is lit by an overhead florescent tube, while the most sensitively chosen designer lamp is no use if you can't see by it to read the newspaper. Successfully balancing the functional and the aesthetic qualities requires thinking about lighting and incorporating it into your earliest plans.

Choice of fixture and light source are integral decisions. Although you may delay the final selection, you should know the type of lighting you require in each area of the home before you begin to furnish and decorate. Planning lighting involves a degree of flexibility, allowing for anticipated different layouts and spatial uses. (For a full discussion of the range of fixtures and light sources, see pages 228-30.)

The best lighting programs offer you flexibility, variety of light level, direction, intensity and fitness for purpose; a new consideration is low energy. The sheer variety and moods of natural light and its partner, shadow, are the secret of its profound appeal. Until really quite recently, artificial lighting did not even begin to mimic this diversity of effect, but technology now allows much more subtle and stimulating interior lighting conditions. Getting this right lies at the heart of a comfortable room.

1 Tube lights and halogen spots are suspended from steel wire running across a double-height space in an innovative and practical arrangement.
2 Modern light sources complement natural light. The clear white light of halogen spots accentuates a dining table.
3 A variety of small light sources provides flexible illumination for a cooking and eating area. Spotlights over the preparation area give bright, shadowless light for detailed work; ceiling spots offer a good level of background light; pendant fixtures add sparkle to the table.

1

2

3

4 Uplights bounce light off the ceiling for a soft, diffused glow. Track lights can be adjusted to highlight display shelves.

5 Lights installed inside these kitchen cabinets are automatically switched on when the doors are slid back, providing discreet accent and information lighting. Halogen spotlights above the island unit offer directional task lighting.

6 Hallways and circulation areas must be well lit. Wall-mounted fixtures illuminate the space with an even wash of light; avoid spotlights in such areas, as they create pools of brightness and shadow.

4

5

6

GENERAL LIGHTING

TASK LIGHTING

ACCENT LIGHTING

PLANNING LIGHTING

Lighting has a dramatic effect on both our perception of space and the way we operate within it, yet it is one of the most economical and versatile elements in the spatial equation. Because it is powered by electricity, lighting should be planned in conjunction with changes to the wiring. In the case of built-in or recessed fixtures, such as downlights, it is obviously less disruptive to fit these features before you decorate, ideally while the surfaces are being overhauled.

Use a basic floor plan to plot out the type of lighting you need in each area. Each room will need a combination of three basic types: general or background illumination; specific task light; and accent or decorative lighting. You can achieve these functions in a variety of stylistic ways; what is essential at this planning stage is to build in sufficient infrastructure to accommodate a variety of light sources.

Background light has been traditionally supplied by a ceiling fixture. In many cases, this solution is ugly and dull, resulting in flat, even and often over-bright conditions. The same level of illumination can be arranged by employing a variety of sources around the room which create overlapping pools of light and shade. Side lights, spots, uplights and downlights are all alternative means of achieving this effect.

1 Natural light is supplemented by a subtle variety of artificial light sources to create a tranquil mood in a bedroom in Provence. Plain plaster uplights, decorated in with the wall, give discreet background light; pivoting bedside lamps provide more focused illumination for reading.
3 A spotlight fixed to a beam lights a bathroom mirror for activities such as shaving or putting on makeup.

1

2 Artificial light varies according to the fixture, and the type and power of bulb. Left to right: recessed incandescent spot; low-energy incandescent pendant; halogen uplight; incandescent multiple spotlight; wall-mounted incandescent uplight; free standing halogen uplight; 'eye-ball' incandescent downlight; incandescent wall lamp.

2

Task light is targeted lighting. Bright, concentrated and directed, it enables activities such as reading, keyboard work and food preparation to be carried out with ease and safety. Spotlights are the classic solution, although there are other fixtures that offer the same result.

Accent lighting operates on a much lower level to enhance the architecture or decoration. Accent lighting which is too insistent or bright defeats the purpose of subtle differentiation and can throw a room off balance. Many kinds of fixtures can work as accents if they are dimmed.

4 Single light sources, such as pendant fixtures, can cast hard shadows which quickly divest a room of atmosphere. A variety of small points of light in this hall and living area have just the opposite effect.
5 A low-level uplight, concealed to one side of the sofa, washes the wall with soft light. Task lighting at the desk is good for working by.

1 Living rooms need varied sources of light for maximum flexibility. The wall uplight and table lamp provide general background illumination, and could be paired with a central pendant light. Spot-lighting in the alcove and a picture lamp above the fireplace give accent lighting, while the anglepoise can be adjusted to give task lighting when reading.

1

TASK LIGHTING IN A KITCHEN

2

2 Halls and stairways require a good level of general lighting. These recessed ceiling lights make locating a book a simple task, whatever the time of day. This corridor – with the desk looking out onto an open-plan layout and with a skylight above the area in the foreground of the picture – is not as gloomy as many in older homes.
3 Outdoor lighting can create dramatic nighttime effects, such as these pools of light in a Japanese-style garden. Inside, high-density general lighting allows the open-plan space to revel in its clutterless simplicity.

Specific lighting requirements include the following:
• Stairs, halls and passageways need to be well lit for safety. Avoid bright, directional lighting which causes glare and deep shadow. Stair treads can be lit individually.
• Exteriors, such as main entrances, front and rear, need to be lit for safety and security.
• Bathroom or dressing-room mirrors need even lighting from all sides for making up and shaving.
• Deep closets and the interiors of store-rooms need lighting to reveal their contents and improve accessibility.
• Bookcases, paintings, display cabinets, and so on benefit from accent lighting.
• Outdoor lighting can be installed to highlight the patio, deck or garden at night, extending the time in which it can be used.

Lighting circuits run around the ceiling, down to wall switches or fixtures, or across to central ceiling points. To install overhead lights, it may be possible to minimize the amount of disruption inevitably caused, by working from the floor above. Otherwise, wiring may have to be routed through a wall cavity or set into the plasterwork of a solid wall. Track lighting can be connected at one single point to a power source, thus accommodating a full range of lights without having to take the trouble to install each one separately.

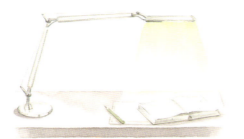

TASK LIGHTING FOR A DESK

READING LAMPS ABOVE A BED

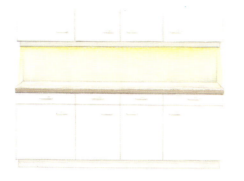

STRIP LIGHTING FOR KITCHEN COUNTERTOP

POINTS TO REMEMBER

When planning the infrastructure for lighting consider:

- There should be more than enough outlets to maximize flexibility and minimize extension cords. This will prevent an excess of loose or dangling wires, which can cause accidents and overloaded power outlets.
- Wall switches – these should be located in easily accessible spots at all main room entrances.
- Individual lamps and lights within the same room can be wired to a single switch for central control.
- Dimmers multiply the effects you can achieve with the same lighting and allow fine adjustment to take account of natural lighting conditions.
- Time switches are useful for security, or safety lighting in circulation areas.
- Some types of light source require adaptors or transformers.

LIGHTING FOR A BATHROOM MIRROR

3

4 An adjustable pendant lamp, preferably fixed to a dimmer, allows you to focus attention on the table at mealtimes, creating a mood of intimacy in an open-plan layout. A reading lamp clipped to the baseboard becomes an innovative uplight, while strip bulbs give accent to the display shelves and spots above the kitchen countertop ensure adequate task lighting. More general light could be achieved by adding ceiling spots or fitting a wall light.

4

Green living

Increasingly, making the most of our homes means making the most of the planet. Environmental issues are complex and often controversial. Solving the Earth's woes can appear too Herculean a task for anyone to believe their individual efforts would make any difference. But the cumulative effect of debates on the state of the ozone layer, the future of the rain forests, the impact of pollution and the depletion of energy resources has been a sure but steady increase in our environmental awareness.

There are many different ways of living green. On the most basic level, you can change the products you consume. It's a logical step to go on to adapt your living habits so that you cut energy use and wastage. More effective is to incorporate conservation principles into the way your home is designed and constructed. Even small changes can make a considerable difference.

Environmental concern is not merely a question of altruism. What's good for the planet is generally healthy for the individual and easy on the wallet. Green-living design uncannily echoes many traditional building methods, age-old and appealing ways of planning layout and responding to the needs of climate and site. Green living is also in tune with our aesthetic preference for natural materials and finishes – back to the fundamental ways in which human beings feel at ease with their surroundings.

ENVIRONMENTAL DESIGN

Environmental design is not merely a question of substituting an eco-friendly product for one that isn't. It involves an intricate analysis of a number of interrelated factors such as pollution, threat to health or toxicity, sustainability and energy costs.

When you turn down the thermostat on the boiler, you reduce the energy you use in direct terms. Environmentalists look further, at the hidden energy costs involved in production and construction. The energy cost of producing brick, for

example, is four times higher than that of wood; standard fiberglass wool insulation costs 30 times as much energy to produce as the insulation provided by recycled newspaper. In addition to these calculations are the energy costs of construction and transportation. There is also the question of how materials are used. 'Low energy' timber construction entails less energy consumed in construction as well as less energy consumed in running the house during its lifetime.

Green designers advocate using building materials such as timber and stone which are found naturally and therefore produce less carbon dioxide. Softwood timber is a renewable resource and managed domestic, mixed-species forestry not only encourages local employment but also reduces transportation costs.

Modern water- and oil-based paints and other petrochemical products are especially wasteful. Some paints produce as much as 90 per cent waste as a by-product of their manufacture, waste which is unrecyclable. Organic paints, by contrast, produce only 10 per cent waste, all of which is compostible; components include pine resin, linseed oil, chalk, beeswax and citrus fruits. Safe to apply, organic paint comes in a range of subtle plant colors, close to those traditional paint recipes much favored by historic preservationists. All organic finishes – paints, stains and waxes – allow the underlying material to breathe, so that moisture is not trapped inside, which means, in turn, that materials wear well.

For those fortunate enough to build their home from scratch, incorporating conservation principles into house design means avoiding plastics, rigid foam insulants and synthetic finishes, using wood and stone wherever possible as well as achieving low-energy use through high levels of insulation and natural forms of design. It starts with the site, tailoring the shape and orientation of the home to protect it from wind and encourage passive sunlight. Large overhangs shelter the house in winter and cool it in summer;

1

1 This Scottish house, by GAIA Architects, was designed to have minimum impact on the environment. A panoramic view of the Scottish countryside is the attractive by-product of positioning the house to make the best use of passive solar heat. The windows have secondary glazing, and the house is built from renewable European softwood, treated with nontoxic borax salts. All of the interior finishes are eco-friendly. **2** Nestling in its wooded site, the house blends well with its surroundings. The highly insulated roof is finished with reclaimed Welsh slate.

2

3

operable skylights allow winter sun to penetrate into the heart of the building, enabling air to circulate freely. The traditional transition areas – sunrooms, lobbies and nurseries – act as a buffer between inside and outside, a natural form of temperature control. Living roofs of meadow grass and wild flowers restore the ground dug for foundations and provide miniature wildlife habitats; they protect the roof membrane from deterioration through ultraviolet light and temperature changes – and, what's more, they look attractive!

Insulation can be provided by recycled pelleted paper treated against rot and fire with borax, a natural nontoxic material. Some designers are experimenting with a form of construction that allows walls to breathe and avoids the problems of condensation associated with modern vapor barrier construction. Wood finished with wax instead of toxic polyurethane, organic finishes and recycled-paper insulation add up to an efficient, healthy building which retains heat and regulates humidity.

In conjunction with modern heating systems, the energy efficiency of such houses can be very high indeed. Equally persuasive is a dramatic reduction in annual heating costs. In these circumstances, low-power individual room heaters provide a heat source that is both effective and surprisingly economical.

There are various devices which help a conventional heating system to run more effectively. Computerized thermostatic controls read air temperature and adjust timing accordingly, working out how long a boiler needs to cycle to reach a given temperature and calculating when the heating should come on to reach this level at a certain time. These 'boiler managers' actually learn your living patterns, ironically reusing microchip technology developed for guided missiles in the Persian Gulf War of 1991.

Heat recovery units are available in the form of individual fans or central systems which constantly suck stale air from each room and eject it from the house, after transferring the heat to incoming fresh air, which is then filtered and ducted into each room. Although not hugely expensive, these systems can only supplement a main heating system, not replace it, and the cost of running the unit has to be considered as part of the overall energy cost. Advocates claim that these devices improve the quality of the air. There are also units that reclaim the heat from boiler or stove flues, as well as heat pumps which can boost the efficiency of heat-recovery units (though the cost of these is high).

SOLAR ENERGY

In northern areas, active solar energy is normally used to supplement water heating, but provides little energy when it is most needed in the winter months, as this is the time when light levels are low.

New forms of solar-energy collection, employing photovoltaic cells on the roof instead of the conventional tubes, may become more popular and could be used to generate a contribution to electric space heating. Surplus energy could be directed back into the power grid.

Passive solar energy can be achieved within the overall design by using south-facing windows and sunrooms to gather the sun's heat and store it within the fabric of the building. Wood-framed houses tend to heat up more quickly and vertical windows are better than roof glazing to trap the weak, low rays of winter sun. It is possible for over-heating to occur in summer, however.

3 This award-winning scheme by Architype Design Co-operative consists of nine self-build houses in a wooded English valley. 'Living' roofs of scabious, tufted vetch, oxeye daisy and bird's-foot trefoil recreate wildflower meadowland, replacing the area lost to construction. Limited soil depth means that the roofs do not require mowing. As well as providing a habitat for wildlife, the roofs help to cleanse the air by absorbing carbon dioxide. Most modern buildings are made out of a variety of synthetic materials such as foam insulation, vinyl floors and petro-chemically based paints and stains, all of which contain toxic chemicals that 'outgas' into the building. Natural materials and nontoxic finishes such as organic paints, stains and waxes work with, rather than against, nature.

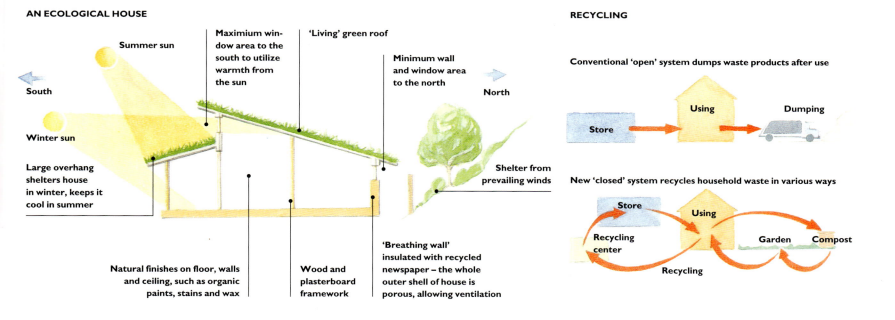

AN ECOLOGICAL HOUSE

Summer sun

South

Winter sun

Large overhang shelters house in winter, keeps it cool in summer

Maximum window area to the south to utilize warmth from the sun

'Living' green roof

Minimum wall and window area to the north

North

Shelter from prevailing winds

Natural finishes on floor, walls and ceiling, such as organic paints, stains and wax

Wood and plasterboard framework

'Breathing wall' insulated with recycled newspaper – the whole outer shell of house is porous, allowing ventilation

RECYCLING

Conventional 'open' system dumps waste products after use

Store → Using → Dumping

New 'closed' system recycles household waste in various ways

Store → Using

Recycling center

Recycling

Garden → Compost

1 Set on a hillside in Queensland, Australia, this steel-frame canvas-clad tent house – the home of architect Gabriel Poole and artist Elizabeth Frith – is an appropriate response to the tropical climate. Louvers over the balcony drive air through the house, cooling it without recourse to air conditioning. The outside walls can be rolled up to merge indoors with out.
2 The tent house, designed by Poole, is cyclone-proof and sits gently on the land, ideal for environmentally sensitive sites where major construction would be too disruptive.
4 An annex, a short distance from the main house, serves as guest accommodation. Mosquito netting provides essential protection from insect life in a house open to the elements.

3 This Swedish vacation house is part of a prize-winning scheme by Norwegian architect Sverre Fehn. Modules for sleeping, living and dining are grouped around an inner patio. The open kitchen is installed in a long corridor running the length of the house.
5 The barrel-vaulted living/dining area contains a fireplace that screens the view of the kitchen corridor.

6

7

6 The bedroom opens on to the outside patio at the heart of the structure.
7 Blending with its site, the house is a wood construction faced in exterior blocks made of dried fine-ground straw mixed with clay, an environmentally friendly material which is also an effective heat and sound insulator. The wood roof is protected with bituminous tiles.

DRAINAGE

An eco-alternative to a septic tank, where connection to a main sewer is not possible, is a reed bed. This consists of passing waste from a house through a series of living ponds, which clean the water using natural biological processes. Obviously, specialist design is required, not to mention enough land to allow for the installation. Soil waste demands a much larger system than 'gray' water from sinks, bathtubs and showers.

Less radical and more affordable solutions include storing rainwater in barrels to use in the garden, or even in toilet tanks. 'Gray' water can also be recycled for garden irrigation.

RADIATION

Electrical and electromagnetic radiation from domestic cables are considered by some people to be sources of stress and ill health, particularly where live cables run in close proximity to sleeping areas – where, after all, we spend nearly one third of our lives. In certain countries, it is common practice to make use of shielded cable as a protection from radiation. An alternative solution is to fit an automatic switch which disconnects the electrical supply when there is no demand (such as at nighttime), but which automatically reconnects the supply as soon as a demand is made (for example, when a light is switched on).

THE GREEN HOUSEHOLD

There are a vast number of ways in which the daily routine of your family can be modified or adapted to reduce pollution and waste and cut energy use. Green housekeeping is often a question of going back to the old-fashioned virtues of thrift and elbow grease.

We've grown accustomed to miracle products which promise all kinds of instant benefits, but the side effects of many common household chemicals pose a long-term hazard. Making a few simple substitutions can improve your health, along with the state of the planet. Read labels and avoid cleaning products that contain toxic chemicals such as chlorine, formaldehyde, halogenated hydrocarbons or pollutants such as CFCs, as well as those in aerosol sprays.

- Choose organic paint and natural finishes – wax and organic wood stains, and natural preservatives.
- Choose natural cleansers – borax, ammonia, vinegar or baking soda.
- Buy furniture made from sustainable woods and natural-fiber upholstery.
- Opt for natural materials – linoleum rather than vinyl, cotton rather than synthetic blends.
- Recycling is the modern version of 'waste not, want not'. Packaging is a great offender – choose loose rather than packaged fruit and vegetables.
- Recycle glass jars and bottles, paper and aluminum cans. Recycling laws are already in place in many areas of the country.
- Reuse plastic food containers.
- Buy rechargeable batteries.
- Buy recycled paper products.
- Recycle old clothes, towels and sheets as cleaning rags.
- Compost organic waste.
- Reuse shopping bags.
- Choose products with less packaging.

In addition to shopping more considerately, you can 'go green' by reducing your energy consumption:

- Insulate your home with non-CFC insulants.
- Put thermostatic controls on boilers and radiators or, better still, use a 'boiler manager'.
- Fit large single-panel radiators instead of air convectors. (Radiant heat provides more apparent comfort at lower temperatures than convected heat, which creates drafts.)
- Choose low-energy compact florescent light bulbs.
- Air-dry your wet clothing.
- Maintain appliances in good order for a longer life.
- Run only full loads in the washing machine and dishwasher.

ALTERING SPACE

1

Decoration puts a smart new face on things, good organization brings order and efficiency to your everyday routine, but spatial changes get to the very heart of the matter. Altering space entails thinking about volume and scale, privacy and openness, natural light, views and vistas. In essence, it means thinking architecturally, which is considerably more demanding than it seems. The biggest hurdle, however, is not lack of professional training, but lack of imagination. It's easy to make small changes to the existing configuration of rooms; but it may be more fruitful to consider the volume of your home in a more abstract way – as a space that must fulfill the various demands and activities you expect of it on a day-to-day basis.

Living in unsatisfactory surroundings doesn't necessarily promote a desire for change; it can just as easily blunt the awareness of how improvements could be made. In such cases, natural caution can be reinforced by the perceived complexity of structural work and the aggravation it can cause. Furthermore, substantial amounts of money can be involved, and there is always the residual fear that change may be for the worse – rooms stripped of their architectural character or 'sunrooms' that are little more than lean-to sheds tacked to the back of a house have, in the past, given conversions something of a bad name.

Overcoming these obstacles and fears isn't a leap in the dark when you take the time to explore all the options and seek professional help to put ideas into practice. Improving the spatial quality of your home may be as relatively straightforward as removing a partition wall to open up internal views and reconfigure your living space, or it may involve more significant alterations, from converting roof space into an extra bedroom or home office, adding a mezzanine level or building an extension.

Ultimately, radical alteration to the structure of your house may be the only means to improve the way you live – to give you more space, more light and a better use of indoor and outdoor areas. You need to weigh the cost of change against the benefits it will bring, both to the way you live and, possibly, to the value of your home. In the long term, the alternative – doing nothing – may work out to be the most expensive course of action of all.

1 The intersecting planes of walls and curved ceiling create architectural interest in this modern hallway. **2** An architect's conversion of a nineteenth-century artist's studio stripped away years of badly considered alteration to make a light-filled gallery for living in. A spiral plaster-shell staircase connects with a U-shaped upper level.

2

3

 3 A bathroom tucked into the roof derives the greatest practical benefit from otherwise wasted floor space. Adding a roof light makes the room feel less enclosed and provides a contemplative view when soaking in the bath. Sliding doors neatly enclose clothes-hanging space.

4 A large pivoting solid wood panel separates a dining area from a kitchen, making a dynamic connection between the two rooms. The thick, roughwashed terra cotta walls contrast with and soften the gleaming stainless-steel kitchen cabinets and appliances beyond.

5 The elemental qualities of light and space are orchestrated to maximum effect in this Majorcan house designed by Claudio Silvestrin.

4

5

Envisaging change

■

■ In a London apartment, juxtapositions in scale create witty illusions in a small space. A low-level bed sheltering under the plane of the roof makes an intimate sleeping space in this imaginative loft conversion. Open and closed storage space is fitted under the eaves.
■ Staircases and hallways in older houses can be exceptionally wasteful of space. This modern open stairway has a graphic simplicity.

■

An architect may be able to imagine your ideal home better than you can. There are many low-key spatial changes which don't require much in the way of professional guidance or only a degree of technical expertise on how to get something done. But if you're planning to make major changes, it's a good idea to consult an architect as early as possible to help you to formulate your ideas.

The conventional view is that the architect is the person who brings the client down to earth, setting limits on fanciful schemes and replacing dreams with sober reality. In practice, many architects find that it is their clients who have the mental brakes on, imagining obstacles to change which don't really exist. The architect's most important role is to envisage what would be the best possible solution to a spatial issue. This isn't a question of talking you into more work than you want done; instead, it is a synthetic approach to problem solving

which enables you to gain the maximum benefits from any change. If your home needs a thorough overhaul of services, an architect can suggest ways of incorporating structural alterations into your plans which won't add much to your budget but may add a great deal to the spatial quality of your home.

BASIC SPATIAL PRINCIPLES

Architects are trained to think three dimensionally, to analyze and plan buildings systematically in terms of layout, elevation and section. You can't achieve such expertise without such experience but an appreciation of some of the fundamental issues will help you to approach the subject more creatively and communicate your ideas better.

Balance between privacy and openness is a major consideration. In general, older houses tend to comprise a series of self-contained rooms, originally designed to accommodate separate activities, all clustered around a staircase. Repetitive and conventional in their planning, these houses can frustrate a desire for more flexibility and communality. Open-plan living has still not really taken hold in the U.S., because builders and developers find the traditional home easy to sell. On the other hand, inspired by the loft spaces that artists thrive in in warehouse districts around the country, this less rigid form of design has made some inroads. Responding to this new spatial freedom, many older houses have been opened up from top to bottom to create large, multi-purpose areas – a dramatic swing from one extreme to another.

It has taken time to appreciate what we've probably known all along, that there should be a balance between openness and privacy. If you take down all the internal divisions between areas, remove doors, knock down walls, integrate stairways and corridors, you may achieve a dramatic new space only to find you don't really like living in it. If all your living spaces bleed into each other, you run the risk of losing your bearings;

there's nowhere to escape to when you need to sit quietly with a book or have a private conversation. Large spaces are exhilarating, but they can also be tiring, noisy and confused, the more so when there are no small enclaves to vary the pace and scale. You may also find that you have lost much usable wall space for storage, for bookcases or simply as an anchor for furniture arrangement.

The same type of approach applies whether you're considering uniting two rooms or converting one large open space into living quarters. You may require privacy for sleeping, bathing and work, but would equally enjoy a layout that allows you to combine living and eating areas, cooking and eating areas, or even all three. Providing a contrast between open and enclosed areas modulates and gives rhythm to spaces, an important dimension that is lacking when every room is either a crushing cell or a vast featureless concourse.

A related issue is thinking about space as volume. It's easy enough to envisage changes to internal planning and layout; what is harder to imagine are alterations that involve changes to levels. Whether opening up space by removing portions of floor, or dividing it by adding galleries and loft levels, these are changes that alter the volume of a space along with the floor area. Such schemes offer dramatic scope for spilling natural light down the center of a building, providing a sweeping, soaring sense of space, creating internal views and vistas that link areas together in visually exciting ways.

Even if you are only moving around partitions, you should never view your home in isolation from its setting. Changes to the inside often imply alterations to the way the interior relates to the exterior, by providing better access to a garden, for example, or by making better visual connections or responding more sympathetically to the site and orientation. You should know which direction the main rooms in your house face, where the light comes from at different

3 A freestanding white panel doubles as a headboard and partition that screens the raised bathroom area from view without blocking light from the rear wall of windows.
4 Converted lofts and warehouses are the ultimate urban spaces – one-room living at its most expansive. Setting up home in a building which was not originally designed for domestic use provides great creative freedom.

times of the day, which rooms are warm and sunny, which are dark and cool. In extreme climates, no home would be comfortable or practical if the design failed to take account of these basic factors. They are no less important in areas of the world where conditions are more temperate. People are profoundly affected by natural light and by the ability to move freely from inside to outside; if you live in an area where there are not many sunny days in a year, it's more important to be able to make the most of them.

Alterations to space can be graded in complexity, with demolishing or erecting partitions fairly low down the scale and adding an addition onto an existing building fairly high up. In practice, however, there may be an interrelated series of changes, some of which are simple and straightforward, others less so. It's more instructive to think about the end result that you are trying to achieve, and to plan backwards from there.

Views and vistas

■

■ The rippled contours of these kitchen doors make a playful contrast with the clean, neat lines of the built-in cabinets beyond.

Perception of space is as important to the layout of a room as the floor area at your disposal. The simple truth is that the desire to increase the 'feeling' of spaciousness probably lies behind many decisions to knock down walls or integrate different areas. Of course, it makes sense to link rooms with related functions. Living and eating rooms, and eating and cooking rooms are prime candidates for merger, with connecting or ante-areas, such as hallways, running a close second. Although practicalities may tip the balance, the sheer expansiveness of a large room constitutes a powerful argument in itself. In a typical townhouse, with rooms running from front to back, breaking through dividing walls provides a dual aspect, with light and views coming into the house from two different directions.

People don't need views, but they crave them. Windowless rooms are the stuff of nightmares and, under most building codes, only alcoves or anterooms can be fully internal. They must be well ventilated but need have no direct visual connection with the outside world. Where the opportunity exists, creating rooms so that light falls from two sides is infinitely preferable to spaces lit by only one window. Better still is to arrange the layout of rooms so that there are internal views and vistas across a space, giving glimpses of outdoor life in different directions. These can be oblique aspects, such as the view from a stairway, landing or from a loft level – vantage points that offer a choice of stimulating perspectives.

Putting in internal 'windows', either glazed or open, can help to spread light around and offer the type of intriguing views that liven up the experience of moving about from room to room. A porthole between an internal washroom and a hall or a serving window between kitchen and dining/living room can help to counteract feelings of claustrophobia while maintaining the separation of private activities from public spaces.

Older houses are often built to turn their backs on the yards that surround them; poorly sited additions may have made access outside even more proscribed. Reorganizing the layout can often improve the ease with which you reach the outdoors, as well as offering the opportunity to bring it closer visually.

New openings, internal and external, have a positive effect on air flow by providing cross ventilation. Arranging the position of windows so that breezes blow through them – and through the house – can cool rooms dramatically and avoid the need for artificial air conditioning.

The overriding caveat is that you must pay attention to proportion, scale and detail when creating any new opening, either internally or externally. Taking out a floor to create a double-height space may mean that existing windows appear too small. It's relatively straightforward to extend a window by lowering the sill – big rooms do need more light and openings of a larger scale. In old houses, taking down the wall between a living room and a dining room, for example, can result in a new room that has two fireplaces and two chimney breasts along the length of one wall; this may prove unsettling, an uncomfortable visual reminder that the space was once divided. It's worth remembering that you can gain many of the most positive benefits of integrating two rooms by retaining a portion of the wall on either side of the new opening, retaining a hint of separation. If you want to maintain an element of flexibility, you can fit the opening with double doors, glazed or unglazed, or shutters that fold back within the reveal. In this case, it's often easier and more economical to find the doors first and then scale the opening to fit them; joinery that has to be custom-made to fit the new opening would add extra expense to what is in other respects a relatively straightforward project.

In the case of external openings, too big can be as unsatisfactory as too small. Picture windows – unbroken expanses of

2

2 Large pivoting windows allow access to a balcony with an enviable view.

3

3 A washing area fitted in a corridor expresses the curve of an exterior wall in a modern Australian house. Panels of mirror reflect the view.
4 Where the climate is hospitable and the view spectacular, large openings bring in light and air and allow free movement between outdoors and in.

4

1

1 A window wall in this Corsican house provides an eagle's eye view of the lush valley.
2 A cylindrical drum containing a deep curved tub is lit by a large porthole window. The circular mirror suspended at right angles above the sink appears to float in the recessed space.

2

3 Massive double doors offer a tantalizing slice of view that takes the eye along the axis of the space into the landscape beyond.

3

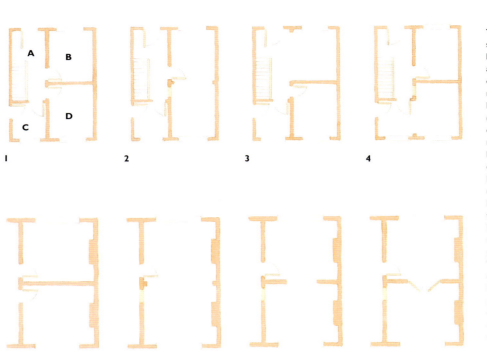

The general layout of a sequence of rooms can be altered by removing an internal wall: (1) a conventional layout might have an entrance hall ('A'), living room ('B'), kitchen ('C') and dining room('D'); removing the wall between the living and dining room (2) or the hallway and living room (3) gives more general living space; removing the wall between the kitchen and dining room creates an open-plan eating room (4). Two separate rooms (5) can be integrated into a single room (6), perhaps retaining part of the dividing wall (7); double doors between such an opening maximize flexibility (8).

plate glass – may seem like a good way of reveling in a view, but they often have a curiously deadening effect especially if the elevation predates the use of such large blank expanses. Windows articulated with panes, or French doors that open onto a terrace often have a greater degree of vitality. Ensure that the view you reveal is worth looking at: a new window which leads the eye straight to the garage won't improve the quality of view from the living room. Work out the best aspects for external openings, and design the landscape and interior to complement each other.

The difficulty of such work hinges on whether structural walls and other elements are involved or not. There may be added complications if the alterations involve changes to services – the loss of a radiator, or changes in sewage, wiring or lighting, for example. If a load-bearing wall is affected, the opening must be reinforced by adding in a beam, concrete support or steel joist. Except in simple cases of extending windows downward, all changes to external walls will entail some form of reinforcement. Inside, it depends on the wall. With structural implications, you will most likely need a building permit. In a landmarked building, it is unlikely that you will be allowed to make any changes to the exterior, but interiors are not always subject to the same protection. Make sure you check with your local preservation agency.

Options for change include:
• Removing a wall between two rooms.
• Making a large connection between rooms, leaving wall area to either side.
• Making an oversized doorway between rooms and fitting doors or a screen.
• Taking out the wall between a stair or hallway and a room.
• Making internal windows.
• Putting in French doors.
• Widening existing windows.
• Deepening existing windows.
• Removing a portion of floor or all of a floor to open up to the roof.
• Adding windows in a roof.

4 The supporting framework of columns and beams provides a hint of separation in a large airy room. Banishing all internal divisions from a house can create 'problem' spaces with no points of reference.

New space for old

Achieving a feeling of spaciousness in your surroundings won't necessarily win you more usable space. If you have a pressing need to house more people, more activities or more storage under the same roof, it may be a matter of redesigning the layout, partitioning a large room to make two separate ones, or of changing levels to insert an extra floor. No-go areas like basements and lofts are often ripe for additions.

Partitioning is simple and normally you don't have to worry about structural problems. Dividing up a large nursery to give the children separate bedrooms, for example, involves a few commonsense decisions about where to place the wall and how to arrange access. The critical issue is making sure each new area has at least one window, and you may lose some floor area in forming separate entrances or lobbies to each new room. You must also consider the proportions of the new spaces; a high-ceilinged room divided in two may look odd unless you also adjust the levels by dropping the ceiling or raising the floor. If there isn't an extreme disparity, you can accommodate the eye to such changes by running a plain cornice or wainscoting around each new room and repeating details such as decorative moldings and baseboards.

Partitions don't have to be full height or full width and they don't necessarily have to follow straight lines. A curved wall that encloses part of a space can be an elegant way of gaining privacy or segregating activities; a half-height wall often makes a useful buffer between an integrated kitchen and eating room.

In an older multi-storied house, where ceiling heights are generous, you can sometimes squeeze in extra rooms by juggling the levels; sometimes a loft bed or office is appropriate. If you've got to rework services anyway, this can provide you with the opportunity to really go to town with your plans, rethinking layout from the ground up. In genuine Victorian townhouses, the kitchen generally occupies the least attractive, lowest

▪

2

level, usually in the basement or semi-basement, reflecting its former status as a room where servants held sway. Moving the kitchen further up into the heart of the house allows you to integrate it more closely with other living areas, releasing the lowest level for more flexible use as an extra bedroom, home office or study, utility room, or that suburban standby, the rec room.

Planning changes to levels entails thinking about 'section', and this is truly an architectural skill. The section, or diagrammatic vertical cut through a building, enables you to work out the best way of using volume, as opposed to planning the horizontal layout of each story. In this context, it is essential to get a grip on the fact that the ceiling is not the floor of the room above. Ceilings, because they are cosmetic finishes applied to the underside of a floor, can be lowered without difficulty to improve the proportions of a room. Lowering or raising a floor, on the other hand, is structural work, because you are moving the position of the floor itself. Adding in a new level – such as a mezzanine in a loft space – also has structural consequences, since you are increasing the load on the main walls.

Basement conversions are not the equal of loft conversions in terms of potential. They are understandably less popular, at least partly because most people find it less pleasant to spend very much of their time underground. Head

height and daylight are the two critical factors. A half-basement on a sloping site, which is deep enough for you to move around in comfortably and which has some form of external opening, offers the greatest potential. You can excavate the ground outside to improve access to a garden or to extend windows to increase natural light. Digging down to create a new basement or extend a shallow underfloor space involves a lot of disruption and expense – underpinning existing foundations, rerouting drainage, waterproofing, substantial building work and all the associated permissions are usually enough to turn most people off. If there is some basement area, but it is not sufficient to make full-scale conversion feasible, you could still look at dropping the ground level as far as possible in order to create more volume in the first-floor rooms.

Changes to levels generally imply changes to stairways, too. You can sometimes gain a fair amount of extra space by relocating and rebuilding an already existing staircase. Old houses tend to waste a considerable amount of space in this department. New stairs to galleries or mezzanines can be exciting and dynamic additions; the thrill of open cantilevered steps or a bold sculptural spiral staircase brings an agreeable theatricality to everyday life, especially when combined with other dramatic features such as roof windows or skylights.

An Edwardian townhouse in west London has been radically remodeled by architects Munkenbeck and Marshall. From the outside, the house is indistinguishable from its neighbors, but inside the space has been gutted to convert the layout of small, self-contained rooms (which themselves had split to form a pair of flats) into a loft-style open-plan layout (see next page).
1 Daylight floods into the first-floor room through a new glass ceiling, the French doors, and a glass landing above the kitchen countertop that looks up through the whole height of the house to a skylight in the roof. Activity areas are zoned by the use of furniture and fixtures: a dining table and chairs; the kitchen island; and (in the front bay window, not shown) two sofas at right angles to the fireplace.
2 From the back garden, a spectacular view of the interior: the maple floor, island unit and graphic staircase add a touch of warmth to the understated minimalism.

1 This unique kitchen, designed by David Pocknell, is fitted into the wall of MDF cabinets, with an inset stainless-steel counter-top. Additional work space is provided by the island unit. Above the gas cooktop, the exhaust hood is housed in an MDF cabinet. On top of this sits a clock which is visible from the glass landing above.
2 At the top of the stairs on the second floor, a glass landing leads to the study, the only conventional room (in the sense of four walls and a door) in the house. The land-ing is a focal point in the reconfigured space, a point from which the opening up process reaches its fullest potential, looking down to the living area, and up to a metal walkway and skylight beyond.

1

2

3 The bathroom on the second floor is the second-largest space in the house. The free-standing bathtub occupies a prominent place, with double washbasins built into the unit beyond it. Hinged mirrors play with the geometry of the room, reflecting back the sleek walls of built-in wardrobes made from varnished MDF; beneath the stairs, a 'wardrobe' door opens to reveal a small dressing room.

3

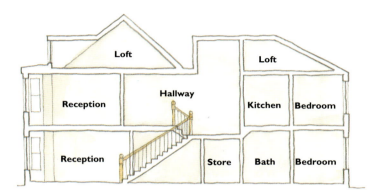

PREVIOUS CROSS SECTION

Loft

Loft

Reception

Hallway

Kitchen

Bedroom

Reception

Store

Bath

Bedroom

NEW CROSS SECTION

Bedroom

Store

Bath

Study

Reception

Kitchen

Dining

4 The bedroom is in the roof of the house, immediately above the bathroom. Low-level shelves form an extended headboard, a place for the owners' collection of aluminum toys and automata.

5 The formal paved garden at the back of the house is dominated by the russet concrete slab, from which spouts a mini waterfall spilling into a trough. The slab, in fact, is a small shed that conceals a barbecue behind it.

4

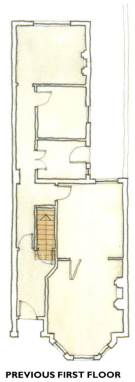

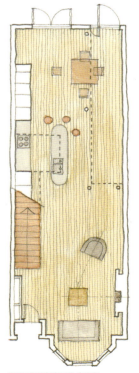

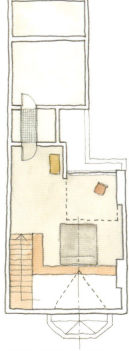

PREVIOUS FIRST FLOOR   **NEW FIRST FLOOR**   **NEW SECOND FLOOR**   **NEW THIRD FLOOR**   **5**

Into the roof

Going up into the roof offers a wide choice of spatial solutions. A loft can often be converted into a habitable room by adding a skylight, lining with new finishes and fitting snug storage space under the eaves where the head height diminishes. The popularity of this type of alteration is evident in the number of companies specializing in custom loft conversion kits which supply you with the relevant components. If you live in the city, and garden area is precious, roof space may be the most feasible way of providing extra room. At the same time, opening up to the roof, by removing all or part of the ceiling, can transform the upper level of your home into a soaring, light-filled space. Loft spaces – with angles formed by the planes of the roof, the potential for toplighting and panoramic views – have their own special appeal. The only drawback is that some people find loft living noisy – in practice, the sound of rain drumming on the roof can prove to be more annoying than romantic. And, unfortunately, this type of conversion is largely ruled out in new houses with preformed roof trusses.

Access is a major issue. If you're going to use the new room regularly, you'll need to install a sturdy staircase, rather than a folding loft ladder. Changes to how an existing stairway works or to the layout of upper rooms may be necessary to fit the new stairway in. You may have to extend the ceiling opening if you plan to move in large pieces of furniture.

The type of window you install should be easy to clean. Windows that pivot on special hinges make cleaning easier; there are also various tools designed for the purpose. Cleaning is not a side issue for a roof window; the pleasure of gazing up at a clear blue sky will be lost if you're forced to look through grimy glass. Any window that can be fitted from the inside will mean you don't have to erect scaffolding to install it. Windows facing the sun will need shades, awnings or covers to filter strong light and keep the temperature within reasonable limits.

Structurally speaking, the work will vary. Ceiling joists in a loft will probably need to be strengthened to support the weight of furniture: double them up by adding extra beams alongside. A rooflight – a window in the flat plane of the roof – is the minimum needed to achieve comfort and livability, and it is advisable to double up roof rafters on either side of it for support. A dormer will increase the floor area with adequate head height, but this may require regulatory permission. Some rafters or beams may have to be removed to gain enough clear space; you'll then have to consider alternative means of support.

1 Converting a loft to a home office can liberate your pattern of work without encroaching on the space of people you live with.
2 In large buildings, the area beneath the roof can be significant. Excellent sources of natural light and the potential for unusual storage arrangements showcase the bonuses of 'loft living'.
3 Loft bedrooms remove the sleeping area from the general domain, enhancing the sense of privacy.

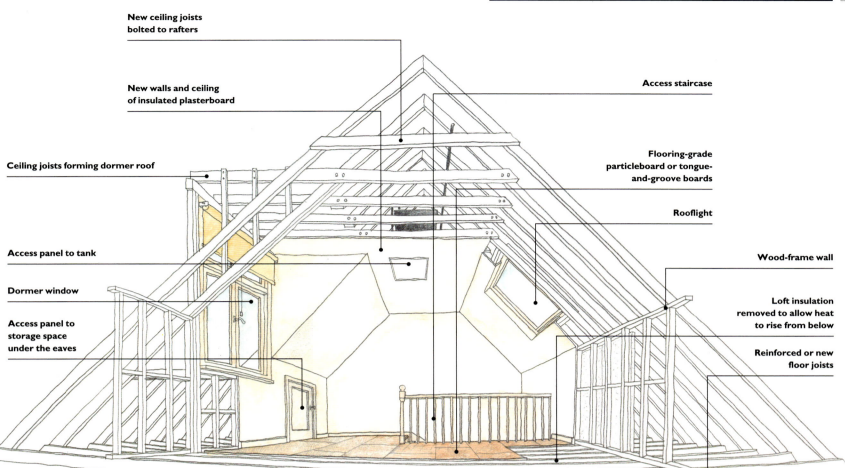

New ceiling joists bolted to rafters

New walls and ceiling of insulated plasterboard

Ceiling joists forming dormer roof

Access panel to tank

Dormer window

Access panel to storage space under the eaves

Access staircase

Flooring-grade particleboard or tongue-and-groove boards

Rooflight

Wood-frame wall

Loft insulation removed to allow heat to rise from below

Reinforced or new floor joists

POINTS TO REMEMBER

- You may need regulatory permission if you wish to split your house into two separate dwellings, for example, by converting a lower level to make a self-contained apartment. If you want to retain a connection between the two units, you will probably need to install a fire-resistant door.
- You may need building department approval for any structural alterations to your home, including underpinning.
- Carefully check where waste lines are permitted to be laid.
- Local historic preservation commissions may have regulations or guidelines governing alterations to your home's appearance, especially regarding changes to window frames, doors and roofing shape or materials.
- Any changes to layout and loft conversions have to comply with local fire regulations. These may specify fire-resistant doors to seal off new areas, type of flooring or size, operation and position of windows as well as locations of doors or fire stairs. The number of stories in your house or, if you are in a loft building, for example, may have key importance in complying with fire regulations.
- Ladders may be acceptable as a means of escape from a loft.

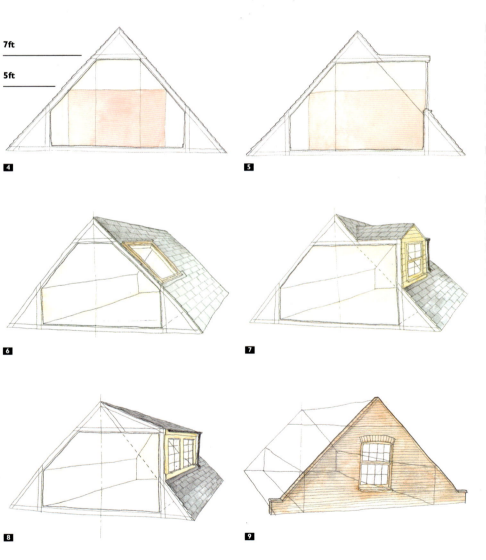

7ft

5ft

4 Floor area in a loft is calculated to be the space at which the roof is 5ft (1.5m) above the floor level. Most building requirements stipulate a minimum finished ceiling height of 7ft (2.3m) over at least half the floor area. **5** The addition of a dormer window can significantly increase habitable floor area. **6** Standard rooflight. **7** Gabled dormer window. **8** Dormer window. **9** Casement or sash window set in gable end.

Conversions

Most buildings outlive their original occupants and, barring natural accidents and planning blight, many go on to outlive their original function. There's nothing new about adapting a structure that began life with another purpose, but in recent times the attractions of living in a converted building have become ever more appreciated, gaining the hip architectural term of 'adaptive re-use'.

The reasons are pretty clear. Whether the house you dream of is a turn-of-the-century Victorian, a 1960s split-level, a contemporary surburban builder's stock-in-trade, or a sprawling pastiche on a cul-de-sac, chances are good that it's in a neighborhood of houses cut from the same cloth. Chances are also good that the layout running through all these developer-driven houses is remarkably similar. The sheer predictability of knowing that the bathroom will be 'first on the right at the top of the stairs' makes many people long for a change. Conversions can offer freedom of layout, and room for the unexpected.

Ever since some country-minded city folk found that life in the barn hayloft was more fun than in the big house, yuppies of all ages and means have been exploring old buildings that long ago divorced their first life. For aficionados of modern design, converted factories or warehouses offer a rugged utility and spare functional beauty; for those more in tune with architectural heritage, there is the opportunity to preserve and cherish unique architectural forms, such as old post offices, churches and schoolhouses. Loft living was a simple expedient for New York artists who, in the late 1970s, colonized the old light-industrial buildings of lower Manhattan and found the wide-open, easily malleable expanses of cheap studio space they were looking for. From these pioneering efforts has come a whole 'loft' style of living, with associated trends in design, such as hi-tech. In the process, a wide range of inner-city buildings has escaped being razed to the ground, recyling useful space and rejuvenating neglected districts from which local industries have long since departed – urban America's 'shrinking industrial base'.

Conversions usually offer more space than the average domestic house. At the same time, they generally encourage flexibility in the layout and arrangement of the space and throw in unusual architectural detail for good measure. You may secure many of these advantages by buying or renting a space which has already been converted, and there are now many highly sophisticated makeovers on the market. True enthusiasts prefer to start with the bare bones. The downside is that, while many of the spatial considerations that apply to an ordinary house are the same, there are extra demands, both structurally and organizationally, and the sheer scale of such projects can be daunting.

First, however, you have to find your building. Unconverted light industrial or warehouse buildings are usually handled by commercial real-estate agents; many

1 Translucent sliding screens section off a sleeping area in a loft conversion. The metal framework of the screens complements the industrial aesthetic of the building.
2 Rough-and-ready plywood partitions subdivide space in a New York loft – a surprisingly sleek use of a basic material.

3

of these buildings, however, are in urban areas that have become derelict and offer few amenities, like basic grocery stores or dry cleaners. If you are a true pioneer, this won't stop you, and it's likely that there are others with the same determination to carve a new residential area to their liking out of the warehouse district.

Depending on the size of the building, the next step may be to find a number of like-minded folks to share the costs of renovating major building-wide mechanical and structural systems. You will need sound advice on financing and contractual matters right from the start.

Even more essential is to secure planning and building permits for both change of use and necessary alterations. If the building you want to live in is in an area designated for manufacturing only, you could be at a dead end unless you can obtain a zoning variance. Buildings are classified according to the functions they fulfill, with 'residential' being only one of many categories. City hall's response to your proposal to set up house in a former piano factory or nursery school will often depend on political issues, such as whether or not the powers that be are trying to encourage new business in the area. If your scheme includes working premises, such as a photographer's studio or a restaurant, you may stand a better chance of success. A prudent course of action is to make the sale or lease conditional on securing permission; otherwise you may find yourself the proud owner of a building that you aren't allowed to live in. Check with community organizations or others that have dealt with the same problems in the same neighborhood, and seek advice from an architect or engineer on the feasibility of your plans. The requirements for adequate fire protection are likely to be stringent. You may have to deal with any number of municipal agencies and bureacracies, from a preservation commission to the planning board.

Naturally, it is easier to bypass such hurdles and look for a floor or loft space

3 Old beams and roof trusses reveal the past in an elegant conversion of an old barn. Disused agricultural buildings provide original and characterful space for those seeking to move away from conventional domestic surroundings.
4 Gridded partitions infilled with glass separate private areas from open living space in a warehouse conversion.

in a building that is already managed by someone else. Whichever route you take, adapting the space to your personal requirements involves the same kind of approach detailed elsewhere in this section, but on a larger scale, suited to an urban enviroment. It is often difficult and expensive in these buildings to create heating and hot-water systems that can be individually controlled, but it is certainly worth exploring. Dividing up space into private and open areas is another exciting challenge. The positioning of existing bathroom fixtures may provide a good starting point. Some partitioning will be necessary, or you may find that your new home has all the intimacy of a football field. At the same time, it is essential to acknowledge the scale and to play up to it; let the original character of the building show through by respecting existing features and structural elements.

4

Putting back the style

1

1 While the practical role of the fireplace may have diminished considerably, the aesthetic and symbolic contributions it makes to the interior are more valued than ever. This empty hearth frames a large ceramic urn, and provides a decorative focus for the room.
2 Paneled doors, architraves and a simple fire surround painted in with the walls lend detail, focus and character without compromising the essentially contemporary mood of this bedroom.

Putting back the style is a moral crusade for some devotees, an enterprise which demands diligence, detective work and spare cash. In such instances it becomes a question of how far to go. It is perfectly possible to restore an interior to a semblance of its original condition, down to historically accurate door furniture and paint recipes. Generally, however, there comes a point when the convenience of modern services becomes too persuasive and period flavor rather than period reality appears more attractive. Others are aware that old houses have been subjected to many changes over the years and that the date of origin carries no special significance. For most people, the main issue is how to successfully reconcile the old with the new.

Period restoration is most feasible, practical and effective on the level of architectural detail. 'Detail', however, is a more powerful element than the word might imply. The aggregate effect of such subtle and seemingly redundant features is easy to judge when you see an old house without them. Detail civilizes proportions, makes sense of scale and adds quality to finishes. Moldings and trim adjust the eye to the breaks between ceiling and wall, wall and floor. Cornices and baseboards edge the plane of the wall, and in the process elegantly conceal the type of superficial cracking which can occur at these major joints. Chair rails, generally positioned about one-third of the way up the wall, were intended to signal the break between the

An old house with a history reveals its character in a variety of ways – through materials and construction, design and layout, and, critically, what is generally referred to as 'architectural detail'. This is a loose term that encompasses all those intrinsic, evocative features, such as moldings, cornices, dados, picture rails, fireplaces and wainscoting, which define, embellish and articulate the plain surfaces of the interior.

Not so long ago, in the frenzied rush to modernize old properties with updated services and more flexible internal arrangements, many such details were unceremoniously stripped off and discarded. The public has, on the whole, been uninterested in these details, and has also been ready and willing to replace them with Postmodern interpretations of historical decoration. But now people have begun to realize what they are missing, and it is less likely that a period house will be stripped of all of its most distinctive features – features which, increasingly, add real value to a home. Coincidental with this renewed appreciation and spirit of preservation has come a flourishing trade in architectural salvage and the reproduction of period detail.

2

3

3 The traditional detailing of this Mediterranean house is subtly emphasized by slate gray paintwork. In the past, doors, paneling, shutters and wood trim were commonly made of softwood which was always painted.
4 Half-height paneling, fine architraves and the glossy polished floor pay homage to early American interiors without resorting to wholesale restoration.
5 An elaborate plasterwork ceiling in a studio apartment is a superb foil to the contemporary design.

4

different types of wall finish – the lower half robust and hardwearing, the upper part fine and decorative. The strip of molding here was originally intended to prevent chair backs from scraping away at the fabric of the wall.

A study of historical interiors can acquaint you with the various forms of these decorative features and their standard positioning. There may be a house in your neighborhood which has retained its details and you might wish to copy these. Alternatively, you might have semi-intact moldings from which you can cast replacements for the missing portions. Synthetic versions are available off-the-shelf; lightweight, easy to install and virtually indistinguishable from the real thing once painted and installed, these can be a practical option.

Avoid period gloss and restore only those elements that make a positive contribution to the interior, either in a decorative or a practical way. If you want to run picture rails around your room, hang pictures from them. You don't have to opt for excessively decorative flights of fancy; a relatively plain molding will do the same job as one with all the curlicues.

Larger period pieces, such as fireplaces, often contribute an important focus to a room. You don't have to be slavishly accurate, but it is important to suit the fire surround to the scale of the room and match its style to the overall character of the space. A tiny cast-iron grate will be swamped in a high-ceilinged room; a baroque marble edifice won't do much for a bedroom unless the decoration is suitably extravagant to support it.

Most of these styling flourishes aren't likely to involve you in much building work, although installing a fireplace does entail opening up a blocked chimney breast. Since chimney breasts form part of the structure of the house, it may first be necessary to get help to establish how far you can excavate.

Removing unwanted features, in the form of modern additions, is another matter. Occasionally something totally unexpected turns up – you may uncover original seventeenth-century features from under layers of Victorian brickwork in the heart of an old farmhouse – but not all discoveries are welcome. Thoroughgoing archaeology on the fabric of your home demands proper surveying, as well as architectural and historical advice.

5

GETTING ORGANIZED

Homes house things as much as they do people. Even the most dedicated minimalist needs belongings, equipment and basic necessities; most of us travel through life with lots more baggage, some of it clearly redundant. When possessions start to get the upper hand, it's time to rethink just how, where and why we hang on to as many things as we do.

Good organization should be largely invisible, whereas chaos and disarray stare you in the face, slow you up at every turn and make aggravating chores out of simple everyday routines. Organizing your home properly doesn't necessarily mandate major upheavals, expense or structural change; it can be as straightforward as reassigning rooms new functions or setting up a special storage area. If you get this right, you'll rediscover space you never knew you had and enjoy using it all the more.

Storage is a workaday word for what is, in fact, one of the key elements in the way your home looks and functions. How and where you accommodate your possessions has a radical effect on the way you use the remaining space, particularly on the ease and efficiency with which you perform almost any task, from getting dressed to cooking a meal, taking a bath to playing with the children. And your basic approach – whether you like to leave everything in view or to banish all your belongings to cabinets and closets – will determine the basic character of your home more surely than any mix of paint colors or decorative style. An entrance hall that is cluttered with bicycles, discarded coats and unopened junk mail speaks volumes about the value of good storage – and the mess has a habit of spreading insidiously throughout the rest of the house.

For all these reasons, it's not an issue which can be approached piecemeal or reactively. You need to look at all the items in your possession, at how often you use them and in what contexts, so that you can then store them somewhere sensible, know where to find them and access them as easily as possible. Good storage also means that your possessions are well cared for and don't get damaged or age prematurely. It's common knowledge that you need twice as much storage space as you think; reorganize your home and you'll probably find it within your own four walls.

1 Kitchens demand special organizational skills. Fresh food, basic provisions, equipment and utensils all need to be stored safely and readily to hand for efficient food preparation and cooking.
2 A well-proportioned storage wall combines closed base cupboards for clutter with open book shelves for display. Framing a doorway with shelving in this way has an appealing solidity and strength.

3 Hide it all from view in floor-to-ceiling closets fitted with shelves at different heights to provide flexible storage space.

4 Plywood door fronts stained in different colors liven up these bathroom units.

4

5 The beauty and fragility of glassware is accentuated by glass display shelves, seamlessly built in to an alcove.

5

6

that it's time for a thorough sort-out and reorganization.

Less is more

Finding space

Home organization tends to lag behind changes in lifestyle or circumstance and if you're feeling the pinch in a particular area, it may be because your expectations or activities have altered. If your culinary horizons have broadened over the years, you may require more storage space in the kitchen; if you now work at home instead of going out to an office, you'll need a place to keep the accessories of your professional life. And if you have children, you'll know how fast their needs change and how important it is to keep a step ahead organizationally.

Micro-planning can get you just so far. Usually what's needed is a more thorough investigation of how you use the space at your disposal. Finding space to put things involves understanding how you use or underuse different areas.

The first aspect to consider is room use. Simple reallocation of space can go a long way to solving many organizational problems. Consider the most common

1

1 As Le Corbusier pointed out, the practice of keeping clothes in the bedroom is neither practical nor conducive to relaxation. Dressing areas can be fashioned from vestibules, box rooms and adjoining hallways. **2** A walk-in closet framed in unfinished plywood makes an idiosyncratic library fitted with floor-to-ceiling shelves.

2

arrangement, with parents in a large 'master' bedroom, the eldest child in a smaller bedroom and baby in a tiny nursery. However, if the children were to share the big room, the parents move to the medium-sized room and the nursery converted to a study-cum-guest room, the benefits for everyone could be wide-ranging. From three rooms dominated by a single use, there would be a new flexibility with positive implications for the entire household. Big bedrooms often make sense for small children, giving them a base where they can play and romp with their friends: if they have their own domain, they are much less likely to invade the rest of the house leaving a trail of Lego in their wake. Similarly, a small study for quiet reading, homework or hobbies, perhaps with facilities for putting up overnight guests, is a positive asset in many families, while a baby will quickly outgrow the confines of a tiny room and will soon be longing for the company of siblings.

Next, consider the 'between-spaces' — such as under the stairs, in landings and hallways – places which have no specifically defined function but which often, especially in older houses, account for a significant amount of floor area. Lining one wall of a hallway with bookshelves or converting the area under the stairs into a study area, play corner or fitted storage space can dramatically benefit the spatial quality of adjacent rooms burdened with too many activities. There's a world of difference between letting heaps of clutter clog up the hall because you haven't found anywhere else for it to go and a wholehearted, architecturally conceived solution that transforms a wasted space into one with its own specific character and appeal. Provided you don't shrink your main traffic routes unacceptably and make it awkward, uncomfortable or even dangerous to move from place to place, decanting storage into circulation areas can be very successful all around.

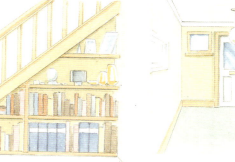

3

4

5

6   7

8   9   10

11

3 The space beneath conventional staircases is often overlooked, but offers great storage potential for shelves of books.
4 Used as bookshelves – rather than for aesthetic display – a wall of shelving makes particularly effective use of space in a hall or landing.
5 If you need a quiet corner for settling checks and occasional work from home, the below-stairs area could be turned into a small home office.
6 Even a small alcove fitted with a shelf at desk height can be put to use as a study area.
7 Fitting a wall of shelving around a doorway can be strikingly graphic.
8 Wardrobe storage can be much more efficiently organized if you think about the types of clothes you own: shelves at the bottom for shoes; full-length hanging space for longer clothes; open shelves for shirts and sweaters; drawers for small items and accessories; and half-height rails for jackets, skirts or other shorter-length items.
9 Stagger the dividing wall between two rooms to provide wardrobe space in the alcoves created.
10 Alcoves on either side of a doorway can be used for open-shelf storage or cabinets.
11 A hard-working corner doubles as a window seat and spare sleeping area, with generous storage space built in underneath the mattress.

An extension of the same idea is to transform partitions between rooms into storage walls, with both inner and outer sides fitted with closets, cabinets or closed shelving. Here is an opportunity to tailor the fitted space to the precise dimensions of what you need to store, which always makes good sense. Storage walls act as buffers to sound and are effective heat insulators, too.

Another way to achieve more storage space is to reorganize the connections between rooms. If you plot how you actually travel around your home, you may be surprised how rarely you use certain entrances to rooms where there's a choice of routes. In this case, blocking up the redundant doorway will win you that much more wall space which can be used for storage needs or could offer the opportunity, for example, to extend a run of kitchen units.

Finally, there is the option of devoting an entire room to storage. Linen closets, pantries and sewing rooms and other areas principally given over to the housing and management of belongings immediately recall the type of planning associated with manor-style households and their legions of servants. Few of us live on such a grand scale but, even when space is tight, fitting out a specific area to house clothes, food or books can make good spatial sense. A separate dressing area can make the bedroom a much more relaxing place; you don't have to sacrifice an entire room for the purpose, a vestibule adjacent to the main bathroom would do. The pantry, the indispensable storecupboard in our grandmothers' day, fell from favor with the advent of kitchen technology, but there is nothing old-fashioned about the benefits of natural refrigeration and orderly keeping of stocks and supplies. With the kitchen often functioning as a family room, separate storage areas are making a comeback. Storage rooms are instinctively appealing, liberating other parts of the house from the burden of catering for too many different needs.

Thinking laterally

1 Storage boxes that slide out on wheels transform wasted under-stairs space into useful cubbyholes. As the stairs go up, the boxes extend to form full-height cupboards. **2** A wooden draining board which can be stacked to one side when not in use maximizes precious countertop space in a small kitchen. **3** Storage on wheels – carts faced in translucent perspex – hides kitchen clutter and look good enough to take up residence in the main living area. **4** A shallow sliding tray fitted with a collapsible ironing board is a space-saving solution for a laundry area. Overhead, a traditional clothes airer can be lowered to provide drying space.

Adaptability is the secret of successful storage; make a sideways step and you can discover unconventional solutions which work brilliantly. Hi-tech style alerted many people to the potential of borrowing equipment and accessories designed for factories, offices and stores; if you aren't enamored of the industrial aesthetic, you don't have to look that far for ideas, you should merely be prepared to consider different uses for fixtures from those for which they were originally intended. A plastic-coated wire mesh container may be on sale as a laundry bin, but if it turns out to be the ideal solution for storing rolled up drawings, then why not make use of it? You could import a serving cart into the bathroom as a home for soaps and shampoos, or fill a log basket with a great many other things besides logs – from the children's toys to dirty laundry.

Lateral thinking also applies to finding new uses for traditional freestanding storage furniture. Chests, armoires, dressers, and cabinets are generally adaptable enough to house a wide range of items, not merely those which their makers first envisaged. Given a face-lift, there's no reason why an old bedroom chest of drawers shouldn't be put to use in the kitchen. Hatboxes can make a good home for needles, thread and other sewing equipment; neatly stacked shoeboxes can store a range of items. Useful items to salvage or adapt include:

• Store fittings, such as display cabinets, hanging rails, banks of drawers
• Wire mesh baskets, carts and bins
• Metal shelving originally designed for catering or industrial use
• School lockers and cabinets
• Filing cabinets, in-trays and other office storage systems.

5 In a kitchen, a compromise is often struck between squeezing in major appliances and allocating enough countertop and cabinet space. This ingenious solution takes the built-in oven and cooktop out of the equation by building them into a wood framework that forms a piece of free-standing kitchen furniture. By incorporating work surfaces to either side, there is still room to rest pots and pans when the food is ready. The wall-hung spice rack and *batterie de cuisine* keep utensils and basic ingredients readily to hand.

5

6

7

6 Ideal equipment for a workshop or studio, this hi-tech storage system with movable shelves and metal bins racked onto back plates – originally designed to store industrial components – can organize a vast amount of clutter.
7 What appears – from the landing – to be a wall of built-in wardrobes in fact hides the staircase up to a loft study. The 'wardrobe' doors do open, however, providing progressively greater storage space as the stairs behind rise. The far door conceals a full-height closet for hanging up coats and stowing away outdoor gear.

ANTON AND COLETTE

Walls shape our lives. Most of us live by house rules in rooms whose nature is dictated by their names. We sleep in the bedroom, we bathe in the bathroom, we cook in the kitchen. Yet, historically, the house has always been a fairly amorphous organism that changes in response to society. In the Middle Ages, domestic activity took place in one room, centered around the hearth (so much for open-plan being a modern concept). Two hundred years ago it was the customary thing to receive company in your bedroom. One hundred years ago it would have been unthinkable not to have a dining room. Times change; walls, metaphorically, dissolve.

The term 'living room' disturbed the status quo when it first entered our vocabulary in the postwar era. Before the coining of this loose appellation, living rooms were specifically defined in a way that clearly denoted their function and, at the same time, the status of their owner. At its crudest, the rich had drawing rooms (literally a withdrawing room) and the genteel poor had what was called a 'front room'. Both terms carried a certain hands-off, Sunday-best implication. 'Living room' seemed better suited to a society that was becoming less class and gender bound. It had an egalitarian ring to it, though for many the lack of definition implied a freedom they could not cope with. Gradually, this strange concept of 'living' in, as opposed to merely inhabiting rooms, spread beyond the former drawing room or front room into the domain of the kitchen. To have your decorating style described as the 'lived-in' look during the 1980s was the ultimate compliment: thus did a practical way of life become a stylistic conceit.

First impressions

From a visual point of view, a home's exterior is felt by many of us to be low on the list of priorities. The money it takes to give the front of the house a coat of white paint could go quite a long way in the living room. Given the choice between a new sofa or a smart façade, most of us would probably plump for the sofa. The longer you live with a shabby exterior, the less you realize it (until, that is, the day you notice it crumbling around you...).

For many reasons, then, the first impressions are often dealt with last. This is perfectly understandable, if shortsighted – you do, after all, spend more time inside, and from a purely selfish point of view it is passers-by and your neighbors who suffer from the visual assault if your house is the one in the street that looks like a rotten tooth in an otherwise gleaming smile. However, as soon as you begin to make improvements you see that it makes a disproportionate difference to the feel of your house: a freshly painted front door can give a tremendous lift to appearance, only you'll then notice just how shabby the door furniture looks.

Even something as simple as a row of geraniums up the front steps can have enormous impact on style. Other improvements may involve more thought and cost. You may, for example, need to claim the front yard back from the street by growing a hedge, or putting up a fence to give a sense of enclosure and privacy. Replacing flimsy wrought-iron gates with a solid, custom-built gate will add to the sense of this being personal space.

However, as with all changes to the façade, the whims of the individual must be balanced against the constraints of the public. Take into account both the architectural period of your house and its surroundings. A row of townhouses can look pretty all painted in different colors if they share the same depth of tone – it's the bay window with bottle-glass panes that strikes the discordant note. In fact, there is probably no quicker way to devalue your house, both aesthetically and in terms of resale, than to mess around with original windows.

1

1 The British habit of giving their houses names instead of numbers – even if it is nothing more original than *Casa Nostra* – is considered to be a sign of affection for the concept of the home. A nicely detailed number, however, conveys the same sense of care with considerably more panache.
2 Not everybody feels the need to shrink anonymously into the urban fabric. Witness this house-cum-studio belonging to London artist, Andrew Logan: forged out of a former garage, it uses a terra cotta render and vivid blue to give the building a strong identity that is neither domestic nor industrial.

2

3

4

3 The range of colors to these San Francisco houses gives them a greater harmony – the differences in detailing would be more obvious if they were all painted white.
4 In London, the same effect is achieved using similar intensities of different colors.

6

7

8

5

5 A long roof unites separate buildings that enclose that most magical of spaces, an internal courtyard. The real beauty of this building, apart from the spectacular location, is the appropriateness of the construction materials: built of wood, the house seems to grow naturally out of the environment.
6 A metal door suits the industrial aesthetic of this development.

10

9

7 Strong vernacular styles of building – such as the richly tiled façade of this house in Portugal – should be tampered with as little as possible.
9 The white stucco front of a London townhouse leaves only the door as an area for experimentation.

8 An imaginative conversion of a small garage has left the original garage doors in place.
10 When the seemingly commonplace doors are opened they reveal a stunning glass-fronted studio. Buildings which retain part of their past have charisma.

Halls and stairways

Entrance halls are important both from a symbolic and purely practical point of view. In a small house, getting rid of the hall to open up and enlarge the living space may seem like a good idea, but stepping straight from the street into the living room is a psychologically uncomfortable experience. It may extend your floor space, but it deprives you of the ceremony of entry, that brief period of transition in which you shake off the outside before you can truly feel at ease in a house. It's almost as if coming straight in from the elements to the living room is too much of a shock to the system, because you are denied that breathing-space in which to adapt

Because a hall is just such a breathing-space, it is best not to clog it up with clutter. If it is very narrow, even coat racks, when fully loaded, can induce a feeling of claustrophobia. If it is wide enough for furniture but it is still very much a thoroughfare as opposed to a room, it is unlikely to feel comfortable as a space for sitting and relaxing but it may be a very good location for purely decorative pieces of furniture.

As an introduction to other rooms it is probably wise to stick with a simple decorative scheme. Fussy wallpapers and dark paintwork give a gloomy over-bearing first impression. Light, neutral colors are best, particularly as the hall-way is often chosen as a gallery space for a collection of pictures.

Floors need to be durable and wash-able: consider the period and character of your house before deciding on the material. Architectural salvage yards are a good source for authentic flooring, but beware of getting carried away. Mellow eighteenth-century Provençal tiles may be beautiful, but they will look totally out of place in a Victorian townhouse. Original encaustic tiles still exist in many Victorian hallways – if there are one or two missing from the pattern there are companies who have revived the method and can produce replacement tiles to order.

1 Barely-there balustrading gives a sense of space. Instead of using wood, many designers choose metal for stairway detailing – rigging wire from specialist yachting shops is particularly strong and effective.
2 A sculptural stair-way in wood and metal is graphic and strong.
3 If a hall is wide enough, a wall of clos-ets is invaluable for storing coats and shoes. Solid doors would be too heavy – louvered panels, as here, work well.

Bear in mind the material and color of floor surfaces in the rooms which lead off the hall so that you can avoid any jarring contrasts. This is one obvious reason why the ever-popular black-and-white tiled floor never fails to look good, as long as you have got the size of tiles in proportion to the floor space.

In a house, the hall is usually domin-ated by the staircase, and this is often the first thing you and your visitors will see on entering. For most of us – living in standard purpose-built houses – a staircase is simply a place that leads up

4

to one floor or down to another, and a lick of paint is about the most it ever receives in terms of decorative attention. But in modern, architect-designed homes the staircase often takes on a much more active part; accorded the status of something of an icon, its important role in linking different levels is given a sculptural form.

However, staircases that make a dramatic statement – which sweep into a room or suggest themselves as places to sit – are comparatively rare, and the potential to make something of the existing arrangement is limited unless you are having work done to other parts of your home. The average staircase is generally undistinguished rather than downright ugly, so beyond replacing missing banisters, it is probably simply a matter of deciding whether to strip, paint or polish the wood.

As for stair treads, if they are in good condition and are of elegant proportion, it is a shame to hide them under wall-to-wall carpet. Bare treads, none the less, are noisy, so a good compromise is a runner. Matting is hard wearing and visually appealing, but avoid materials that are too tough and unyielding – they will be difficult to fit properly and are often scratchy under foot.

5
6

4 Conventional stairways use up a huge amount of floorspace: where this is restricted a spiral staircase is the obvious solution.
5 The hall is a linking space: vistas from it should be an integral part of the design.
6 Any horizontal surface becomes a natural dumping ground in the hall – a cunningly placed glass shelf prevents people hanging their coats on the art.

Living in the kitchen

1 The slick workmanlike lines of a compact built-in kitchen are softened by its relationship to the living room.

1

2

Liberated from negative associations we are free to enjoy the kitchen as never before. Where once it was barely considered as a room, it is now felt by many to be about the most important space in the whole house – a place where we are sustained both physically and emotionally. Although it is primarily functional, a place in which to cook, it is also, in practice, an informal living room; in many ways it probably plays the role of the eighteenth- and nineteenth-century morning room where visitors were received in the daytime, so that its style and comfort are almost as important as its functional layout.

Our kitchens give out signals to other people, both about our character and our attitude to food. This may be only a stylistic front. Take, say, what can loosely be called the farmhouse kitchen, where a central table doubling as a work surface is the focus of a generally cozy-looking space – lined with cupboards, shelves and perhaps a hutch – that conveys a welcoming air.

Undoubtedly, this look involves a certain amount of self-deception. There is something slightly ludicrous about the idea of a farmhouse kitchen in an urban environment, but this probably reflects a general escapism: the harder the outside world gets, the worse the economy, the bleaker the news reports, the cozier the kitchen becomes.

If you take the farmhouse kitchen as your basic format or guiding inspiration, you should work with materials that are suited to your house. Fitted kitchens can disguise themselves as an ad hoc arrangement of cupboards which look back, stylistically, to a gentler age. A farmhouse kitchen does not have to be nostalgic. You can still follow the pattern that has proved to be the most practical and successful way of combining general family life and cooking, but use ultra-modern furniture and fixtures or a contrasting combination of old and new. The table does not have to be a scrubbed pine, antique refectory table; it could be glass, metal or laminate.

This ideal of a large, hospitable 'lived-in' kitchen depends on a generous allocation of space. If you try to cram farmhouse style into a poky modern room, the creature of your dreams who

3

4

5

6

7

2 A fresh color scheme of blue and neutral injects vitality into this practical kitchen, where a butcher block adds an extra work surface.
3 With its tiled walls and high ceilings, the old-fashioned air of this room is emphasized by the free-standing furniture. Roller shades half way down the windows afford privacy without sacrificing light and ventilation.
4 A separate utility room means there is nothing to disrupt the tonal harmony of this studio kitchen, where color and texture are aesthetically blended.
5 The message of the lived-in kitchen is that cooking is a pleasure. Attention is focused on display and presentation, with clever use of mirror in the elegant wall of shelving.

inhabits this space – the one who gets back from a hard day's work and starts calmly baking bread while four angelic children create brilliant collages on the kitchen table – is likely to end up screaming and burning the meal.

If you have the space, then the most workable solution is what the French call 'le living' – an open-plan area with cooking facilities and a table at one end, a chair or sofa, shelves for the children's toys and the dog basket at the other.

But this is a look that needs to be done with conviction. Cheap, badly planned kitchens which take up a corner of a square, carpeted room do not have the same atmosphere as 'le living'. The classic architecture and planning textbook, *A Pattern Language*, sees in this half-hearted measure 'the hidden supposition that cooking is a chore and that eating is a pleasure. So long as this mentality rules... the conflict which existed in the isolated kitchen is still present.'

6 Last night's wine bottle and this morning's jellies cohabiting on the table spell the ultimate Bohemian dream for some, nightmare squalor for others. Of course, it helps to have signs of faded grandeur: remove this scene to a small, one-room apartment and it can lose its charm.
7 Different ceiling heights and the use of units to break up space create areas with a defined sense of their own while retaining the open plan.

The self-contained kitchen

1

3

2

4

Naturally there will always be those who do not look upon cooking as a spectator sport and who prefer to practice their craft in solitary confinement. For these reclusive cooks and also for those who simply do not have the flexibility of space to allow for combined living and cooking areas, there may be no alternative to the small, but not necessarily isolated, kitchen.

Even if there is no room for anything other than functional essentials, the kitchen does not have to feel cut off from the lifeblood of the home. If it opens onto a corridor, a double door may make it seem less like a cell. Look at how the kitchen relates to the spaces around it – perhaps you can open up at least partially to the living room.

Styles of cooking have some, but not a major, impact on design. Consider planning and efficiency before getting bogged down in matters of style. It is best to choose a fairly basic style of kitchen and then dress it accordingly. Be realistic, too, about your culinary expectations. Seductive as they may be, sophisticated pieces of equipment will not turn you into a brilliant chef. An unused kitchen has a dead feel to it, so if you see food as only a means to an end, you are likely to be far happier in a farmhouse-style kitchen than in a kitchen-as-laboratory which puts the spotlight on performance.

Of course good cooks do not need an ostentatious kitchen. Custom-made kitchens have become so sophisticated that we have tended to lose sight of the basics. Cooking only demands ingredients, heat, water, a sharp knife and a set of saucepans. But by the time you

2 Even the paintings are freestanding in this low-tech kitchen, which gives a new slant on twin ovens.
3 The hatch hits new heights of sophistication in this 'machine for cooking in', to misquote Le Corbusier, where the work surface doubles as breakfast bar.
4 A high counter with shelves above shields the kitchen from the dining area.

5

6

5 A high kitchen counter screens culinary clutter from general view.

6 A serving hatch can be closed off or open as convenience and sociability dictate, the perfect antidote to culinary claustrophobia.

7

8

9

7 Kitchens come alive as rooms when furniture, such as this grandfather clock, are used out of context.

8 The hard lines of a professional stainless-steel restaurant kitchen provide a good model for the compact domestic kitchen.

9 Where a galley kitchen extends off the main living room a shared color scheme works well.

have been through all the brochures, you can easily convince yourself that life simply isn't worth living unless you have a wire drawer for potatoes and an aluminum-lined one for bread.

If you are on a limited budget, look for creative solutions rather than the cheapest thing available. You may find it works to buy a range of inexpensive stock cabinets and replace the doors with ones made up by a local carpenter. Painted tongue-and-groove, for example, can give you the custom-made look at a fraction of the price.

Kitchen planning

Good planning is the key to a successful kitchen, but don't be intimidated by its seemingly technical nature. Basically, planning is a question of assessing your requirements in terms of equipment and storage space, and balancing that against the architecture of the space you have available. There is no exact prescription because people's priorities are different. One designer's clients living in the country were concerned that the refrigerator should be acoustically isolated so that its humming would not spoil their rural peace and quiet. Le Corbusier apparently thought it would be a good idea to put the kitchen at the top of the house to do away with the problem of cooking smells.

However, there are three fundamental factors in kitchen planning – where to site the sink, cooking facilities and refrigerator. Once you have established these it is relatively easy to design the kitchen in a logical fashion around them. Most kitchen designers base their plans on the 'work triangle', an imaginary line drawn between the three work centers of sink, stove and refrigerator. Ergonomically speaking no two centers should be more than a double arm span

apart or so close together as to cramp your movements. Individualists might balk at this prescription, but ergonomics is as much about common sense as it is about scientific precision. You may think it is no problem to walk from one end of the kitchen to the other to get something from the refrigerator but repeating that sequence time and time again, day after day, will eventually wear down your resilience.

The placement of the sink is where you should start. Traditionally it is placed in front of a window. There is no law about this, and sometimes the layout of the room makes it impossible, but it does feel distinctly odd to stand in front of a sink without a view. And it makes sense to put the area of the kitchen where you are likely to spend most of your time nearest the source of natural light. If window space is unavailable, the next best thing is to have the sink facing outward into the room – on an island, or peninsula layout. If none of these choices is feasible, at least try to avoid having cabinets above the sink; claustrophobic working conditions are certainly not going to increase the appeal of working there.

1 In this single-line kitchen, bulky cooking equipment is stored in the cabinets below the countertop, while ingredients are neatly displayed above on glass shelves.
2 A combination of built-in and freestanding equipment allows for optimum flexibility in the layout of room, provided you have enough space. High-tech stainless steel appliances are moderated by the washed blue walls and the pink and yellow trim.

3 The classic L-shaped configuration, with a kitchen table providing an additional work surface.
4 Storage cabinets on wheels are incredibly versatile. When not in use, this impressive kitchen is hidden away behind the wall of sliding doors.
5 In a large family kitchen, the island counter is invaluable, acting as breakfast bar, food-preparation surface and room divider all in one.

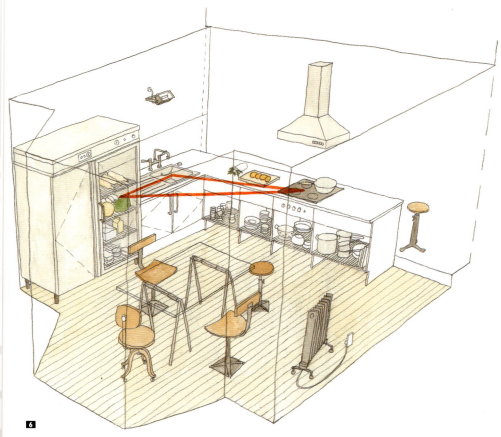

6

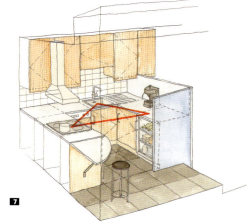

7

9 The galley kitchen is the most efficient use of space, with counters running along two parallel walls. There should be a minimum 48in (1200mm) between facing units to allow easy access to under-counter cabinets.
10 The island kitchen requires plenty of floor space. Islands create a separate work area at the same time as opening up the kitchen. An island cooktop requires dedicated worktop ventilation or an exhaust hood.

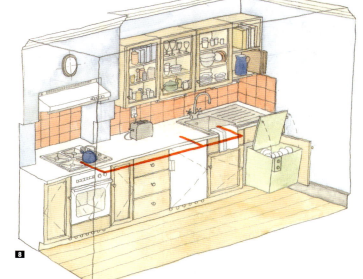

8

For practical purposes dishwashers should be located near the sink. Placement of the oven is not so crucial; anyone with young children, and older people who want to avoid too much bending down, will probably choose an eye-level appliance. Don't choose a stranded position; you will need a surface close by for resting hot dishes.

Disguising appliances as cabinets – the built-in look – is a hotly debated question of aesthetics. Many designers dislike the dishonesty of it, and put it on a par with hiding the television inside a fake antique cabinet. On the other hand, a run of units, unbroken by knobs and dials, has a certain neatness. You can celebrate technology by choosing appliances in stainless steel or gleaming enamel; or you can compromise – hide some, display others.

Portable appliances which are likely to stay permanently on the countertop must also be taken into consideration; toaster, microwave, food processor and espresso machine all eat up valuable space. You also need to take the height of these into account when allowing for clearance between countertops and overhead cabinets.

6 The L-shaped kitchen allows ample space for a dining table without interfering with the routes between the elements of the work triangle.
7 In a small U-shaped kitchen, a flap-down countertop provides useful extra work space. Positioning the refrigerator at the end of a run allows easy general access to it.
8 The single-line kitchen works well in any room with a run of at least 10ft (3m). It should be carefully planned to provide as much worktop space as possible.

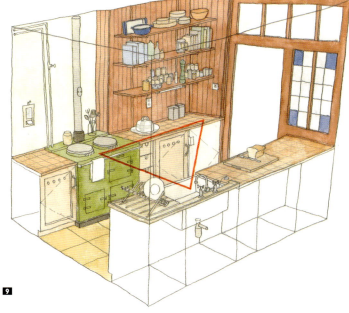

9

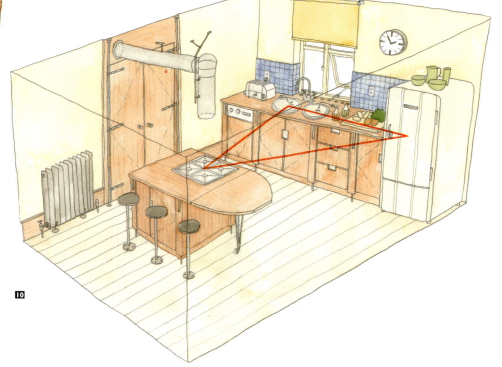

10

EATING

The demise of the dining room has been one of the most dramatic changes in the way we inhabit houses, and when we trace its death throes we see it goes hand in hand with the renaissance of the kitchen. The dining room is not totally extinct; in grander houses, and more formal families, it would – even now – be unthinkable not to have a separate room for dining. But in most houses where there is space for one, the dining room now doubles as a recreation or work space.

Early in the twentieth century domestic wages and working conditions were generally so pitiful that even fairly modest households could afford at least one maid. For as long as there was no real alternative to domestic work, there was a ready supply of labor. But during and after the First World War, jobs for women in factories – with better salaries and shorter working hours – became available. Thereafter, those that remained in domestic service were in a stronger position to demand higher wages and regulated working conditions so that only the wealthiest people could afford to continue employing servants.

New books like *First Aid to the Servantless* and *The Servantless House* made housework seem like rather a jolly adventure and extolled the virtues of extraordinary cleaning machines like the 'Ukanusa Drudgee' and the 'Dreadnought' dishwasher. But when the first flush of enthusiasm had died down, people began to look much more seriously at the practicality of their houses. When servants had been taken for granted the kitchen was often positioned some distance from the dining room. During World War I many families – 'though respectability might hardly countenance it', wrote a shocked Randall Phillips in 1921 – were actually eating their meals in the kitchen. Having broached the subject Phillips goes on tentatively to suggest the idea of 'eliminating the sitting room from the middle-class house and having instead one large living room – large enough, indeed, to allow a dining table to be set comfortably at one side of it, leaving plenty of space around for sitting, writing or reading.' The dining room was not yet dead, but there were certainly signs of its mortal decline. Seventy-five years later the dining room as a formal, monolithic space is probably only seen where old habits die hardest.

Eating is about more than just physical sustenance. Meals can be an intensely social occasion, a chance for family and friends to gather together. Whether the main eating room is the kitchen, living room or a separate dining room, we require the space to be relaxed, congenial and adaptable to various moods and occasions.

The open plan

1

2

3

The open-plan kitchen is brilliant for rushed family breakfasts and relaxed suppers but it has one huge drawback – the formal entertaining side. It requires formidable powers of organization and tidiness to present an impressive three-course meal within the same space that you have produced it – particularly if the table doubles as a work surface.

In an ideal world, you would not have people come to dinner whom you felt it necessary to impress. But in real life it happens, and even the most relaxed among us feel the need to change tempo and have the kind of refined evening that demands something more exotic than pasta and candles in bottles. There is also the cynical but historically justified view that perhaps the open plan is fashion-motivated, and that we shall all soon revert to more formal lifestyles.

Whatever the reasoning, it is sensible to make your eating spaces flexible. If you are restricted to eating in the kitchen this will largely be a matter of styling – replacing the cereal-splattered plastic cloth with white linen and dressing the table accordingly. Lighting is an essential factor in defining spaces and orchestrating mood. In *A Pattern Language*, Christopher Alexander advocates a low-hung light, central to the

4

5

2 Varying the height of the ceiling and using different materials creates interesting pockets of space within an open-plan structure. A sunny enclosed verandah makes a perfect dining spot.
3 Use of a single color brings unity to a small, open-plan area. It also helps to have dual-purpose seating: this table can be moved across to the built-in sofa at mealtimes.
4 An enclosed room works well within open-plan space only if it asserts itself boldly.
5 A countertop creates extra space for the kitchen.

1 What a room gains in space from an open plan it can lose in intimacy. The natural inclination is to move table and chairs into an area with some sense of enclosure, such as under the sloping ceiling, as here.

6

7

table, with dark walls around so that the light acts as a focal, gathering point. In the farmhouse-style kitchen this has the added advantage of de-emphasizing the work surfaces and drawing the eye to the decorated table. The same effect can be created using modern, low-voltage downlights: position a narrow-beamed spot over the center of the table with wide-beamed spots providing more general illumination. The ultimate, low-tech solution is soft, flattering candlelight.

In a room where there is only space for a large table with chairs drawn up to it, the transition from formal to informal is difficult to make. A room that is elegant by candlelight and perfectly suited for dinner can seem cold and uninviting at breakfast. Even when the kitchen is cramped, people instinctively gravitate there in the morning. In a large room it might be possible to create a more appropriate ambience by setting up a smaller table in an alcove or by a window that catches the morning light.

By using different flooring materials you can give some sense of demarcation to cooking and dining areas. It can work well, for example, to have the eating area fitted with wooden floorboards while the cooking and preparation space has some kind of tiled or stone floor.

8

6 A steel kitchen needs to be balanced with equally strong statements in the dining area. The false ceiling over the kitchen neatly conceals the workings of the lighting and ventilation, an essential consideration in open-plan layouts.
7 In an artist's studio the boundaries between work and relaxation are effortlessly blended.
8 Semi-open plan, where enough of the dividing wall remains to form a partition, may be more suitable in an older house. The exposed pipes add to the charm.

9

Breaking down barriers

Furnishing

1 Pick-and-mix Arne Jacobsen chairs, designed in the 1950s but having found their true niche in the '90s, bring a splash of contemporary color to an open-plan kitchen and eating area.

2 An eating alcove, with a custom-built bench and cantilevered seating, makes effective use of a small space.
3 In our less formal society, matching sets of dining chairs are no longer *de rigeur*: in fact, they can look positively overbearing. Complete sets of chairs, with carvers, can fetch a fortune, whereas you can buy odd pairs of chairs quite cheaply. From a psychological point of view, dinner guests may feel under less pressure to conform when seated on mismatched chairs.

The trend when furnishing eating rooms tends to fall into two distinct categories – humble in the kitchen and monumental in the dining room. Even the most unlikely people choose rich wood or its simulation for dining rooms. In the kitchen, old chairs are chosen because they are cheap and suitably rugged for family use, if not the height of comfort.

This doesn't have to be the rule. Going up the scale halfway in price and comfort, the armless dining chair with tall back and upholstered seat is good for its elegance in the dining room or for dressing down with simple slip covers to protect against accidents in the kitchen. If space is tight then folding chairs are a practical solution – instead of chairs left

getting in the way around the table, they can be folded away in a closet; or you could adopt the Shaker solution, hanging ordinary chairs from a peg rail.

The shape and position of the dining table is another vexed issue. A round table is considered more sociable and democratic than a rectangular one: there is no 'head' of the table and therefore no need for power-statement chairs with arms. This arrangement fits with the opinion of Archbishop Grantly in Anthony Trollope's *Barchester Towers* that 'there was something democratic and parvenu in a round table'. But if you are serving more than six people, the proportions of a large rectangular table are easier to live with than those

1

2

4 Gravitating towards the light of the French windows, the positioning of this dining table frees up the rest of the room for other purposes. The directors' chair is immensely versatile: it can be used inside or outside, and folded away when not in use. However, it is not a long-term solution: after a year or two they tend to look the worse for wear.
5 Curved chairs have been cleverly designed to fit a round table.

3

4

5

6 Simple slip covers can transform directors' chairs into something more ceremonial, and they have the advantage of being washable. **7** Bentwood chairs have been fashionable since Le Corbusier controversially used the traditional restaurant chair in a domestic setting.

6

7

of a large round table. Most tables now incorporate ingenious leaves to tailor their size to the number of diners and make them compact when not in use. If your dining table doubles as a play surface for small children there is no point in letting them practice their artistic skills on a wonderful piece of designer craftsmanship. Make do with a practical laminate or junk-shop table – no one need know what lies beneath the white damask when it comes to entertaining.

There is an accepted convention that the center of the room is the right place for the table – and for fairly compelling reasons. The wall space is freed for other uses and, in a kitchen, the centered table can serve as an island work surface. If, however, the room is so small as to impede circulation around the table, it is better to have the table close to a wall, which will also enable you to make use of bench seating on one side.

Contrasts of style work very well in a kitchen dining area. A bland backdrop of modern kitchen units can be lifted by an old, characterful table. And while good modern lighting is essential for work surfaces, an antique chandelier, by being taken out of context, adds surreal glamor to an earthy kitchen.

RELAXING

Even the best modern designers and architects have a problem with their living rooms. Closely allied to the dictate that form should follow function they are happiest designing bathrooms and kitchens because both have a clear function. But what is living – relaxing with a book, sprawling in front of the television, thinking, dreaming, talking, loving, playing with the kids? It is difficult to express this with only four walls and a three-piece suite, particularly when you add the desire for some kind of individual style, an expression of personality. Moreover, this problem is partly restricted to modern society. In previous eras living rooms were subdivided and given spurious functions. There was the morning-room where the lady of the house would spend her mornings, receiving company or perhaps writing letters. There might have been a parlor or sitting room reserved for the afternoons. The drawing room was for more formal occasions – for withdrawing into after dinner or for entertaining company too grand for the morning room. When living was such a circumscribed affair, the decoration of these rooms was probably an easier task.

Today most of us view home as a place to which we retreat, a sanctuary from the stresses of working life. In fact, as Adrian Forty has pointed out, individualism in decoration is strongly linked to the growth of industrial society. For those who are subjugated at work, a style statement at home becomes 'a sign of being capable of independent thought and emotion, of having a life apart from the mill-wheels of the economy.'

The living room should be a place where we feel totally at ease – a temple of the soul. It will also be a place in which other people can feel relaxed, too. However, the desire to impress others, tempting though it may be, should never override personal style and comfort. Whether you express yourself in white walls and architect-designed chrome and leather, wall-to-wall carpet and flouncy chintz, or bare boards and distressed antiques, the true test of the success of such a room is whether or not you choose to spend time there. If you retreat to the bedroom or kitchen instead, then something has gone very wrong. Perhaps it is a showroom or a dead area? It certainly is not, in the fullest sense of the word, a living room.

Relaxing, whether alone or with family and friends, is an essential antidote to daily stress. From a quiet corner where we can curl up with a book to a place where we can entertain friends, our living spaces need to be flexible, personal and, above all else, comfortable.

Setting the style

1

2

Adhering to a preconceived, self-conscious style is the very antithesis of relaxing. If you take comfort as your starting point, and let the style evolve naturally from what you feel comfortable with, you are more likely to end up with a look that inherently 'gels'. Whereas if you set out with the aim of reproducing a 1950s living room or a Colonial look, it will always have a forced air to it.

As Edward Gregory wrote in 1925, 'a really interesting drawing room is very rarely perfect in style.' Gregory castigated rooms decorated in the 'painfully proper' style of Louis XV: 'You cannot walk into them yourself without shyly glancing in the mirrors and feeling that you are an anachronism. . . Yet the room is in most delightful taste. You cannot find fault with it. You only feel just a little bored and rather overcome.'

Anyone who has sat in some fogyish room that looks like a museum will know what Gregory means. A room that forces you to behave out of character, that inhibits your actions or your dress may be a dazzling example of period accuracy, but if style hijacks comfort it can never be considered a success. On the other hand, at least the fogy's room is usually done with some passion. Too often people choose what

1 A stylishly eclectic room pays due attention to the vaulted ceiling and unusual proportions without taking them as a stylistic lead for decoration and furnishing.
2 A restricted color scheme gives this elegantly constructed room a restful air.
3 Rooms need not be all of a period: this one is unified by a love of art: from 1950s chairs to a collection of turn-of-the-century vases.

they consider to be the 'modern' look – usually dating from the 1930s – because they believe it delivers effect for very little effort. Paint the walls white, add a large photographer's light and a black, leather Eames chair and finish with an abstract rug – a Modernist's room, totally devoid of feeling.

There is no reason why you shouldn't indulge a certain style of decorating. But if you can discern which elements of the style appeal to you, and adapt those to your own way of life, you are more likely to be successful than if you try to fit the style into an environment for which it was never intended.

3

A living room is more than just an assemblage of objects – it needs some sort of foundation. This is not to be confused with giving a 'theme' to a room. Look at the space you have, commune with its architecture and work with it instead of trying to superimpose flimsy notions of decorative style. You need to work out what it is you want from the room – whether you want it to be warm and cozy or light and airy, a daytime or a nighttime space. It is no use adopting someone else's style from a magazine because you probably have different needs and priorities. By all means take inspiration from books,

5 Cozy rooms do not have to be small, dark and cluttered. The symmetry and ordered neatness of this room does not impose a stiff formality on its occupants: window seats and cushions invite a more casual, relaxed way of life.
6 Comfort is not an abiding priority for everyone: this room is an ode to '50s design, each piece existing in spectacular isolation, and yet drawn together by the obvious passion that lies behind them.
7 Cross-cultural influences are more effective than attempts to recreate a particular national style, as in this cool Western interpretation of Asian design.
8 In some cases, interiors are led by the outside environment. The cool white and blue of this beach house are an obvious response to the view, while slatted furniture is a perfect complement to the climate.

4 When work is an all-embracing obsession it can enhance – rather than intrude upon – the living room. In this living room-cum-studio, the work of an artist is complemented by the comfortable curves of the furniture.

4

6

5

7

8

magazines, fabrics, paintings, museums and other houses, but do not use these as the starting point. The foundation from which you must always begin is your own lifestyle, an honest appraisal of your needs. Taking style as your foundation will always result in a room that has a kind of emptiness to it.

Gregory was very good at defining what it is that makes rooms which are in 'perfect taste' so peculiarly unsatisfying to be in. 'The fact is,' he wrote 'that there is nothing in sight which suggests an idea; nothing which sets one's wits working, or stimulates an entertaining train of thought.'

A calm retreat

For social relaxation the drawing room lives on in spirit if not in name. Today, perhaps, we make the mistake of equating relaxation with mess and clutter – wading through plastic toys and dolls in order to clear a place on the sofa. In fact it is incredibly stressful not to have somewhere calm and peaceful to retreat to. Houses need to be able to accommodate changes of mood and at least one room, particularly in a raucous, family household, should supply this need.

Having child-free zones tends to smack of Victorian values – Muthesius noted that 'children are on the whole not allowed into the drawing room except as visitors in their best clothes.' It needn't be the children who are excluded, just the things that go with them. Children are just as capable of appreciating the different moods of different rooms as are adults – and it's a good opportunity to instill in them an appreciation of finely made pieces. If they have adequate space to play elsewhere then the living room can become the special place where they have a bedtime story or for quiet times – perhaps

1 In Victorian times it was common practice to change curtains and slip covers twice a year as the dark, heavy upholstery which contributed to a cozy warmth in winter could feel stifling in summer. A cheaper modern equivalent is to use dust covers which, apart from the practical application of hiding ugly upholstery, give rooms an ethereal, floating quality.
2 Our concepts of comfort have changed radically over the last few decades. Many people feel more comfortable with sparse elegance than wall-to-wall carpet and overstuffed chairs.

6

3 Most people do not have unerring, one-dimensional taste that they apply throughout their homes. They like different things to suit their different moods, and so will feel most relaxed in rooms that reflect different facets of their taste. Bold and comfortable, this room has both coziness and coolness, antiquity and modernity, meshed together in the general ambience of relaxation that comes from its owners' confidence in their own taste.

4 The drawing room traditionally pays homage to the notion of social relaxation, and is laid out in the classical configuration of chairs and sofas drawn up to each other to facilitate easy conversation. Here, a chair and footstool turn their back on company to allow a bit of solitary communion with the view.

for watching television. If, however, the living room has to double as playroom and family room, then make sure there is a large basket or chest into which all the toys can be thrown when it's time for the room to make the transition to grown-up space.

Criticisms of the formal living room voiced down the century are that its decoration reflects what goes on there, that somehow the triviality of conversation seeped through to the furnishings. 'It [the drawing room] has the least style of all the rooms', was Muthesius's verdict at the beginning of the century. He felt it suffered 'from having too many odds and ends packed into it and the deliberate informality all too often degenerates into confusion.' Edward Gregory, however, felt obliged to defend it from 'reformers' who believed the drawing room encouraged snobbish ostentation: 'They point out that a house is to live in, not to pose in, perhaps forgetting or ignoring the fact that it is just as easy for the superior person to tilt the nose while wearing homespun garments and occupying an Arts and Crafts "houseplace" as to condescend in conventional evening dress surrounded by the decorative accessories of a drawing-room.' Gregory's argument was that even if the drawing room did lead to 'an artificial, self-conscious propriety', at least such a room 'prevents the household degenerating into slovenliness, which is even worse.'

Gregory's words may now ring rather severely, but they are worth thinking about. Today we are altogether more circumspect in our criticism of others' taste but it remains true that environment affects behavior to a profound, usually subconscious, degree. Certain living rooms – those that are a spontaneous expression of the owner's taste and personality – instantly put you at ease, while others – perhaps because the seating is wrong, perhaps because the room is living a lie – make you feel awkward and uncomfortable.

5 A tranquil room, unfettered by any needs other than somewhere comfortable to sit and something beautiful to look at. No colors are better suited to express the feeling of calm, unhurried living than white and cream.

6 Port-hole windows, white walls and a couple of sofas and an armchair contribute an understated calm.

7 In vacation houses and weekend cottages decoration is best left underdone: improvization, with cheap but striking fabrics, is both more effective and appropriate than full-scale, overblown decorative schemes.

7

Comfort

3

2

1

Making comfort the priority for your living space is neither as obvious, nor as simple, as it might appear. Physical comfort – somewhere soft to put your bottom, somewhere supportive to lean your back – is a comparatively modern concern. It did not really figure in domestic life until the eighteenth century; until then, home was not much more than shelter for the poor, while for the rich it was a means of conveying status.

When we talk about comfort now, we don't just mean a physical sensation; it has a much wider definition which takes in a range of sensory satisfactions. Comfort, as Witold Rybczynski has pointed out, is multilayered: it involves 'convenience, efficiency, leisure, ease, pleasure, domesticity, intimacy and privacy – all of which contribute to the experience.' Today, comfort, wholesomeness and honesty are packaged as a fashion commodity and labeled 'natural', hence the wool throw for the sofa, the sisal matting for the floor, the beeswax candles for the mantelpiece.

1 When the interior architecture of a space is as spectacular as this, it is wrong to try to cover it over with the conventions of comfort like curtains. Heavy, dark furniture would have weighed the place down, whereas the white sofa and chair with the checkered rug echoing the small square window panes keep the visual flow of the space perfectly balanced.
2 Another space in which the decoration is a response to the architecture. The sloping walls and beamed ceilings are complemented by the simple, unpretentious furniture and fixtures.

4

5

 3 A room where, apart from the chair, comfort is probably more visual than physical. Nothing jars the eye in this natural color scheme.
4 Comfort and order are not mutually exclusive as this snug but stylish living room proves. Yellow makes a perfect background for the warm, earthy tones and green accents of the confident color scheme. The ladder leads up to a loft level.

5 Tall ceilings can make a room seem austere. Here, the sociable seating arrangement gives intimacy, while the indoor tree breaks up the distance between chairs and ceiling and provides a point of focus as an alternative to the fireplace.

It is difficult to predict what is going to make you feel comfortable – especially since you may know what you like without knowing why. People recognize comfort when they experience it. Rybczynski says that 'this recognition involves a combination of sensations – many of them subconscious – and not only physical, but also emotional as well as intellectual...' Given that comfort is a multilayered thing, it is probably best to start with the most tangible layer – physical comfort. Establishing your needs in this sphere gives you a good foundation on which to build.

6

7

The essentials are warmth and light. In planning where to site heat registers, you need to take into account architectural and functional considerations, but you must also have some idea of seating arrangements. If you put registers against walls where you are likely to want to place sofas, the heat will be wasted. Under windows is ideal because the warm air, hitting the cold coming from the window, is well circulated. However, from the point of view of light, this is also a good place for a sofa.

Lighting is fundamental to comfort. The need to alter it according to mood and the time of day corresponds to human physiology as well as to the biological clock. In a living room you need general, ambient lighting, along with task and spot lighting. A low-voltage lighting system requires professional installation, but the flexibility it offers is worth the expense. If you are stuck with a central pendant light fixture, at least install a dimmer switch, which will allow you some mood changes.

6 The human instinct to gravitate towards a fire is supplemented in this room by the provision of alcoves which, semi-enclosed, give a sense of security, the perfect place to curl up with a book.
7 A room at ease with itself and the environment, its palette of natural colors and materials blending with the landscape outside.

Seating

1

Seating affects behavior. You can see the truth of this in any waiting room with its hard, straight-backed chairs set in rows against the wall which force you into an alert, expectant posture while discouraging socialization. Historically the design and placing of chairs has been determined by the mood of society. Sitting only became a recreational pursuit (as opposed to a statement of authority or a means to an end) in the more leisurely eighteenth century when many different types of upholstered furniture were designed.

The grouping of chairs to aid conversation was something of a social skill in the eighteenth century. Mark Girouard details the 'formal circle' arrangement in *Life in the English Country House*. Maria Edgeworth describes this as 'of all the figures in nature or art . . . universally the most obnoxious to conversation' in a contemporary novel. This circular grouping reigned supreme until about 1780 when a more informal grouping to accommodate different clusters of people found favor.

1 A huge, deep sofa is the epitome of luxury if you have the space to take it. Socially, however, it only works if the company is relaxed enough with each other to sprawl across it. Perching on the edge of a large sofa intensifies any feeling of unease and discomfort.
2 Versatility is a key consideration of seating arrangements: a cool grouping of designer classics is the perfect accompaniment to the bare architectural lines of this space, but a stone ledge for display can be commandeered for extra seating when entertaining large numbers of people.

2

Girouard quotes a wonderful description by Fanny Burney of being entertained in the 'new style' by an anxious hostess. 'When some other guests came in and instinctively started to form the traditional grouping of chairs, the hostess exclaimed: "My whole care is to prevent a circle," and, hastily rising, she pulled about the chairs, and planted the people in groups with as dextrous disorder as you would desire to see.'

Today we are rather less artful in our social manipulation but most people instinctively arrange furniture so as to facilitate conversation and make others feel at ease. Grouping sofas and chairs loosely around a focal point such as the fireplace works well – as long as you remember that in a social situation a sofa never pulls its full weight. Unless you are on intimate

3 The success of this banquette seat lies in its organic curves which make it both visually and physically comfortable.

3

4 With such striking upholstery, these sofas need to keep their distance, but are linked by matching side tables.
5 In a fairly confined space, two small sofas may work better than one sofa and a couple of chairs.

6 Modern sofas come in all shapes and sizes, not necessarily with arms and a back. Such sculptural seating works well in a contemporary interior.
7 Cushions and throws add exoticism to plain sofas.

terms, a two-seater sofa will only accommodate one person who can then spread; two people sitting side by side are forced into a formal pose. Similarly, even a large three-seater is awkward for any more than two. In conversation people like to turn their whole bodies towards each other and furniture should not inhibit body language. There can be something too confrontational about two sofas facing each other.

Furniture can also be used to 'zone' areas of the room for different types of activity. For example, if you have a television in the room, don't arrange the seating in such a way that everyone is forced to watch it. If the television is set up in a corner in front of a sofa or chairs it should be possible to make another grouping of seats that relate to each other to facilitate conversation or for solitary occupations such as reading.

A mixture of sofas and armchairs is good both visually and psychologically. The combination breaks up the space of a room in an interesting way and allows for differences in sitting style – upright and more sprawling – in addition to permitting different levels of intimacy. If you are entertaining an insurance adjustor you would probably prefer not to have to cozy up on the sofa. On the other hand, a room with only single chairs can seem rather unfriendly and distinctly formal.

The tyranny of the three-piece suite, however, is probably over. Its smug respectability hampers the flexibility of a room, and does not sit well with the new informality. A mixture of seating – the strict, clean lines of a modern sofa, perhaps, set against the voluptuous curves of an antique chair – can lend a stylistic signature to the whole room.

Recreation

When the television first became widely available, nobody tried to conceal the fact that they had one. The television took pride of place in the living room, an icon of a new age, and less fortunate friends and neighbors – without a TV of their own – were invited round specifically to watch it. The change from black-and-white to color broadcasting simply reinforced its standing as a status symbol. If the TV was housed in an elegant wooden cabinet, this was not so much to hide it as to honor it. In most Western households television became a kind of altar, a place of honor – until the advent of 24-hour broadcasting.

Today the question of where to put the TV is not so simple, bound up as it is with increasingly ambivalent feelings: perhaps we watch it a lot, but wish that we didn't; maybe we watch it but don't want other people to know that we do; maybe we watch it so seldom that we don't want it dominating the room.

Where the television is placed affects your viewing habits so it is best to start from a considered position. Now that many homes have more than one television, and it is turned on rather as a radio used to be, the television is an appliance that needs to be integrated into the room so that viewing is comfortable but the TV does not unduly dominate. For passive viewing while going about household chores, it might be better to mount the television to a bracket on the kitchen wall or to buy a miniature portable set.

Hiding the television does not need to be furtive or dishonest: it is a very good means of restricting yourself only to programs you genuinely want to watch. Freestanding television cabinets have a bad image; they are expensive and pretend to be something they are not. It is probably better to find a well-designed television set.

Fortunately music systems come without any cultural hang-ups and value judgments, and as most modern stereo systems are neat and compact, they rarely cause too much visual disturbance. For a state-of-the-art sound system – speakers in every room of the house, for example – it is probably best to consult an expert.

You may survive happily without a stereo or television but a living room without books or pictures is a barren place. A few purist souls consider books too untidy and hide them in cabinets or remove all the dust jackets so that the colors don't jar. But a lot more common is the 'displayed reading' style with books used as decorative objects – a forgivable conceit, really, when books are visually so luscious.

1

1 A less furtive alternative to hiding the television completely is to use sliding screens which, when closed, give the room a clean, uncluttered look.

3 Is the television, after all, such a visually contemptible object? As a plain, black square, it is no less offensive than a hole-in-the-wall fireplace, and it does not appear incongruous set between the pile of logs and display of ethnic baskets in this room.

3

2

2 The solution favored by those of the 'honesty' school of design is to bare all. The living room and bedroom televisions here are unashamedly displayed, while the downstairs TV is even flanked by candlesticks as if it were a modern-day altar.

4 In ultra-modern interiors, too much new technology can look like a parody of itself, or overly ostentatious: this is an artful blend of high and low tech, with its modest floor cushions and old-fashioned telephone.

4

5

5 With one-room living it is hard to be discreet about television viewing: when your bed-making technique is on full view, why worry about hiding the speakers? In fact, this style perfectly suits the stripped-back architecture of the room.
6 Recreational icons: why should only vases of flowers and works of art be viewed as suitable objects to display, when some people may feel just as passionate, if not more so, about their bicycle or electric guitar?

6

Special places

Like the siting of sacred buildings in auspicious landscapes, there are corners of most houses where areas of seating have become firmly and permanently established. It may be a window seat that gets the morning sun, a quiet alcove or a front porch – but there is something almost magical about these places which draws us to them. One of the worst things about modern estate houses is that they can be so bland and featureless, that they are completely lacking in idiosyncratic space.

As with all magic, however, the appeal of these special places is founded in logic. These are places which have become fixed refuges because they are in a favorable position regarding light and sun. Or perhaps there is a wonderful outlook from them. Christopher Alexander believes that alcoves are fundamental to healthy living spaces from the point of view of relationships between the occupants of a house and their need for a degree of privacy. 'No homogeneous room, of homogeneous height, can serve a group of people well. To give a group a chance to be together, as a group, a room must also give them the chance to be alone, in ones and twos in the same space.'

Alexander suggests that what he calls 'window places' are not just the luxury that modern costcutting house building would suggest them to be, but are, in fact, a necessity. A room without a window place, he believes, keeps its occupants in a 'state of perpetual unresolved conflict and tension – slight, perhaps, but definite.' This is not as crackpot a theory as it might at first appear for, as Alexander goes on to explain, we are naturally drawn towards windows for the light, but at the same time we have an equal need to sit somewhere comfortable and if all the comfortable places are situated away from the windows there is a conflict.

In a very old house, the chances are that these places will already have been established by history and human inclination. Otherwise you may need to seek them out and build on their potential. Windows, as Alexander points out, need to be 'taken seriously as a space, a volume, not merely treated as a hole in the wall.' A bay window, for example, is the perfect place for a window seat; topped with a comfortable cushion along its length and built-in cabinet space below, it doubles as useful storage space. If your budget does not run to

built-in cabinets, a simple bench or an extended windowsill with a curtained skirt concealing the clutter underneath has a cottage-like charm.

If no such place suggests itself to you, it is worth considering adding a sunroom. These always work best if they are seen as an extension of a room; too often they are indiscriminate additions, perhaps a dining room, that relate badly to the rest of the house. You may find that adding a glass alcove to an existing room gives you as much useful extra space as a whole new room.

Many townhouses often have a corridor of outdoor space running between them and the neighboring house which seldom gets used because it is too narrow – no more than a pathway to the back of the house. Local zoning ordinances permitting, this is an ideal area to convert from dead space to a living alcove with a skylight to let in as much light as possible. As the external wall is always structural anyway it makes sense to use this to partition space rather than trying to open out completely. In most houses the room that it adjoins will be the kitchen and it may be just wide enough to make into a cozy sitting space or a study area.

1 Landings are often wasted space. A chair and small table have turned this into a quiet reading retreat.

2 A bedroom open to the countryside is the ultimate room with a view.

3 What patio umbrella could possibly compare with the romance of sitting in the shade of an ancient tree? It only takes a few floor cushions to turn dream to reality.

4 Alcoves are magical spaces for adults and children alike. It may seem indulgent to squander storage space, but measure that against quality of life. The owners have niftily incorporated storage potential above and below this alcove.

5 You may not share the idyllic setting, but sunroom furniture on a deck makes the most of summer just as much in Poughkeepsie as paradise.

6

6 Though the raised platform was probably added to improve the wall-to-floor proportions of the high-set window, it has also created a cozy nook.

7 Window seats provide a pleasure quite out of scale to the space they take up. If they are not incorporated into the architecture of your home, it is worth investigating the possibility of building some in.

8 The tropical equivalent of the sunroom is a cool, shady verandah.

7

8

S L E E P I N G

Bedrooms are probably the most neglected area of any house. True, we spend a third of our lives there, but most people require only that the room contains a comfortable bed. After all, the reasoning goes, if the greatest proportion of that time is spent visually unconscious, who cares how the room looks?

In fact, through pressure on space, the bedroom is gradually becoming a room with multifarious purposes, often combining as a study and personal living room. But even when it retains its single, primary function, it should not be undervalued. We don't, after all, drop into sleep from a vacuum. Those moments just before we go to sleep, taking stock of the day and winding down, and when we wake up recharged are, or should be, prime time for reflection and contemplation. How you wake up can affect the whole of your day. So your sleeping environment needs every bit as much, if not more, consideration as your living room.

A bedroom is usually a fairly good indicator of the inhabitant's self-respect. People are generally happy to put all their energy into decorating a living room because they believe by that they will be judged. In some cases living rooms are decorated purely with other people's perceptions in mind. But a bedroom, usually out of bounds to others, is selfish space at its purest. It is a shrine to the personal and the private. It is where children can create their secret world; teenagers can make rebellious statements; adults can seek sanctuary. There is no more depressing sight than the institutional bedroom, devoid of personality. This is why many homes for the elderly allow residents to have treasured pieces of furniture in their rooms.

Even in the houses of people we know well it feels like trespassing on intimacy to go uninvited into the bedroom, though in the seventeenth and early eighteenth centuries the bedroom was used as a reception room. It seems that the bed is the object of embarrassment – not necessarily because it is the most usual place for lovemaking but because it is witness to all our most private thoughts and dreams. This is why, when a bedroom doubles as living room its owner usually goes to some effort to cast off slumbering associations and disguises the bed as a sofa. Nighttime must be welcoming, but easy to banish by day – that is the real dilemma of the bedroom.

Sleep recharges the body's batteries. It is a universal need, one of the great levelers. Yet if the basic requirements of shelter and a bed are fairly simple, we nonetheless personalize our sleeping spaces as much as we do any other area of the home.

Orientation and position

The history of the bedroom and the history of privacy are closely intertwined. Domestic privacy did not really exist until around the beginning of the seventeenth century: people ate, entertained and slept in the same rooms, with much use made of collapsible beds. As Philippe Aries points out in *Centuries of Childhood*, people rarely slept alone; there might be several beds in one room, but the fact that a room contained a bed (or beds) did not make it a bedroom – it was still a public place. When beds became less mobile in the seventeenth century they were fitted with curtains to afford a degree of privacy, but often servants slept alongside masters on trundle beds. Hard as it is to imagine now, 400 years ago 'nobody was ever left alone . . . people who managed to shut themselves up in a room for some time were regarded as exceptional characters'.

It was in the eighteenth century, when the notion of family life and privacy took root, that rooms with specialized functions took over from semi-public arrangements of space in a house. Most notably, bedrooms moved upstairs and became citadels of privacy.

The bedroom is beginning to revert to a less isolated position but it is not likely ever to become as public as it once was. Many people feel uneasy in groundfloor bedrooms, possibly because they feel more vulnerable sleeping at ground level but also because the upper floors – particularly of houses in built-up areas – receive more morning light. Christopher Alexander believes that natural light is crucial to healthy architecture: taking it even further, he – along with a new generation of eco-designers – prescribes sleeping in rooms orientated towards the sunrise so that people wake up naturally with the sun. The theory is that our

1 A bedroom with the contemplative serenity of an abstract painting... unless there are children around, in which case the inviting open window becomes a nightmare of dangerous possibilities.
2 Despite the itchingly prosaic reason behind its existence, the mosquito net exerts a powerfully romantic pull through its colonial and bridal associations.
3 Another escapist's idyll – with its connotations of innocence, of lost childhood play in the garden shed – this look relies on total authenticity, though something of the effect could be recreated with painted tongue-and-groove boards in a loft bedroom.

5

6

bodies are attuned to the sun's cycle, and if you are gently nudged awake by the sun immediately after a period of REM sleep you are more likely to emerge refreshed and energetic; whereas if you are woken artificially in mid-sleep cycle you will have to drag yourself out of bed with bleary eyes and a heavy head. Certainly the idea of sleeping facing east has prevailed through different periods and various cultures. Some early twentieth-century cribs had built-in compasses, presumably so that the baby could be healthily positioned.

Modern houses built on the principle of lateral space seem less odd with bedrooms on the ground floor, perhaps because they have been designed with good natural light. Also, they are not circumscribed by age-old conventions; freed of the restrictions of an outdated architecture, more of us might look at our bedrooms without sleep in our eyes.

4 In rural locations where no interior should compete with the view, simplicity is the rule. By minimizing furniture and pattern, the inside takes its cue from outside.
5 In a sparsely furnished bedroom, a row of shirts provides a decorative focus. The shirts may not be neatly pressed and could not be accused of wearing their relationship with the laundry on their sleeves, but this is more than simply an artful conceit.
6 A feminine bed, with lots of frills and flowers, can emasculate its male occupant. Here, a comfortable compromise has been struck between feminine 'prettiness' and masculine sobriety.

Using the space

In many ways, those bedrooms that operate purely as a room for sleeping in do not make sense in an age where space for many people is at such a premium. The bed is the dominant feature of the room and the space around it often tends to be rather awkward and unfocused. For most of us, in average-sized bedrooms with a double- or king-size bed, the space we negotiate is that around the bed; quite often the fact that there is no easy circulation flow turns out to be what makes a bedroom such an uninviting, dead space during the daytime.

What can you do about it? Some futon mattresses can be rolled up and stowed away and sofabeds have the benefit of versatility, but as a permanent arrangement these alternatives are both time-consuming and demanding. Also, denying the existence of the bed is ultimately counterproductive – you have to work with it. The solution might be as simple as moving the bed to a different position in the room, though you will probably find that your options are fairly limited. Pushing a double bed into a corner may give you a more manageable space, but it makes access for one person difficult, is awkward when you come to change the sheets, and limits space for a bedside table – though there are built-in alternatives such as a shelf or small alcove in the wall.

Psychologically, most people seem happier with their bed cater-corner to the door: half concealed behind it, rather than facing it. In the West this is a hazy notion, but in China it is formularized in the ancient science of *feng shui* which guides building and interior design, and behind whose often mystic-sounding dictates usually resides much rational common sense. The bed, it is believed, should be positioned so that its occupant can see anyone entering the room; and the headboard should rest against a wall, not float in space, since the bed's occupant will otherwise feel similarly unanchored in life.

1 In a high-ceilinged room, a platform level gives a sense of enclosure around the bed, at the same time as providing valuable storage space so that the floor area can remain uncluttered.
2 The bedroom in this converted warehouse has the luxury of plenty of floor space around the bed. This, together with the huge expanses of window flooding the room with natural light, make it a wonderful place to occupy during the day as well as the night.
3 If your bedroom is going to accommodate activities other than sleeping, it is best kept cool and uncluttered, with furniture that does not look too cozy.
4 A tranquil room focused on relaxation.
6 Bright colors need not be reserved exclusively for children's rooms: waking up to this wardrobe every morning should ensure the day at least starts on a cheerful note.

4

5

8

6

7

5 The bedroom is a good place for fantasy furniture: one avant-garde chair can have enormous impact, particularly where the bed is quite simple.
7 Washbasin units have a slightly out-moded feel, but a more workmanlike sink opens up the room to new possibilities.
8 When there's no room for harboring sentimental feelings for a bedroom, this is an efficient solution for a work-dominated environment: the bed folds away into a wall of closets.
9 High-tech hanging space: these wardrobes on wheels form an impressive wall of clothes storage.

Perhaps the main problem with bedrooms is that we try to cram far too many functions into them so that they fulfill none of them particularly well. These functions – from dressing and toiletry through general storage and maybe even work space – carry with them bulky, often ugly pieces of furniture – wardrobes, dressing tables and the like – that clutter up the traditional bedroom. Where possible it is best to shift the emphasis of some of these functions to other rooms. Many of us, for example, dress in bedrooms simply from convention; it may make sense to make hanging space elsewhere.

A combined study and bedroom is a practical combination. The space is used day and night, though some believe that it is unhealthy to keep a computer in the bedroom because of electromagnetic radiation. There is also no doubt that electrical office equipment attracts dust, which certainly does not make for the healthiest sleeping atmosphere.

For some, the ideal sleeping space is an elevated platform, accommodating only a bed; this works well in a large open-plan space, but is not a solution for the average house.

9

Setting the style

1

2

The modern 'healthy' bedroom is as much about the visual as the physical conditions. Just as the late nineteenth-century obsession with hygiene hinged on the visible notion of cleanliness and resulted in furniture designed to have no hiding place for dust, one modern ideal of the bedroom rests somewhere between Scandinavian and Mediterranean style – bare boards, wafting muslin drapes and crisp white sheets.

Fundamentally, we associate sleep with purity – 'the sleep of the innocent' – which is why we are so concerned about sleeping in a benign atmosphere. At the same time, however, the bedroom has a sensual side, which some prefer to emphasize and which can be at odds with the pure, virginal look. Sex in a white and airy bedroom might be of the health and efficiency kind – an athletic tangling of showered and shiny, perfectly toned limbs – while the dark and exotic bedroom, with its curtained four-poster, advertises a more sultry, possibly more experimental, coupling. Perhaps this is why people don't often show off their bedrooms – it gives too much away. Small wonder that so many opt for the 'polite' bedroom which yields no clues – the floral, frilly affair deemed 'feminine', yet curiously sexless.

In the late nineteenth century the bedroom became the focus of an intensive campaign of dust- and germ-busting. Papers written at this time on the 'healthy house' are similar to articles written about household pollutants today. In the 1880s, bedroom floors were to be made of wood and left mostly bare: wall-to-wall carpeting was considered a dusttrap, so rugs were used and shaken out daily. Washable silk and cotton were recommended for curtains. Much the same advice is given by eco-designers now, though to the old enemies of dust and dirt they have also added the specter of chemical pollution from synthetic materials.

1 Pristine and pure, the sharp lines of this bedroom are softened by the mosquito net.
2 Art as furniture: an extraordinary abstract assemblage in wood and metal forms a dramatic headboard against which no patterned bed sheets could compete.
3 The monastic cell has long been associated with cerebral personality, though this raw-textured bedroom perhaps owes as much to the aesthetic of the bounty hunter.

3

4

4 When a room is devoid of architectural features, be brave and go all out on color.
5 Beamed ceilings have such a strong presence that most people opt for submissive white walls; but here, painted Shaker closets make a bold statement against the bare wooden beams.

5

6

7

6 Ship-shape and streamlined, this room hints at both nautical and log-cabin associations, but arrives at uncontrived simplicity.
7 Remember when we weren't so sophisticated that we couldn't just hang things from a nail in the wall?
8 A tall room is given more comfortable proportions with fabric hangings that make a private haven of the bed.
9 Bare brick and a rustic headboard are balanced by the bold color scheme.

8

Certain colors seem particularly well suited to the bedroom, depending on whether the room comes into its own for you in the morning or at nighttime. White remains popular for its pure and romantic elegance while yellow – in spite of the late John Fowler's stipulation that it should not be used in a lady's bedroom because it made her complexion look sallow first thing in the morning – is a wonderful color for making a room sunny, even if the skies are pewter. But those who make a point of never welcoming the morning light and who come alive at night choose dark, jewel-like colors to intensify a warm, enclosed atmosphere.

9

The bed

1 Allergic to dust or allergic to decoration, this is a room in which the purity of the space speaks for itself, a place for the committed minimalist.
2 This unusual antique boxbed gives wrap-around painted decoration and a sense of security.

1

When people say that a bed is the most important piece of furniture you will ever buy it is not strictly true: it is the mattress. Anyone who has spent a tortured night on a soft or lumpy mattress won't need to be told about the wisdom of buying the best you can afford. Sleeping night after night on an inferior mattress will result in back trouble in later life. A mattress should be firm enough to support your spine but not so hard that it throws the hips and shoulders out of their normal curvature. If it is too soft, rolling from side to side is difficult, impeding the natural movements you make during healthy sleep.

This does not mean that you are restricted to characterless beds. If you have a wonderful antique bed, you can have a mattress made to order; if you want to commission an iron four-poster, you can have it made to fit the mattress of your choice. Alternatively you can customize basic beds simply by adding an unusual headboard.

The importance of the bed does not merely lie in physical comfort. It has a symbolic significance we have sadly lost sight of. In the past the 'marriage bed' was a status symbol. In the Austrian Tyrol, for example, a carved and painted bed, often with the couple's initials worked into a highly decorative scene, formed part of a bride's dowry. The American architect and writer, Christopher Alexander, mourns the loss of the kind of bed 'which nourishes intimacy and love'. He envisages a true marriage bed, one with a headboard that can be carved and painted over the years as a kind of celebratory testimony to a couple's relationship. A little fanciful, maybe, but he has a point – we have lost the personal touch in our bedrooms. When it comes to buying a bed, back problems, house-dust mites and allergies have all but obscured the romance.

However, the enduring appeal of the four-poster bed is rooted in romantic notions. Although it lost favor in the hygiene purge of the late nineteenth

2

3

4

3 A bed with powerful symbolism stands out from the bland places where most of us sleep. This is a monument to its owner's passion for tribal art.
4 A platform bed provides extra storage underneath.

6

5

5 Modern versions of the four-poster bed tend to trade the traditional heaviness and draft-excluding properties for a feeling of airiness and curtains that are more decorative than functional.

7

8

9

10

century – it was considered unhealthy to sleep within the confines of a small, heavily curtained space – the four-poster is now considered a stately touch to bedrooms. This is fine where a stately touch is appropriate, but too often they look slightly ridiculous, dwarfing the proportions of a small room and aping grandeur in a way which diminishes natural style.

Modified versions of the four-poster often work better in modern rooms. There are some minimal black iron four-posters or pale wood frames over which a simple length of fabric can be hung to great effect. Alternatively, do without the posts and hang a lightweight fabric canopy from ceiling-mounted rods.

From a stylistic point of view, one of the problems of 'historical' beds is that the comforter looks out of place. Some people conceal the practicality of the comforter under a bedspread, while others are returning to the comfort and nostalgia of crisp sheets turned over wool blankets. It is all very well to sneer at the comforter as the furnishing equivalent of fast food, but who is going to make the bed and iron the sheets?

6 Beds can be islands of individuality. This one uses a clash of materials and styles to stunning effect. The base, which incorporates a decorative brass grille, has echoes of a classical *bateau au lit*, while the skeletal metal top is uncompromisingly modern.
7 The celibate single bed always looks good because its proportions are often easier to work with than those of a double bed.
8 The rustic feel of this simple bedroom is reinforced by the old timber bedframe and the farm-gate style headboard.
9 Upholstered headboards may conjure up visions of pink button-backed nightmares, but they can be as cool and simple as this.
10 Iron and steel frames are increasingly ousting the more dated brass bed.

Children's bedrooms

1

It is part of cultural mythology, perpetuated in films and books, that when a baby is expected the parents 'prepare the nursery'. Some blame it on hormones and claim it is a pregnancy-induced psychosis that results in a frenzy of furnishings and fluffy mobiles. Others believe that it is a way of distancing ourselves from our natural instincts – for the first few months of life all a baby wants is to be held and fed. Spending vast sums of money on nursery furniture is totally unnecessary, though it undoubtedly assuages guilt about spending less time with the baby than nature intended.

When the child has a sense of its own identity then a separate room becomes appropriate – or at least a room shared with siblings. Giving small children a room of their own is the adult's idea of a treat – to make them feel 'grown up'. And yet preteenage children generally prefer the comfort and security of others sleeping in close proximity. At the same time they do like to have some kind of base or private place where they can keep their special possessions or hide away. Slumber play tents are perfect for children who love having their own hideaway; bunk-beds also give a good sense of territory.

1 In a vacation house, building platform beds across the entire width of a room economically accommodates four children. Wall-mounted reading lights are a necessity, and some might say a safety rail for the top bunk-beds is, as well. Although this sort of sleeping arrangement is an adventure on vacation the lack of privacy might be a disadvantage on a more permanent basis and lead to squabbles between siblings.
2 An ingenious solution to accommodating the maximum number of children in the minimum amount of space, this loft conversion allows a couple to have all their grandchildren to stay for the weekend.
3 Mosquito nets add romance to the prosaic bunk-bed, enthusiasm for which has normally worn off by the age of ten. A room divider and muslin-swathed doorway gives the illusion of privacy for an older child.

Stringent safety regulations govern the dimensions of bunk-beds, particularly with regard to the safety rail on the top bunk, which should not have a space large enough for a child to slip through and then get its head stuck. If you look at the room through a child's eyes – as an exciting adventure playground – you may spot other potential hazards.

One can, however, become paranoid about safety. It is really not necessary to build special low children's beds in case they fall out at night: when children make the transition from crib to bed they inevitably tumble out a few times, but injury is rare. If you pre-empt your child's every move, you may well stifle the growth of self-confidence and self-motivation, and dull their own innate sense of danger.

3

In a house with limited bedrooms and more than a couple of children it makes sense to sacrifice the main bedroom to them. Often it is the room that receives the best light in the day, which will be wasted if it is only used for sleeping rather than for playing, too. A couple of bunk-beds leave plenty of floor space for toys which can be neatly stacked under the beds at night in boxes. Communal sleeping for children means that other bedrooms can then be put to other uses – at least until the teenage years when a 'room of one's own' becomes an issue.

Devoted parents are often tempted to indulge their children with decorative 'themes' – whether it's the very latest cartoon-hero wallpaper or converting the room into an authentic wigwam. This should be resisted: the wallpaper will inevitably be uncool next year and specific themes limit creative play. Far better to paint the walls a cheerful color which will not have you gnashing your teeth every time they decide to personalize it with stickers and posters.

A bed; some good, ample storage; perhaps a small table – a child needs very little else in a bedroom. It may not be so much fun for parents, but ultimately the best thing they can provide in a child's bedroom is potential.

4 More than two beds in a row may revive memories of school dormitories, but few can have been as stylish as this. The hand of an adult is evident, though: parents like their offspring's things to match; children prefer to express their individuality.

5

4

5 Most small children's clothes only need folding away in drawers; a row of Shaker pegs is perfectly adequate for the few which need hanging.
6 By the time children reach the age of 11 or 12 they need their own space, particularly somewhere to do their homework. A bed draped in a throw with cushions to match becomes a makeshift sofa, and may even encourage them to make their own bed.
7 A platform bed (with all-important safety rail) makes room for storage and play space beneath it.

6

7

8

8 Bookshelves double as room dividers to give a sense of enclosure and privacy.
9 Children's bedrooms are irresistible for the adult decorator, though once a child reaches a certain age it's impossible to maintain the order and tidiness evident here.

9

WASHING AND BATHING

The history of bathing is not necessarily synonymous with the history of cleanliness. Though personal hygiene played a part in the rise of the bathroom, the bathing ritual is a more complex process, and the room in which it takes place is often referred to by such inflated titles as 'the temple of ablutions'.

The idea of cleanliness being next to godliness is a fairly modern one: in the early Church bathing was frowned upon. St Francis of Assisi considered dirtiness to be one of the insignia of holiness and St Agnes is said never to have washed. Until the move towards more hygienic surfaces at the turn of the century, people tended to furnish their bathrooms much like other rooms in the house, with bathroom fixtures treated like pieces of furniture, often encased in fine dark woods such as mahogany. With the drive against dirt the bathroom became rather less hospitable, with hard tiled surfaces and free-standing white cast-iron bathtubs.

Interestingly, the entire concept of the bathroom began to change in the late 1920s. In a technological breakthrough, engineers perfected a previously impossible process, that of color-matching products made of different materials – the enameled cast iron used in tubs and the vitreous china used to make toilets. Suddenly, the bathroom became a place worthy of attention, where status could be conveyed via the color of its fixtures.

Using the bathroom as an arena of status and style has continued unabated – from gold-plated taps to the latest whirlpool technology, from suites in designer colors to the inconspicuous opulence of all-white rooms. Stripped of our outward vestments of status, reduced to the democracy of nakedness, perhaps the need to surround ourselves with the reassurance of material wealth has become all the more intense.

Recent thinking on the bathroom, however, is more concerned with its therapeutic value. Pope Gregory the Great thought baths were permissible only if they did not become a 'time-wasting luxury'. For today's generation this is perhaps the whole point of the exercise, with cleanliness merely being a by-product. In the history of contemplation, from the first 'eureka', the bath must rank at the top of inspirational locations. The bathroom is still a place for the quiet luxury of comfort and style.

Washing is about more than physical cleanliness. Soaking in a hot tub after a hard day's work, ruminating on the oddities of life, we are afforded some time on our own. It is little wonder, then, that the bathroom is decorated both to accommodate planning needs and to reflect personal comfort, a haven of peace and privacy.

Planning

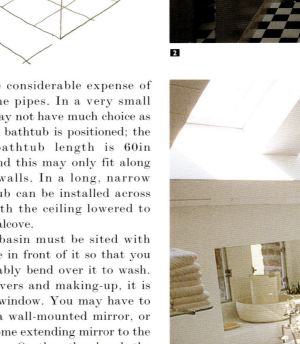

The bathroom needs more planning than any other room in the house after the kitchen. Options are more limited, and mistakes as costly. Added to this, the room often tends to be what is left over after everything else is housed – a small, often windowless space. Once bathroom fixtures have been installed, they are semi-permanent, and you are unlikely to want to change them as this will entail both considerable expense and a lot of disruption.

Planning a small bathroom is like working out a puzzle. There is probably only one solution, given that you have to site the minimum of three important items – bathtub and/or shower, toilet and sink – within a very small space, taking into account the position of architectural features such as windows and doors, and not forgetting the plumbing and drainage pipework. Think very carefully before putting your plans into action.

In some ways planning restrictions can work to your advantage; this gives you a starting point. Before beginning, check local building ordinances to make sure the work you are planning doesn't violate them; building and plumbing codes vary from community to community. The toilet should be placed close to the existing soil stack, unless you plan

to go to the considerable expense of rerouting the pipes. In a very small room, you may not have much choice as to where the bathtub is positioned; the standard bathtub length is 60in (1524mm) and this may only fit along one of the walls. In a long, narrow room, the tub can be installed across one end, with the ceiling lowered to make a cozy alcove.

The washbasin must be sited with enough space in front of it so that you can comfortably bend over it to wash. For wet shavers and making-up, it is best by the window. You may have to do without a wall-mounted mirror, or attach a chrome extending mirror to the window frame. On the other hand, the windowsill can be used as a shelf and you can always replace the glass panes of the window with mirror glass, which will give you an illusion, at least, of space. Leave yourself plenty of elbow-room either side – it is difficult to wash in comfort if the basin is jammed right up against a side wall.

The toilet requires the same forethought. Make sure that there is enough room between the rim of the seat and the wall in front so that your knees are not forced up under your chin. A bidet needs space to the side and back to make room for your legs.

1 A bidet needs 24in (600mm) clear space in front of it, and a minimum ceiling height of 6ft 6in (2m).
2 A dado works to counteract the tall, narrow shape of this cloakroom.
3 Placing the sink near the light would have obscured part of the window; the alcove instead makes a blissful spot for a tub.
4 A bath needs its width again for comfortable maneuvering.
5 The classic line-up for a narrow room.

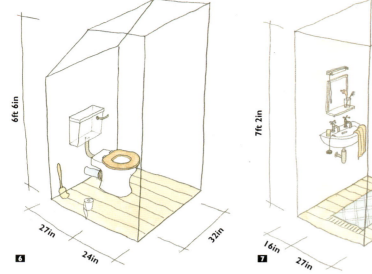

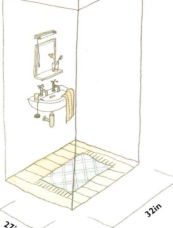

6 A toilet needs 24in (600mm) clearance space in front.
7 A sink needs slightly greater clearance to either side.
8 The requirement of two sinks has left a rather tight fit in this bathroom, but the glass tiles dispel any claustrophobia.

In a small bathroom, an inward-opening door can limit space even further. You can rehang the door to open out, or fit a sliding door to free up usable space. An outward-opening door will work very well with a bathroom attached to the bedroom, but it is not practical if the door opens out on a narrow corridor.

Even an average-size bathroom will need precision planning to fit everything in. As with kitchen planning (page 128), it helps to draw up a floor plan, cut out bathroom fixture shapes to scale and fit them into the space on paper.

In a large bathroom, space may not seem such a problem. However, large bathrooms often leave a vast expanse of empty floor in the middle. The answer may lie in placing a free-standing bathtub in the center of the room; a raised platform can equally break up floor space and provides space for a sunken tub which is still easy to clean.

It is essential to have enough bathroom storage space if you don't want cleaning products on display. If you are concealing pipework under the sink, this is an ideal opportunity to create storage. The sink can be set into a counter-top surface with cabinets beneath, while open shelves or a small storage cabinet can be mounted over the toilet.

9 In a small loft bathroom a shower enclosure may fit where a tub would not, provided there is sufficient pressure to maintain a decent water supply. This can be a problem with top-floor bathrooms if the water tank is kept in the roof, but a special pump can be installed to remedy it.
10 Any less space than this in the bathroom would feel extremely cramped.
11 Separate showers need clearance space as shown if washing is not going to be a contorted affair.

Fittings

Bathroom humor is proof of an almost universal embarrassment about bodily functions. So excruciatingly embarrassing did the turn-of-the-century British find the whole notion of 'toilets' that, supposedly, there were strict rules governing the placement of the ground-floor facilities. A toilet had to be always tucked away in an inconspicuous position and access must be through another room. But nor must it be too difficult to find, the prime requirement being that anyone should be able to slip in unobserved, with minimal fuss.

Today there are plenty of toilet styles with plain unembarrassed lines in classical and modern designs. However, as of January 1st 1994, Federal law mandates that manufacturers cannot produce toilets that use more than 1.6 gallons of water per flush. Toilets that meet these new requirements rely on gravity-operated or pressure-assisted flushing mechanisms. Neither requires special plumbing, and both can be hooked up to existing supply lines and drains. The high efficiency pressure-assisted and gravity-fed toilets come in sleek one- and two-piece models. Other new ways to conserve water in the bathroom include low-flow showerheads and faucets with ceramic disc valves.

Washbasins come in pedestal and wall-hung styles which conceal some of the plumbing; less dependent on the aesthetic skills of your plumber is the built-in sink in an all-concealing vanity that will allow room for cleaning fluids.

1

1 An unusual shallow, trough-like sink.
2 Raised sides and built-in backsplashes were a sensible feature of older sinks, copied in good reproductions.
3 Old-fashioned faucets and fittings are increasingly popular, rather more so with home-owners than with plumbers.
4 There is no need to match sanitaryware: most styles of sink go well with the traditional Victorian-style bathtub.
5 An interesting *ménage à trois* of washbasins built into a wall unit.

2

3

4

5

6

7

10

11

8

9

There are many designer toys for the bathroom, such as glass sinks, though these should only be considered for obsessively clean individuals. If you opt for fancy equipment, the style may date quickly. Tasteful luxury is a standard tub shape, but big and deep; anything too adventurous – round, sunken, triangular – runs the risk of looking like something out of a James Bond movie. For the same reason, whirlpool baths can have an image problem, though it is possible now to buy whirlpool baths in standard tub sizes. If you prefer the safety of nostalgia, there are modern versions of the Edwardian claw-foot tub or you can have the genuine thing re-enameled, though this may cost as much as a good-quality modern tub.

A shower offers manufacturers less scope for vulgarity, though some prefabricated shower enclosures can look like alien space capsules in an otherwise well-designed bathroom. The most important aspect is sufficient pressure to deliver a shower worth having; for this you may have to install a pump.

6 Side-mounted faucets work best on round-ended baths.
7 Cedarwood tubs, inspired by Japanese tradition, are undeniably elegant, but they are expensive and require maintenance, needing to be filled every day to prevent them springing leaks.
8 A school sink is set in to a wall of marble which also conceals the radiators.
9 Soap dishes come in a range of striking contemporary designs.
10 A towel rail gone crazy, windows on the slope and a basin set into a sculptural rock: who says there's no room for individuality in the bathroom?
11 Sanitaryware design is entering a new era, with the big companies taking the lead from individual designers.
12 A plain glass screen makes an economical shower cabinet.

12

Mood, atmosphere and privacy

1 If cleanliness is next to godliness, you're just that bit nearer on an urban rooftop. But al fresco bathing is sadly a rather idealistic notion, brought down to earth by considerations of plumbing, drainage and load bearing.

1

2

Functionally the bathroom may have changed little over the past 100 years; the fixtures and fittings are more sophisticated but they still perform the same function. It is the spirit that has changed. Today we take hot and cold running water and the daily bath or shower for granted; relaxing in the bathroom has become a personal retreat devoted to luxury and contemplation.

Unwinding from the stresses of the day with a long soak in a hot tub is a simple luxury available to most people. Inevitably, then, some people will want to differentiate their bathroom, making it a personal haven of privacy and contemplation. In the last century you could be superior by having a bathroom instead of going to public baths. In the twentieth century you could distinguish yourself further by having a bathroom attached to your bedroom, emphasizing the privacy aspect.

Some feel that this bathroom obsession has gone too far, that it is a further step in the process of giving our houses the luxurious but bland uniformity of the international hotel. Architect Christopher Alexander decries the trend: 'These separate, efficiency bathrooms never give the family the chance to share the intimacies and pleasures of bathing, of being naked and half-naked together.' He is one of the growing group of architects and designers who, perhaps inspired by trips to Japan where, at least in the traditional houses, bathing is not a private ritual, are exploring the bathhouse or communal bathing idea. But for most people, this runs counter to the cherished concept of the bathroom as a place for private contemplation in peace. Some of the Japanese techniques of bathing are gaining ground; the idea, for example, of showering the dirt off first and then

relaxing in a hot tub. Deep cedarwood tubs can be used but, like wooden rowing boats, they have to be filled every day to keep them from springing a leak.

In some households the question of whether to house the toilet in the bathroom is a contentious one. A bathroom without a toilet does look deprived. The reason for putting it with the other bathroom fixtures is largely one of convenience, so that all bodily functions can be dealt with in one room, without having to put clothes on, or take them off. Those who favor the separate toilet think that it is more hygienic and causes less traffic jams in the morning. The problem with lonesome toilets is that they tend to be housed in narrow claustrophobic rooms and are often overlooked when it comes to decorating. If the toilet is situated next to an existing bathroom, it might make more sense to knock it through.

2 Modern plumbing need not restrict you to soulless acrylic sinks: here a shallow stone trough, echoing the shape of the porthole and slotted into a window recess, turns handwashing into a spiritual experience... But note the washbasin unit in the background for more prosaic everyday use.
3 The toilet as sculpture: one man's mission to put art into the cistern.
4 What more invigorating way to start the day than in a deep tub in front of windows flung open to welcome the fresh air.

4

3

5

5 The cozy, lived-in bathroom, with its freestanding tub, comfortable chair, even, perhaps, the ultimate luxury of a real fire. A large, freestanding bathtub can look a bit like a beached whale, but here it is visually integrated by the simple means of color.

6 Privacy is a cultural norm, not an absolute. For a more brazen approach, choose bathroom fixtures that are good looking enough to bare their all.

7 The bathtub as icon in a minimalist bathroom, a shrine to purity and cleanliness.

6

7

Decoration

1 White tiles graphically grouted in black, and shiny exposed plumbing give this bathroom a crisp, masculine air.
2 Mosaic tiling, particularly in this watery blue, is the perfect material for bathrooms.
3 A bathroom in a Gothic house built by Lord Ellenborough for his mistress is given an ecclesiastical theme.
4 A brass curtain rail turns the tub into a shower and lends an air of Edwardian opulence, toned down by the simple Shaker pegs above the toilet and sink.
5 Back-to-basics bathing: soaking up the atmosphere in an antique copper tub.

A bathroom can be the most satisfying of rooms to decorate: because it is usually fairly restricted in size it offers the chance to indulge in schemes and materials – a shell-encrusted grotto or a mosaic tiled hammam – that you might feel to be excessive in a larger space.

Just as the style of bathrooms in the early twentieth century was a reflection of society's emphasis on hygiene and cleanliness, today's interiors convey images of relaxation and escapism. Stretches of pristine white tiles or gleaming marble suggest a kind of cerebral hygiene, while the trend toward Edwardian-style fixtures and large bathrooms with armchairs to lounge in is the nostalgic face of escapism.

Certain practical considerations have to be taken into account, but none are particularly complicated. Obviously, surfaces need to be water resistant and easily cleaned, so wool carpets should be avoided as they rot easily if allowed to get wet; synthetic carpets with rubber backing can be used if you like the idea of padding on to a warm floor in the mornings, but on the whole a hard surface – marble, tile or vinyl – with the option of soft rugs is preferable.

Good lighting is essential for grooming tasks in the bathroom. The sparky white light of halogen downlights recessed into the ceiling works particularly well here, but you may need to add extra 'task' lighting for shaving and make-up areas. If you prefer a more traditional lighting scheme, remember that for safety reasons light-bulbs have to be enclosed within shades that fit flush against the walls or ceilings: pendant light fittings are not suitable. Switches need to be operated by a pull cord or to be situated outside the room.

Wall treatments should be practical – but this need not cramp your style. While uncoated wallpaper and matte latex paint are ruled out, you can use ceramic tile, glass mosaic tile, eggshell paint, tongue-and-groove boarding, marble or granite. Bare plaster, sealed with a matte varnish, gives a kind of raw warmth to the room – you can embed jewels into the plaster for a touch of exoticism – while painted tongue-and-groove has an elegant simplicity that works particularly well in the bathroom. Using mirror as a wall

6 A huge panel of glass makes a simple backsplash with strong visual impact. Old-style bathtubs look particularly good when contrasted with contemporary accessories and fixtures.

8 Saunas do not have to be all scrubbed knotty pine.

7 For the minimalist, space and clean lines are more of a luxury than the most opulent fixtures. Shower enclosures are seen as ugly intrusions, and if you have a sloping floor with drainage at one end they are unnecessary anyway.

9 A marble-topped Edwardian washbasin together with the color scheme and mosaic detailing give a turn-of-the-century accent to this room.

10 Decorated with paintings and furniture, bathrooms can be just as homely as any of your other rooms.

surface gives the illusion of space and is often used to suggest luxury, but you may find that large expanses of mirror, as well as being a pain to clean, throw back too many unwanted reflections.

Accessories can follow any theme set by your choice of materials. If you have plaster walls a bit of glitter works well as a contrast, whether it is punched aluminum cabinets and ethnic mirrors or the clean lines of chrome-and-glass shelves and trolleys. With tongue-and-groove boarding, slightly rustic cupboards and mirrors with wide wood frames look good; chair-rail-level beading should be wide enough to provide an ideal opportunity for displaying pretty glass bottles or sea shells. As a general rule, the more clean-cut image of marble or granite is best left uncluttered, though you can soften the look with luxurious thick white towels.

Showers and storage

Until quite recently a dressing-room was seen as something that only those with large houses or no children could aspire to. However, if a bathroom is large enough and there is another elsewhere in the house, it can double as a dressing room, though it will also double the time you spend in there at peak times. Take care to ensure that the room is well ventilated; a steamy room is far from ideally suited to clothes storage.

The ideal is a small, separate, well-lit room, reasonably close to the bathroom and bedroom. As well as clothes-hanging space and drawer space, you need 6ft (2m) square for dressing. If your funds don't run to custom-built closets, you can create some very effective ad hoc solutions; use a dress rack for clothes and baskets on shelves for small garments and accessories. You can curtain off the area if it's part of another room.

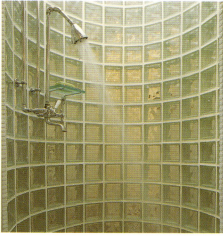

4

5 For the world-weary soul, and for the child within us that never grows up, a brilliantly improvized high-tech-meets-rustic shower enclosure.
6 Aluminum wall-mounted fixtures have an almost surgical appeal that works well in a confined space.

5

6

7

1 The general aesthetic standard of store-bought shower enclosures is fairly abysmal. Many designers prefer to make their own, despite the problems of sealing. Here, a sand-blasted sliding door has a clear square of glass for *Psycho*-phobes.
2 An integral sunken tub doubles as a shower tray.
3 A sylvan shower fitted in an old sunroom is a wonderful *folie de grandeur* that few of us would take further than an idle fantasy. In fact, it's more practical than it might appear, and the plants get watered at the same time.
4 A sweeping curve of glass fire bricks makes a stunning shower enclosure.

8

9

10

Some people would rather sacrifice the dressing room for a shower room if there is space. While the tub is for relaxing, a shower cleans and energizes; it is probably a more appropriate and efficient way to start the day, whereas a tub comes into its own in the evening. A separate self-contained shower unit is infinitely superior to any half-hearted measures. If you have two bathrooms it make sense to turn the smaller one into a shower room. Alternatively, a shower room could be situated on the ground floor, for use by someone coming in from outdoor exercise.

A downstairs bathroom with a toilet and washbasin is perhaps a luxury in terms of space, but it can double as a laundry room and a useful place for keeping outdoor boots. If possible allocate a 'dead' space under the stairs or in the hall to hang coats and hats.

7 A corner of the bedroom can be given over to a shower.
8 Baskets with tie-on labels are an effective means of storage.
9 Built-in cubby holes integrate more neatly than wall-mounted soap racks.
10 Generous towel rails make for easy airing and drying.

WORK AND PLAY

Whenever we consider ourselves radical in the way we live, there is invariably some long-distant precedent to remind us that nothing is ever new. Over the last twenty years, new technology has revolutionized the work field and meant that the option of working from home is available to administrative workers as well as creative artists. But, despite all the sophisticated equipment – the faxes and the desktop computers – that have allowed this to happen, we are merely coming round full circle to an older model of living whereby work and leisure were all based under one roof. A room of one's own is both a necessity and a luxury. Even in the most intimate household there is a need for individuals to be able to retreat to their own space. Christopher Alexander argues that all members of the household need their own private space, that it is necessary for psychological health, and that 'it helps develop one's own sense of identity; it strengthens one's relationship to the rest of the family; and it creates personal territory, thereby building ties with the house itself.' Virginia Woolf in her book whose title is perhaps better known than its contents argued that a room of one's own was a vital precondition of creativity.

When the idea of working from home began to take shape in the late 1970s, 'home offices' strived to be simultaneously 'hi-tech' and low cost – not a happy combination. It was almost as if the worker needed reassurance that this was really a place of work. In a commercial office the design and layout of furniture gives out subtle but unmistakable messages about the workers' status and authority. Many home workers may still feel unsure about their place without the security of an established hierarchy, and something of this insecurity manifests itself in the home office, giving out confusing signals. There is a need to separate working life from domestic routine, yet at the same time the office must be integrated into the house. As people become more relaxed about their working life, so this will be reflected in a confident handling of the design of their working environment. Certainly it seems ridiculous not to capitalize on the comforts of working from home – there is no point in abandoning a city office only to recreate exactly the same atmosphere at home.

Working from home frees us from the dull conformity of office life. Whether it's a room in daily use or a quiet corner for dealing with monthly checks, it need only look as formal as you want it to be. And if the children have their own playroom, why shouldn't you also devote a space to a favorite pastime?

Choosing the space

1 For designers, the choice of where to work is fairly simple. All they need is a drawing board and good light: with windows on two sides, this is an ideal location.
2 Sitting in a leafy sunroom makes work hardly seem like a chore at all.

1

2

3
5
4

Choosing the best room in which to work from home involves several considerations. In a family house you need somewhere quiet, away from the main flow of household traffic – not the room through which the children trudge to the backyard – but you also need good light and, if possible, a pleasant outlook. If you receive clients or colleagues at home, the space should be distanced from your domestic life. It is hard to keep up a professional front if you have to negotiate a path through drying underwear or past an unmade bed.

If your house is large enough, you may have the luxury of a whole room. As this is obviously the best option, it is worth trying to reorganize your living space to allow for an office – sacrifice the dining room or turn the biggest bedroom into a communal sleeping space for the children so that you can use one of the smaller bedrooms as an office.

3 Even if you do no paid work from home it is good to devote a quiet corner to private study or domestic paperwork.
4 The otherwise-wasted space under the stairs is a popular location for a small personal office. The only drawback is that it might be short on natural light so you need to ensure good task lighting.
5 It may be important for professional credibility to give your office a commercial look distinct from the rest of your home.
6 Work space can be created from even the smallest room; but in a bedroom, as here, try to use bright furniture that does not have an office feel to it.
7 An office environment does not have to be visually barren: objects that give you pleasure are as important here as anywhere else in the home.

8 A window alcove makes a perfect mini-office. At home you are free to explore unusual filing solutions.

6

7

8

The next best option is a room with dual functions. The bedroom tends to be unused space in the daytime, but unless it is a very big room, the bed will dominate the space, though you could consider a sofabed or a futon. It can be depressing to sleep in the same space that you have worked in all day, so it is important to separate – psychologically if not physically – the two functions. Try to create a fairly self-contained work area, by the window if possible, with your back to the bed. Under these circumstances, it is very important to take regular breaks from your work and have a change of scenery.

The other room which is often only in part-time use and therefore makes a good working base is the dining room. The dining room table can double up as a desk or work area although this is obviously not ideal if you have to keep putting your work away.

Creating a work area in your living room may not work well from a visual point of view, but you may be able to create a suitably self-contained working area. In any event you will need good storage and filing systems to keep unsightly paperwork or work samples under control. It may be worth having special cabinets made into which your equipment can disappear at night. Or, if your work is reasonably contained and not too dependent on high technology, an old-fashioned bureau or writing-desk may adequately meet your needs.

If nowhere suggests itself inside your home, perhaps you should look to the outside. Sheds have always had a romantic allure – even an extremely prosaic prefabricated one can have its magic. This is a place to indulge your dreams, to revive the childish art of make-believe homes and to release your decorative *alter ego*!

Perhaps we need to rethink our whole attitude about the division of work and 'life'. For many people work is not a chore, but a part of their life from which they gain a great deal of enjoyment. In this case you may not feel like hiding your work as if it were something to be ashamed of. Equally some people feel that their work actually benefits from being in the hub of domesticity. Where would we be, after all, without the kitchen-table novel?

Planning the layout

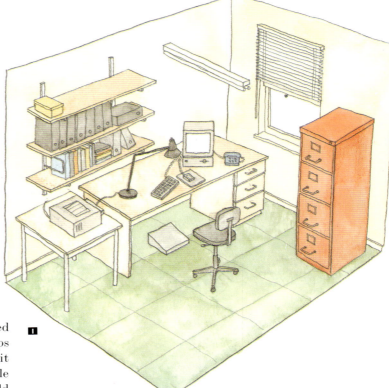

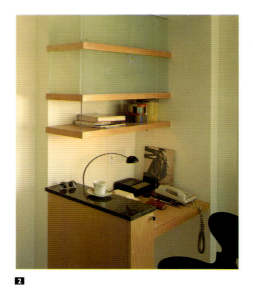

One of the joys of working from home is that you can plan your office to suit your particular way of working as well as your personal foibles and preferences. There is no office manager to dictate that your filing cabinet must be gray to match the carpet squares. In fact there is no reason why your work space should resemble an office at all, unless you need the status-support of an important-looking desk. Provided it is a comfortable height and stable – particularly important with computers – any work surface will do. But you cannot allow yourself so much freedom with the chair: a dining room chair is fine for the limited amount of time you are at the table, but when you are seated at a desk for hours everyday you are placing considerable stress on your spine. So buy the best office chair you can afford: there are a few designs available which have a more 'domestic' feel than the bureaucratic gray swivel chairs.

If the work area can be partitioned off, even if only by suggestion – perhaps by the arrangement of furniture – it may restore equilibrium to the whole space. In converted warehouses and old factories with high ceilings, it does not make sense to divide the space with full-height walls. Often moveable partitions and storage systems work best, creating a wall on one side so that you still keep the flow of space, but with some sense of division. Different floor levels may help to orchestrate the space, and a sleeping platform is worth considering; psychologically it might be helpful to sleep at a distance from your work. If possible consult an architect or interior designer – a professional evaluation of the space and its potential will probably produce results you had not dreamed possible.

You don't have to endure utilitarian metal storage systems and filing cabinets either. You could use baskets to file papers in, while office supply stores

make good hunting grounds for containers to house stationery and papers. If there is no alternative to living on top of your work then good organization is vital. Make storage for your work apparatus a priority, so that you are able to put things away neatly at the end of the day. If a table has to function as work surface and dining table, make sure you have large tablecloths to transform it from workhorse to centerpiece.

Take advantage of the comforts that working at home can offer but also try to insulate yourself against the temptations and diversions. For instance, if you have to go into the kitchen to make yourself a cup of coffee you may find it difficult to ignore the unwashed breakfast dishes or the mountain of laundry. You could buy a coffeemaker or you could go even further and install a mini-kitchen – a sink, small refrigerator, microwave and pantry – preferably one that can be neatly closed away behind cabinet doors.

1 The minimum requirements for an efficient work space are a desk, easily accessible shelves, a filing cabinet, ergonomically designed chair and good light. Ideally, natural light should come from the side, particularly if you work with a VDU.
2 Good planning makes the best use of even the smallest corner. In a tight space like this, a raised side to the desk encloses the work space as well as providing extra work surface.
3 Industrial work space often has its own raw aesthetic which it is best not to tamper with: trying to tame the space with domestic imagery will be doomed to failure. Less than perfect walls give you the advantage of being able to knock in nails or extra shelves as the need arises.
4 Only a totally self-denying workaholic would turn their back on a view like this. The computer, however, is positioned away from the light source, and the shutters and venetian blinds are essential to cut down the glare and heat of a hot summer's day.

4

5

6

7

5 If working from home deprives you of a spare bedroom, it makes obvious sense to invest in a sofabed. As a bed it will enable you to accommodate guests, while it can be used as a sofa for periods of relaxation during the day. If the idea seems too dangerously domestic, stick to plain-colored upholstery while it is in office use – you can always add an exotic throw to brighten it up for guests.

It is impossible for any human being to work at a consistently high level of concentration without taking a break. Most people go through a natural 'low' in the early afternoon. If we obeyed our body clocks and took a 10-minute nap at this time, we would probably be more productive. Anyone who has nodded off, chin in hands, while pretending to read a report will know that it is simply not permissible in a commercial office. But in your home office a comfortable sofa or armchair can provide a haven for a rest or a change of pace – not all work needs to be done sitting at a desk.

There is no reason why your office should not be a joyful and pleasant place, where you enjoy spending time. Give shelf space to objects which you enjoy looking at, enliven the walls with favorite photographs and paintings. Capitalize on the visual quality of the things you work with: tools, brushes, fabrics can be both functional and a decorative display when not in use.

Lighting can be your most valuable ally in delineating work and leisure time, though one advantage of working from home is that you can juggle your hours to include nighttime work. For work you need maximum voltage. But when you want to relax, it is important to switch to a gentler, mood lighting.

6 Even the most utilitarian furniture can be given executive status with a little imagination. Painting the trestles to match the filing cabinet transforms a cheap option into an elegant solution. The printer is raised on a small color-coordinated shelf while the paper tray is an ordinary box given glamor with a simple coat of paint.

7 For some people – notably writers and young fogys who hanker after the days of Dickensian clerks – the appeal of high-tech is entirely resistible. An uncluttered table, good light and a sharp pencil may be all you need to write that masterpiece.

Playrooms

1 Children need very little to fire their imaginations. Fashionable, expensive climbing frames may have far less play value than a pretty garden pavilion. A dump to adult eyes is paradise to children, where an old iron bed doubles as den and trampoline.

Play is essential to the development of children – without it the spirit of childhood shrivels up and dies. Children need play space of their own with some sense of independence from their parents. For babies and toddlers play is a valuable prerequisite to more formal learning. But where there is potential space for one, the separate playroom has quite probably been squeezed out by the home office, and the takeover by television now means that in too many households passive entertainment has replaced active play.

While children are at the baby and toddler stage, their playroom may be a portable basket of toys which means they can play under the watchful eye of a parent. But once they get past the stage of swallowing marbles whenever the opportunity presents itself, they benefit from some independence. If you do not have the space for a separate playroom, the bedroom usually doubles up as one. Children seem to have no problem in dissociating the space from sleep: as soon as the first rays of daylight hit the room it readily takes on its daytime role – with a vengeance. But children also like to be near, so a room three floors up probably won't work until they are at least seven or eight.

Generally, children's playthings fall into three categories which need to be considered when it comes to storage. There are board games which are probably best stacked in vertical piles on shelves with the names on display. There are all the pieces which go together to make a whole – Lego, bricks, plastic people, etc. Keep these in brightly colored plastic storage boxes – shoe boxes are also useful for keeping the smallest pieces together. Hardback books obviously need shelves but you may find that a large basket on the floor is more useful for the paperback picture books of early childhood so that the children can flick through by themselves to see the covers that might be overlooked on bookshelves.

2

3

2 Teenagers living at home need somewhere to call their own – and somewhere free from the decorative influence of their parents. If you have the space to indulge them, a bedsitting room is ideal – with sofas and chairs to accommodate their friends – because however groovy you may feel yourselves to be as parents, they really do not want to sit around the kitchen table with you. With their constant craving for clothes, it does not make sense to waste space on a wardrobe which will soon be crammed to overflowing – a hanging rail will be able to take the load better.

3 Easily cleaned floors with soft rugs are best in a playroom.

4

5

4 A loft level in a child's bedroom conveniently separates sleep from play and makes going to bed more of an adventure than an affliction – at least until the novelty finally wears off.

5 Many children feel liberated rather than repressed by a certain amount of order and discipline in an area set aside for quiet, creative activity. A healthy play environment, however, should also include a less structured area for dressing up and pretend play.

Generally speaking when it comes to children's toys, storage and display should be one and the same. Toys should be accessible and safe – don't keep them in heavy-lidded chests which can be dangerous. Make sure shelves are firmly bolted to the wall: children will inevitably climb them when trying to reach something on the shelf above.

If you are lucky enough to live in a house with nonstandard features – deep windowsills, small alcoves and pockets of 'awkward space' – children will make a beeline for them. This is where they can spend the most valuable currency of childhood – their imagination. Be wary of buying things where the adult designer has done the imagining for them – the darling little lipstick-pink Chesterfield sofa, for example. For the same money you could buy or make them a real outdoor playhouse.

As children get older they need more space – whether for watching television, making model airplanes or homework. Where there is not much floor space a loft bed which houses a desk, drawers and wardrobe underneath is useful for this age group. The disadvantage is that they are difficult to move around for cleaning and may be considered deeply uncool by the teenager.

Accepted wisdom about teenagers seems to be to keep them as far away as possible from their parents. A mobile home in the backyard, as some advocate, may be a little excessive, but they do need somewhere private to go and listen to their loud music. The mutual revulsion between teenagers and parents is much exaggerated; like all of us teenagers need to be given a degree of freedom. If you have the space and funds, a finished loft or basement retreat is probably the ideal solution.

Individualizing personal space can counter an increasingly stand-ardized world. This section provides a visual sourcebook that shows the range of materials and finishes available to enable you to custo-mize your surroundings. Since most of us are allergic to design that looks good but doesn't wear well, the text notes how different options combine form with function, design with economy. Character and a sense of budget are not mutually exclusive terms when it comes to remodeling or redecorating. While our homes are the perfect vehicle for expressing individuality, they must also be within our means. So in addition to the relative merits and mainte-nance of design options, the text also considers the practicality and relative costs to enable you to make the right choices for your home.

In the section on walls and ceilings, the emphasis is on decorative treatments that support style and substance. Without lifting a ham-mer, you can use materials such as paint and paper on walls and ceilings to make rooms wider and taller, in appearance, if not in fact. Textural surfaces, ranging from commercial sandpaper to concrete to natural fibers, grow more tactile at close range.

Flooring is a room's home base; always underfoot, acoustics and sense of touch enter into consideration. Choose a gently massaging surface – carpet for instance – and you cross a room as silently as if on tiptoe; a wood floor that feels cool and smooth will have you marching. Materials that complement the use of the room and the other elements in the space is another factor of a good choice. If you increasingly find that the generic simply won't do, read on and open you sights to the range of options now open to you.

Keeping the elements of a room simple allows you to exploit the potential of color. Here, bare wood floorboards and white walls provide a neutral foil to the vivid blue of the upholstered armchair. The simple yellow sliding door draws the eye through into the next room and makes more of a feature of the staircase.

WALLS AND CEILINGS

Walls are boundaries that enclose a room and ceilings are the lofty extreme. Exploiting the decorative potential of these basic elements can dramatically affect the apparent proportions of a room and radically determine its overall character and mood. Backgrounds are not insignificant; the sheer area involved lends impact to any choice of finish.

Plain white walls and ceilings have become the trademark of contemporary interiors. If you're unsure how to proceed and need time to evolve your decorative instincts, there's nothing wrong with this tried-and-tested formula. But even the most hesitant decorator should eventually be liberated by the huge range of of techniques, materials and finishes. From silky smooth gloss paint to broken-color effects, bold patterned papers to matchboarding, it is easier and more economical than ever to put decorative ideas into practice.

Color, pattern and texture are the fundamental variables. Color generates an almost emotional response, from the quiet contemplative quality of chalky whites, serene blue-grays and gentle greens through to the electric jolt of sunshine yellow, scarlet or marine blue. If a room seems bland and characterless, these basic associations can help to lift it out of the ordinary. Dark rich colors and dense pattern draw in the boundaries of a space, making it warm and enclosed. Light fresh color allows walls to recede and promotes an airy, expansive quality. Pattern offers similar potential, but requires sophisticated handling. The scale of the repeat and type of design must be tailored to the proportions and size of the room: large-scale prints with a high degree of contrast will overwhelm a small, enclosed space; tiny, subdued motifs will fade to insignificance in a big high-ceilinged room. Texture is a vital component of any finish, bringing a tactile quality and a material expression which adds depth and character.

When you begin to draw attention to the walls, it's worth remembering that any applied treatment will only ever look as good as that which underlies it. In spatial terms, decoration can disguise and distract, but it can be cruelly revealing of substandard surfaces. Preparation may be dull and time consuming, but it constitutes the essential means to your required ends, enabling you to gain maximum benefit from your decorative efforts.

1 Decorating doesn't have to be terribly costly or time consuming: even the simplest walls look better for a couple of fresh coats of white paint. Neutral colors focus attention on simple touches such as a vase of flowers in dappled sunlight.
2 Primarily used in the construction industry, simple builders' planks have been used to form a partition wall.

3 A dramatic plane of strong color – as on this ceiling – can make a room seem larger by drawing the eye away from the enclosing walls.

4 Concrete blocks follow the subtle curve of this window, and are juxtaposed against the smooth surface of the traditional plaster wall above. Concrete walls and floors are most feasible in new constructions or when adding an extension.

5 A wall of glass brick filters light from upstairs, refreshing the rooms below.

4

5

Making a choice

1

2

The walls and ceilings of your home have to withstand considerable wear and tear. They should be able to weather the dirt of day-to-day living and sustain the occasional knock; they need to withstand condensation and, within reason, be straight – though no house is made up entirely of right angles.

Before you even begin to consider a new decorative scheme, you need to check for (and, if necessary, eliminate) any structural problems: no finish can cover up a damp wall or a ceiling in poor condition. Injecting foam insulation into the wall or ceiling cavity reduces heat loss and can mitigate condensation problems.

If heat loss remains a concern, consider warm, thick finishes such as plaster, wood and padded fabric panels. If noise pollution is an issue, walls of stone and fabric are better than plaster or wallpaper at absorbing sound and providing privacy. Paint and wallpaper are versatile, and generally cheaper and much easier to change than tile, stone and wood paneling, making them good interim choices.

ON THE SURFACE

One of the first things to consider is a general color scheme, either for a particular room or for the whole of your house or apartment. Do you want the walls to be a muted background to furniture and furnishings or do you want them to be bold in their own right? Do you prefer solid color or pattern, a silky smooth gloss finish or a rougher texture? It is a good idea to concentrate on playing up good features and minimizing those that are less attractive. Different rooms have different moods: think in terms of the overall feeling you want to achieve, the function of the room and its contents.

When a room has disparate or dominant features – walls at odd angles, sloping ceilings, a staircase, more than two entries – a single decorative treatment or pattern often helps to unify the space. Alternatively, you can highlight irregularities by distinguishing between one plane and another with different shades of the same color, by using the same color but varying

finishes and textures, or with complementary colors. A block of bright color on one wall articulates the space by making that particular wall the focus of attention. Using color to pick out architectural details brings definition to a room, and can be a useful means of drawing the eye away from less than perfect finishes elsewhere. Pale wall finishes extend the boundaries of small and plain rooms by reflecting light; similarly, pastels and soft colors will make you less aware of narrow confines.

Picture rails and chair rails provide an obvious boundary for different wall treatments. If they've been removed you can reinstate them with new moldings or simply by painting a stenciled border, dado or stripe. Trim gives structure to a room: picture rails in tall rooms make the walls a more manageable proportion; omit baseboards and walls appear to float.

Glass walls and ceilings filter and diffuse natural light. Glass is not an expensive material to work with and can be used as a layer over plaster or MDF (medium density fiberboard).

Setting up a dialogue between the walls and the upholstery works best when you stick to simple applications and clear color as a foundation. Using color that appears nowhere else but on walls or the ceiling can be clean and modern, but you need to have a good eye to know that the colors you've chosen will work together in a bold way rather than result in a migraine-inducing clash. A close harmony between the colors and textures of a room is the more obvious route for most of us.

Decorative paint effects – such as sponging, stippling or dragging – add depth to flat walls and can help to disguise uneven surfaces and poor plasterwork. You need to practise first on a patch of wall to ensure you have the necessary skills to apply the technique to good effect.

Bear in mind that whatever decorative treatment you choose should easily accommodate doors, windows and other built-in features such as shelves or a fireplace. The proportions of a room can be made to look very different according to the way in which walls are decorated.

1 Contrasting colors of paint on the walls and ceiling of this kitchen add wit and depth to a small space.
2 Old and new – in this case sheets of aluminum, ceramic floor tiles and a slatted wood floor – can make an aesthetically pleasing combination.

3

4

CEILINGS

A ceiling is like the lid of a beautiful box. There are times when a white ceiling is appropriate, especially when the room's contents are what warrants notice. Ornamented ceilings, even those given a coat of high-gloss paint, are uplifting. Generally, the higher the ceiling the more reason to give it some texture, depth and reflectiveness. Silver and aluminum leaf, Adam-style plaster moldings, thin beading and rough-hewn wood are possible effective choices. Picking out molding in contrasting colors is one way of adding interest at ceiling height, especially if the walls and ceiling are painted the same color.

To unify a room with several ceiling heights, you can establish a horizontal line around the space – perhaps at picture-rail height – and use a different finish above and below the line. In upstairs rooms, skylights and dormer windows open up not only the ceiling but the whole room. In converted roof space, the pitch of the ceiling is a positive feature to exploit.

PROPORTION

If the ceiling of a room is nearer to eye level than the floor, the room may feel particularly claustrophobic. Windows can reinforce this telescoped effect by drawing attention to the room's mid-section. By fiddling with the information walls and ceilings display about their size, you can control how the eye takes stock of space and fool it into reading rooms differently. Shifting the design focus to neglected wall areas or the ceiling through decorative treatment can make rooms perceptually more desirable.

Pattern and texture expand the horizons of walls and ceilings visually, creating a variety of moods and, if needs be, an illusion of spaciousness. Stripes can act as a frame, defining the boundaries of what they enclose. Vertical stripes, in either wallpaper or paint, direct the gaze up and down, which seems to raise a low ceiling. Horizontal stripes painted on walls effectively anchor a ceiling that floats too high. The thickness and spacing of stripes should broadly reflect the size of the room. If you

are painting quite broad stripes, it's best to plan quite carefully in advance so that features such as doors and windows are taken into account and the stripes aren't broken up in a complicated and visually distracting manner. Unless you want the illusion of living in a tent, stripes are best avoided on ceilings and crooked, imperfect walls whose faults will only be emphasized.

Horizontal patterns lead the eye around, visually broadening a small room. Painting in a chair rail below waist height, devising one from molding, or using a wallpaper border at chair-rail height helps widen a room by drawing attention downward and making walls seem farther apart. Long, narrow rectangular panels entice the eye upward; squat rectangles below a chair rail anchor the scheme.

Continuing the ceiling color or material down to picture-rail height or painting it a darker shade than the walls are ways of lowering the apparent height of a ceiling. Tenting a ceiling with fabric or applying a rich color makes a room seem wider.

3 Home improvements are often more about knowing when to leave well alone: these renovated oak floorboards and window shutters are complemented by the bare brick wall.
4 Dividing up part of a room with painted particleboard partitions and damask curtains also lends a warm touch to the concrete walls.

Paint

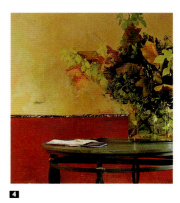

Paint is incredibly versatile, relatively cheap and offers an unbeatable immediacy. With a little practice, you can achieve exactly the color and texture you want.

Though on the surface paint doesn't appear greatly to change things, appearances are deceiving. With a few tricks of scale and the sorcery of color, a room can be made to appear larger or smaller, wider or taller. Horizontal patterns broaden and vertical designs seem to lengthen walls. You can lower the

1 Latex painted walls with contrasting trim on window frame and above picture rail.
2 Paint effect on ceiling.
3 Broad latex painted stripes.
4 Contrasting glazed walls above and below chair rail.
5 Paint effect carried over from wall to door.
6 Rough textured plaster walls.
7 White latex walls against contrasting wall of rough plaster colored yellow.

ceiling of a room by painting it a color other than white or off-white. When the ceiling and molding are painted the same color, the eye lingers where color changes between the walls and the molding, not at the true ceiling line. This also serves to lower the ceiling and instill architectural definition.

CHOOSING PAINT

Latex and solvent-based paints, also referred to as oil-based paints, come in five finishes from dull to shiny: flat, eggshell, satin, semi gloss and high gloss. The shinier the paint, the easier it is to wash, but the better the finish has to be. Modern additives speed drying, inhibit mildew and improve surface appearances. High-gloss paints are the most wear- and moisture-resistant, containing a high proportion of resin that produces a tough film. They are recommended for fingerprint-prone doors and scuffable trim. If you prefer a less obtrusive shine on woodwork, semi-gloss paints work well and provide moderate durability. Latex is water

based and the least durable, but is suitable for walls and ceilings since it both covers easily (though several coats will be needed) and dries very quickly. Solid latex paint is sold in trays with a roller; it is as near to non-drip as you can get, which makes it particularly suitable for painting ceilings and other inaccessible areas.

Water paints and milk-based paints made from natural pigments bring warmth, earthy colorations and a chalky quality to wood, plaster or wallboard. These paints come in a variety of colors in powdered form. Rubbed down with steel wool, walls finished with water paint or milk-based paint have an instant patina. If a very fine sandpaper is used, the finish looks polished; using a soft cloth produces a burnished effect.

The best paint is costly, made from high-quality ingredients such as long-lasting pigments, pure oils and solvents. Look for titanium dioxide on the label; paints with it may need distilling, but those without it can clump, adhere poorly to surfaces and tend to yellow in sunlight.

You can also use paint to make up glazes and washes. A glaze is a mixture of turpentine and solvent-based varnish, usually in the proportion of 2:1, to which solvent-based paint is then added. Glazes are slow to dry, but give walls a rich luminous sheen.

A wash consists of water-based (usually latex) paint diluted with acrylic varnish and can be applied instead of or over an existing paint finish to add depth and texture. The translucent wash of color brilliantly reflects the light and opens up even the smallest and darkest of rooms.

COLOR

Thinking of a wall, ceiling and trim as architectural elements can provide guidance for choosing one or more colors. Painting the walls a deep matte and the trim in a contrasting high gloss, for example, would bring out the depth of the walls.

For older houses there were conventions of the day for painting interior and exterior architectural elements that can be easily researched. Visual sources, such as paintings of period interiors, provide wonderful clues.

Another way of choosing a color is to approach paint the way an artist approaches a canvas. Adding colored pigment to an eggshell suspension with varnish is a technique painters use to give a burnished depth to the canvas. When this sort of glaze is applied to an eggshell undercoat it gives a wall extraordinary depth of color. Instead of coordinating walls with your furnishings, you could paint them in a color that complements those of the furnishings. Literally mixing complementary colors, such as pink and blue, produces a rich 'bruised' shade. When in doubt, however, show restraint – remember that you will have to live with the results!

White walls are a tried-and-tested convention. Ethereal white, tinted with a hint of vanilla or cream, is more inspired and has a greater richness than plain white. Painting different rooms in a house with five or six tones of softly contrasting shades of white and gray provides a neutral backdrop for belongings, and the walls will reflect light in interesting ways.

If you are moving house or apartment, the best initial response – if it is feasible – is to paint the interiors white and allow your design ideas to develop over time. However, in a gloomy basement or in a small room, white isn't always going to give you light or make the area less insipid. It is sometimes better to exploit the situation and use dark, rich colors. It's not always necessary to use the palest colors in order to create a feeling of space and light. Soft blue and creamy yellows, for example, work particularly well in dark rooms.

Choosing a paint color from a paint chart or numbered chip is never an adequate gauge as to how the paint will look on a wall. It is worth the expense of purchasing a single quart first. Color changes during the course of the day, according to the source of light. A sunny exposure makes any color appear more yellow; cold winter light is whiter and less distorting, while rooms with eastern and western exposures fluctuate through the day according to the position of the sun.

Incandescent light is yellower than sunlight; halogen is white and tends to sap warmth away from paint hues; the new flurescents come in many colors ideal for home use.

To test paint samples, buy a can of each chosen color and brush a patch of pure white primer on a window wall, which is typically the darkest, on the wall where sunlight lands, at floor level and under your lighting, then apply a coat of your chosen color on top. Look at these swatches under artificial light in the evening and at various times during daylight. Is the color giving the effect you want it to? Try to picture the painted wall when furniture, window treatments, a rug and people are in the room.

Custom mixing enables you to achieve any color you've seen and loved. You need to take care to mix up enough paint to cover the surface: if you run out of paint half way through the job it may be very difficult to match a new mix exactly. Many paint manufacturers now offer a color-mixing service themselves.

5

6

DECORATIVE PAINTING

Using paint instead of molding to create wall details has a venerable history seen in eighteenth-century Scandinavian cottages, Mexican haciendas and Medieval paintwork on half-timbered houses. The look is fresh and painted details are easy to amend. Painting the wall below a chair rail, for example, draws the eye downward and makes walls seem further apart. This is a useful trick for hallways and other narrow areas.

Since their heyday in the early 1980s, some decorative techniques now look a little tired: sponging and ragging are both over-exposed, while marbling requires a deft hand if it's going to have the desired effect. Distressed surfaces call for a subtle approach and plenty of practice beforehand. More versatile and easily mastered methods such as graining, however, still have life left in them and make inexpensive ways to conceal flaws and gain texture. Today, decorative painting remains a fun form of camouflage.

With any decorative paint effect, it is important that you restrict your palette. Methods such as ragging and graining that involve broken color generally work best when the base color is close in tone to that used for the effect. If the tones are not carefully matched, the effect will look clumsy. Pattern and texture will partly be determined by the print left by whatever tool or material you use to apply the paint finish. You should always practice first on a piece of lining paper so that you familiarize yourself with the technique and also so that you gain some idea of how the finished room will look. (For this reason, it's not a good idea to try out the technique on a small piece of paper, as you'll not get a very good idea of scale.)

Almost any paint effect can be used on woodwork as well as walls, but you should resist the temptation to go crazy with a new-found technique. A grained chair rail or carefully placed stencil will have much greater effect than a room in which every surface has been subject to one special effect or another.

7

If you are painting in or adding wall details, keep your design in proportion to the scale of the room. If you are unsure about the results a scheme may have on the room, transfer your idea to a piece of tracing paper, then sketch possible schemes on the paper with colored pencils and tape these to the wall to see how it looks. Bear in mind that any design should take doors, windows and other built-in features into account. Use a metal ruler and carpenter's level to ensure that the lines on the wall are accurately marked out. Before you start painting, lightly tape along the proposed line and view it from a distance. If a wall slopes badly or is settling, a straight line may actually accentuate the problem and unbalance the room. 'Straighten' the line until it looks right.

Start from a point in the room that will not be the center of attention, and use a good-quality paint brush. Chinese bristle sash brushes are best for enamel paints and nylon bristle brushes for latex.

PLASTER

A lot of new construction and renovation in the interior is made from MDF (medium density fiberboard) or particleboard. When you paint either of these materials, the finish is often lackluster, offering little in the way of depth and richness. If your budget allows, you can remedy this by applying a skim coat of plaster on new walls so the paint will have greater resonance. Plaster is a durable and relatively inexpensive finish spread on walls. It has the material quality of chalk and, unlike flat latex, it doesn't scuff.

Plaster is traditionally made of layers of lime and rough sand troweled onto wire mesh. Its surface can be striped (by running a plasterer's comb over wet plaster), sparkled (by working in marble or metallic powder) or textured (by rubbing straw or sawdust into the surface). The most understated white plaster is produced by burnishing a plain plaster skim to white iridescence with kaolin from Germany, the substance that makes porcelain whiter than fine bone china. Bare plaster is such a lovely buff-pink color that it can be worth leaving uncovered in some rooms.

PREPARATION

Proper preparation can add years to your paintwork. Make sure the walls are washed clean and have been lightly sanded, and that uneven surfaces have been patched before they are primed and sanded prior to a main coat. Gloss paints require undercoat; latexes generally don't. Professionals recommend sanding between coats for a smoother finish.

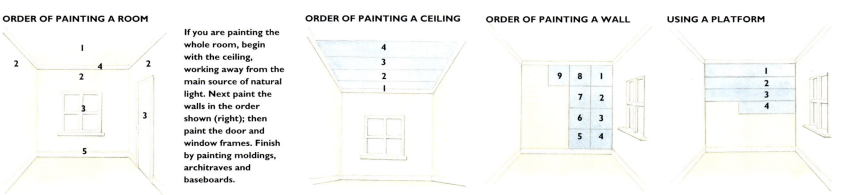

ORDER OF PAINTING A ROOM

If you are painting the whole room, begin with the ceiling, working away from the main source of natural light. Next paint the walls in the order shown (right); then paint the door and window frames. Finish by painting moldings, architraves and baseboards.

ORDER OF PAINTING A CEILING

ORDER OF PAINTING A WALL

USING A PLATFORM

Wallcoverings

WALLPAPER

Potentially less anonymous than plain paint or plaster, wallpaper is a popular choice for decorating walls, offering plenty of character and style. The texture of some wallpapers can help to disguise a wall's flaws, while a wallpaper mural can deceive the eye about the proportions of a room. People have a tendency to forget how well wallpaper works on the ceiling. An architectural paper and border, perhaps illustrating *trompe-l'oeil* plasterwork, for instance, give a ceiling wonderful depth.

WALLPAPERING A ROOM

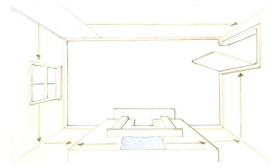

If you are hanging wallpaper with a large pattern, you should begin by centering a piece above the fireplace or other significant feature of the room. For all other wallpaper, hang the first sheet in the corner of the wall adjacent to the window wall and work away from the source of natural light.

Wallpapers also work well in combination with one another or with paint. Using one paper under a chair rail with a different design above, or using contrasting patterns in a room gives you a real feeling of dimension. These days, patterned wallpaper is not just huge floral bouquets and flocked Victoriana; contemporary patterns, stars, stripes and elegant repeat motifs lend vitality and boldness to a material that has not always been held in esteem.

The perceived wisdom is that you should hang a large-scale wallpaper in a large-scale room, and a small-scale paper in a small-scale room. However, small rooms can be given style with a large-scale paper. Choice is governed more by personal taste than proportion and by how much you want the walls to be a backdrop to the rest of the room.

Before buying a wallpaper, invest in a large sample. Pin it to the wall and view it night and day, in natural and artificial light. Florals are easier to pattern match than plaid papers and natural fibers. Delicate and difficult to clean papers, such as grasscloth, woven raffia and foil papers, are only really suitable for walls that are not going to be subject to rough wear and tear. Vinyl wallpapers are the best choice for busy, trafficked areas such as the hallway and kitchen.

PREPARING WALLS

Before wallpapering, strip the existing decoration down to the base wall, and then apply a coat of wallcovering primer to seal the walls. Hanging paper directly onto impervious painted or plastered walls requires high-contact adhesives. If the walls are in poor condition or contain lime, it's advisable to line them first with an inexpensive lining paper to provide a base of uniform porosity and color. Lined walls give a smooth and less patchy finished result, and the wallpaper will adhere for longer than if it were applied to an unlined wall.

Generally, heavy wallpapers last longer and are easier to hang than lightweight papers. Always use the paste recommended by the manufacturer. Wallpaper shouldn't be hung immediately after it has been pasted; most wallpapers expand after pasting, a process which takes at least three to five minutes. If the paper is still expanding while it is hung, it will dry unevenly and shrink, leading to badly matched seams. Some professional paper-hangers also apply paste to the wall as well as the paper for better bonding. Follow the directional arrows (printed on the back) when hanging wallpaper to ensure that patterns are not hung upside down.

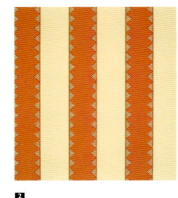

TYPES OF WALLPAPER

There are two basic categories of wallpaper – handscreened and machine printed. The labor-intensiveness and quality of the finish is reflected in the cost of the paper. Handscreened wallpaper is the costliest variety. Designs are cut into wood blocks, and these are then dipped into chalky paint and applied by hand to heavy paper. The paper is then hung up on rollers to dry between each color print.

Handscreened paper is more difficult to hang. The longer pulp fibers of the strong paper (used to prevent tears during the printing process) make it prone to stretching and curling when it is wet with paste. Bought from source, handscreened paper can be printed in colors of your specification, and can last up to 30 years without the colors becoming dull or the paper worn.

Machine-printed papers are either spongeable, washable or scrubbable. Spongeable papers wipe down gently with soap and water. Washable papers are covered in a thin acrylic film that allows washing with mild detergent and water. Vinyls have a tough, thick plastic coating and can be scrubbed. Most machine-printed wallpapers today incorporate vinyl, making them less vulnerable to wear than the paper stock used for handscreened varieties.

What can be classified as wallpaper often goes beyond the inventory of design retailers. Brown kraft papers (the sort that are used in the manufacture of brown paper bags and commercial sandpaper) are brilliantly inexpensive alternatives to traditional wallpaper, and they don't look cheap or makeshift. Brown paper is simple and sophisticated; sandpaper reflects light beautifully and is a tactile surface. The biscuity-ocher color of both becomes a neutral and warm backdrop. They both work particularly well when counterbalanced with white-painted trim and light wood floors.

NATURAL FIBERS

Natural fibers have a powerful, understated beauty. Their simplicity appeals to the eye. Wood veneers, woven raffia and dried grasses are backed with paper to make them easier to hang. The effect is as varied as the materials, from the luxury of silk to the rough appeal of hessian. Paper covered with a thin cork veneer can be used on the walls of a child's room for posters, though most of these materials are delicate and won't withstand much wear. Natural materials cannot be matched: panel seams may be noticeable; conceal them with borders or, alternatively, incorporate them into the design.

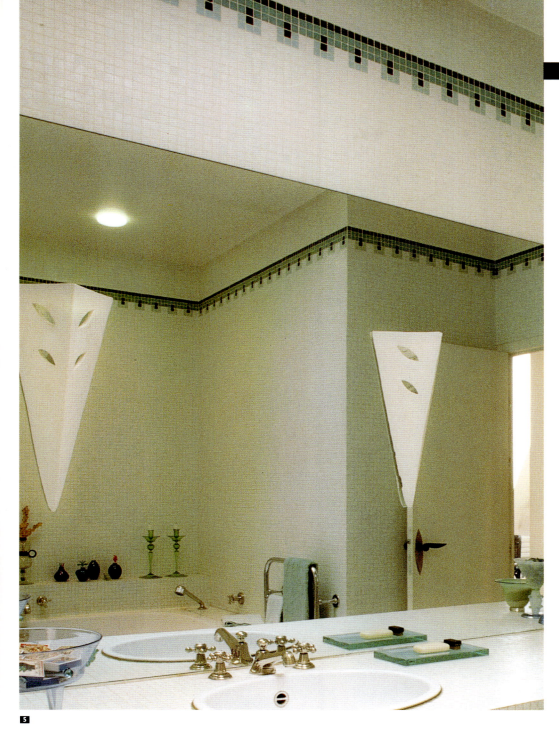

5

8

putting up wall tile, don't attempt to align borders or dadoes with the grout seams of fixed tiles. It is historically incorrect and may lead to practical problems and superfluous cutting. Grout joints can pick up dirt, though new stain-resistant grout compounds and grout colored to match tiles makes maintenance easier. Cutting tiles to fit around electric outlets, pipework and the like requires some skill.

Tile designs range from vibrant panels on Aesthetic Movement

6

7

FABRIC WALLS

If walls are pitted, the plaster is flaking, or you need to muffle sound, covering walls with fabric involves less headache than calling in builders. Fabric can be pasted like wallpaper, paper backed, sewn together, or put up in a panel system. The traditional style of fabric walling is to lay wadding or interlining on bumpers which are attached to battens nailed to the walls. Pattern-matched fabric is then sewn into panels and stapled

to the top and bottom of the walls. Glued strips of piping or a braid hide the staples. Fabric can be gathered into casement curtains and hung from rods at ceiling and baseboard. Since fabrics are not required by law to be labeled regarding flammability, you should check. Make fabrics flame resistant by coating them with a flame retardant solution.

Felt, cotton, linen, wool and any other light- or heavyweight fabric can go up on the walls. Generally, the

more body and stretch a fabric has the more it requires professional fitting to conceal seams and match the pattern. Thin silk dupioni, which tears and gives, and plaids, which tend not to match particularly well, are less suitable than other materials.

TILE

Tiled walls can be beautiful and resilient. There are rich possibilities in size, color and finish, from iridescent to crackled, matte to metallic. Varieties include glazed and unglazed porcelain, vitreous glass, terra cotta and clay. Handmade, customized tile is available from artisans, while antique tile salvaged from old houses is obtainable from secondhand shops and architectural traders. If you hanker after the luxury and intense color of hand-glazed tiles but are put off by the price, think of incorporating them to maximum effect, as a border or to form a focal point.

Tile comes in batches and can be subject to color variations; buy extra to use as replacements later. When

fireplaces to 1920s tiles comprising a field of plain tiles – a reminder that plain white tiles can be laid to great effect, perhaps at an angle, or in staggered rows. Among the authentic touches that you can revive is Victorian wafer-thin grouting, though a return to the traditional method of polishing unglazed tiles is ill-advised since modern polishers do the job much better. Tiled surfaces in older homes were frequently obliterated with paint or wallpaper as taste of the period dictated. Since they are hardwearing and durable, many tile walls will have survived relatively undamaged, waiting to be rediscovered and restored.

Unglazed tile is best if it is sealed to protect it. Wax is a more time-consuming process, but is more color-rich, wears better and produces a deeper patina than emulsion polish or acrylic varnish. Wall tiles should be applied with a faster-drying adhesive than floor and countertop tiles. Handmade tile is uneven and looks best if grout joints are not too tight – about $\frac{1}{8}$in (3mm).

1 Handscreened wallpaper with large repeat motif.
2 Machine-printed striped wallpaper.
3 Machine-printed paper with small design.
4 Machine-printed wallpaper with repeat motif above a dado.
5 Small ceramic mosaic tile.
6 Natural fiber.
7 Ceramic tile.
8 Glass brick.

Wood and metal

WOOD

Wood paneling guards against heat loss and insulates noise, conceals uneven or crumbling walls and can be crafted anew or recycled. As the cost of hardwood rises and forests continue to be depleted, there is an increasing need to use wood that is not endangered. Period wood paneling can be found at architectural salvage yards and given new homes, often for less than the cost of new paneling. Hardwood doors and pieces of armoires and tables can be recrafted into wood paneling. Timber bought from ecologically farmed plantations provides an excellent substitute for mahogany and ebony, and is no more expensive.

Wood wall paneling, historically referred to as 'wainscoting', has been used as a lovely and practical wall lining for principal rooms since the fifteenth century. As with most wood wall finishes, it is mounted on battens fixed to the wall. Modern tongue-and-groove end matched paneling – simpler to construct – often features beaded molding. Though it was originally used in country homes,

batten board and wood veneers avoid period clichés. Tongue-and-groove boards can be nailed to wall battens vertically, horizontally or diagonally. Depending on the quality of the wood used and the pattern of its grain, the surface may be stained, varnished or painted.

Tongue-and-groove paneling is popularly used in bathrooms, where it can be painted in seaside colors or to complement bathroom fixtures. Wood paneling also makes good, practical sense in a hallway, since it is well able to sustain knocks and blows. Plywood makes inexpensive paneling and, when stained, the wood grain comes through beautifully – this can make an excellent treatment for studies and home offices, where it creates the look of an old-fashioned library. Battens are used to cover the seams between pieces and to create the paneled effect. Plywood is also a good surface for paint, particularly light colors such as khaki, olive green, wheat and white. Hand-rubbed stains and glazed finishes enhance doors and walls.

Seal wood wall finishes as insurance against dampness and stains and insulate them with metal sheets or fireproof material if they abut the oven or cooktop in the kitchen or the fireplace in the living room or family room.

DADOES

Dadoes are decorative wall treatments of wood, paper or paint that stop at chair-rail height. The Victorians used dadoes made of frame-and-panel and tongue-and-

groove boards to protect walls from being damaged by chair backs and general traffic. Today, dadoes can be just as useful in protecting walls and/or breaking up the monotony of the bare background of a large expanse of wall. Stock architectural molding, paper and paint can be used expressively to give the impression of a period dado.

METAL

Sheet metal is chic but expensive. Copper, brass and aluminum are costly wallcoverings but work well as panels under chair rails. Stainless steel is even more of a luxury. Most metals dull easily, needing frequent polishing. They come in sheet or tile form and veneer molding, and should be adhered directly to smooth plaster or wood panels. Pressed aluminum ceilings, left bare or painted a pale color, are an inexpensive way to add texture. Steel diamond plate, used on fire engines and for commercial floors, adds modernity to a room. Painted white and glazed with a glaze coating, the wall or ceiling neatly diffuses light.

1 Sheet-metal cladding screwed to wall.
2 Tongue-and-groove boards used to create a dado.
3 Wood paneling.
4 White-painted tongue-and-groove walls.

Doors and openings

1

Doors introduce rooms or close off space, and they vary in importance. Doors to closets can be very different in material, trim and hardware from doors leading to private rooms, which in turn differ from those opening onto public spaces. The way a door looks hints at the pretensions, scale and purpose of the room behind it.

All doors should be appropriate in style and proportion to the architecture of the house and the

2

corresponding room. Today many door manufacturers sell a range of surrounds and trim options to complement their doors. If doors are very large, they will have a much greater sweep, forcing a certain amount of the floor space to be left unoccupied, doubly emphasizing the room's grandeur. Exaggeratedly big doors shepherd you into a room, while small and narrow doors are more intimate.

INTERIOR DOORS

In most instances, new or old, plain, hollowcore doors need rescuing from banality. People tend to hope they will just fade into the background, but simply by adding an interesting door knob, a new trim around the door, or raised panels you can enhance their appearance for minimal time and money.

Flexibility is a good idea. When doors recess into the wall, the space is opened out. Unfortunately they are not always easy to operate. Doors that reach to the ceiling, such as pivot doors, interact with the room in a much more dynamic and

conscious way, and occupy more space than those of standard height with a frame. Pivot doors have one edge which rotates around a pin to swing the door open or shut. Ceiling-height doors add presence to a room, drawing attention to its height and playing with its proportions.

Since a door interrupts the view from one room to another, it is by its nature a focal point. With a little forethought, doors can add interest to boring and plain walls; depending on their style and treatment they can generate warmth or a cool demeanor, make a room appear large or cozy. Painting the door and doorframe contrasting colors exploits the tension between these two architectural components. Painting the door a dark color in contrast to white or pale walls and using stenciling or *trompe-l'oeil* decorative painting gives a door impact and a colloquial drama. Veneering doors with wood, or covering them with thin sheets of stainless steel or *découpage* are among the many decorative options.

3

It is a good idea to de-emphasize doors with matching paint when they are not in alignment or if there are too many. It is also a sensible strategy for undistinguished doors and those in rooms with chair rails or other architectural features that might otherwise be overwhelmed. Glass doors offer acoustic privacy without closing out light or views and provide a continuity from space to space. In narrow houses, glass doors prove far less claustrophobic than wood doors. The patterning and

1 Flush interior door.
2 Sliding partition door.
3 Glass rear door.
4 Traditional front door.

size of the glazing creates decorative effects as well as welcoming light into the room. Interior French doors can seal off the living room and let in light from other sources.

Folding doors solve space problems. A folding door can create a room within a room, closing off a kitchen, for example, when the cook is hard at work, but folded aside to open it up to the general living area at other times. Doors originally designed for industrial or commercial use, such as for diners, restaurants or boats, can be just the quirky jolt a room needs. Space is made totally flexible by the retractable or movable walls that are designed to divide up offices.

For some homes nothing is as commendable as an old door. Dutch and French doors, porch and screen doors can be found secondhand, probably covered with layer upon layer of paint. Depending on the decoration of your home, you can strip the doors completely (it is easiest to have this done professionally) and then stain or repaint, or you can rub back the paint layers using wire wool to create a 'distressed' finish. Recycled pine, oak and cherry doors of varying degrees of age and pedigree can be found in architectural salvage yards.

PAINTING A PANEL DOOR

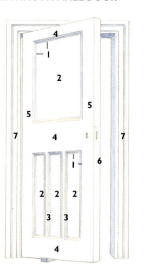

Wedge the door open before starting to paint it. Tackle the job in the following order: (1) moldings; (2) panels; (3) uprights between panels; (4) horizontals; (5) outer uprights; (6) door edge; (7) frame.

EXTERIOR DOORS

The front door gives a home focus. Traditionally, the grander the house, the greater the emphasis on the entrance. A front door with side lights creates a paneled door with columns and a pediment. Painting the front door in a contrasting color to the façade gives it impact. Coating a front door with firehouse red enamel – as scandalous Elsie de Wolfe did to Manhattan houses in the early 1900s

4

and designer Brian Murphy does on white stucco Los Angeles bungalows – is an immediate way to articulate an entry. Conversely, painting a front door the same color as the exterior reduces its impact.

Safety glass is required by Federal law in all doors that function as passageways. This includes: exterior doors with fixed glass, framed and frameless glass doors, two-panel storm doors, and sliding glass doors.

Many manufactured exterior doors now come ornamented. Unless it is appropriate for the period of your home, avoid beveled glass, columns and pressed wood grain on sheet metal – they all look inauthentic. The simplest door with good hardware is far better than a door that pretends to have been crafted 100 years ago. For exterior doors, choose wood that can withstand weathering, such as oak or teak. Unless the front door is protected by a deep porch or awning, stain or paint doors rather than varnish them. Door frames can be painted to match window frames, with the door a contrasting color.

FLOORING

Floors form a large part of the surface area of any room, so the way in which they are treated will determine – or at least affect – other decorating and furnishing schemes. Different materials offer different results in terms of color and texture as well as having properties that make some of them more suited to certain applications than others. In addition to finding a flooring material that complements the room and that falls within your budget, you need to consider your choice in terms of the functions it will need to fulfill. A soft wool carpet, for example, feels luxurious underfoot but will quickly wear in high-traffic areas such as entrance halls, and will prove a mean surface to keep clean in the kitchen; ceramic tile, by contrast, is cold to the touch (unless paired with underfloor heating) but wipes clean more easily. Still other materials – notably marble and various stone floors – need a solid sub-floor or heavily reinforced floor to take their weight.

Whether you are reconditioning existing floorboards or entirely reflooring a room, the financial outlay will be considerable. Whatever choice you ultimately make will be with you for many years to come. If in doubt, opt for a fairly neutral shade and material which won't interfere with other elements in the room and which, broadly speaking, increases the impression of space – you can always add color and interest using rugs and other furnishings. Fairly neutral flooring will also keep your decorative options open, accommodating future changes of stylistic direction.

Another important consideration is the junction between different types of flooring. Make sure the transition between rooms is not too jarring and that joins are neatly finished. You can mix and match different flooring materials in the same room, perhaps to define different areas of activity – say, terra cotta tiles in the kitchen area and wood floorboards in the eating area of an open-plan family room. As long as there is some sort of tonal or textural harmony, such combinations can be both visually stimulating and highly practical. The range of options may seem vast and overwhelming, but a careful analysis of your own requirements and the relative merits of the materials available should result in you making a choice that is a pleasure to live with for many years to come.

1 Ceramic tiles – both water- and stain-resistant – make a practical floor.
2 Juxtaposing different flooring materials can add texture and interest to views and vistas. The rich glow of oak floorboards segue into muted flagstones in the adjacent hallway. Rugs delineate the living area and harmonize tonally with the wall finish and the upholstery.

3 Slate floors – whether tiles or slabs – come in a range of hues including purple, red, gray, blue, brown and green.

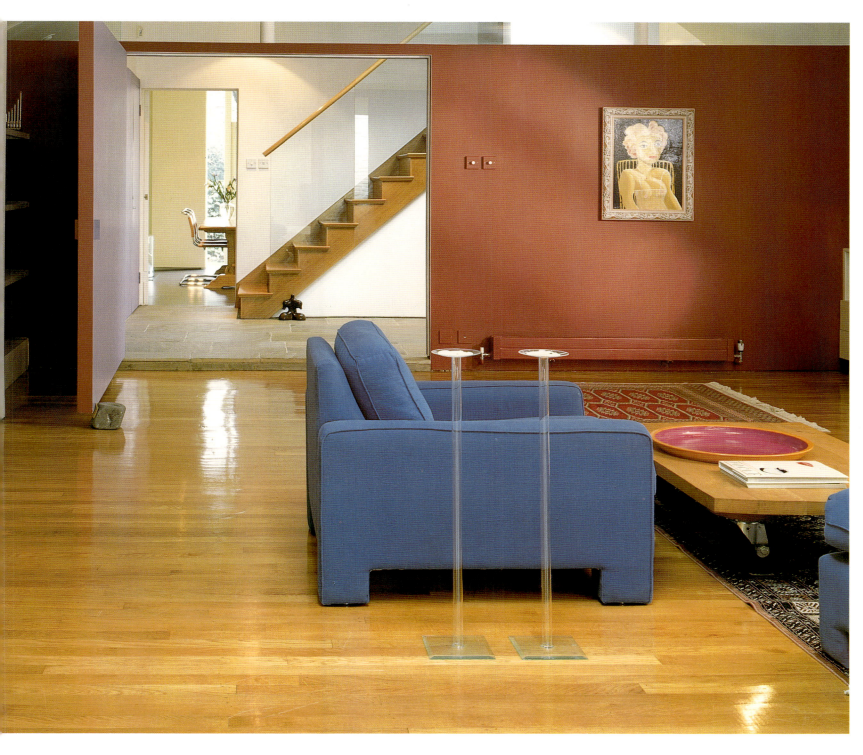

4 Genoa marble tiles have an understated elegance that works equally well in traditional and modern interiors.

4

5 Square ceramic tiles shouldn't necessarily limit you to rectilinear floor patterns. Contrasting colors follow the curve of the bathroom wall, forming a witty sea of water around the tub

5

Making a choice

1 Painted concrete walls and handmade terra cotta floor tiles possess both sophistication and an inviting ambience. Scattered kilims and slip covers add comfort and warmth at relatively little cost.

1

The ground rule when deciding on a floor is to select the right material. Base your decision on price, wear and tear, upkeep, comfort, how the room will be lived in and the type of atmosphere you want in the room. Ensure floors are sufficiently robust and adaptable for the demands of daily use. Is your floor going to see children and pets bringing in dirt day in and day out, toddlers experimenting with food or crawling about? Terra cotta, flagstone and wood are durable, natural materials that will stand up under these sorts of demands. The manner in which they wear with age is all part of their attraction. If it's an exterior floor, will it be subjected to freezing and thawing or exposure to rain? Some floors – such as stone or concrete – will withstand brutal weather; others – like some types of tile – will crack or lose their glaze when exposed to the elements.

Granite and flagstone combine function with patina, but are less sound insulating than carpeting and vinyl, which are easier to install and cheaper. Concrete, aluminum and

rubber are also durable, though the acoustics caused by a stainless steel floor mean they should always be used with discretion.

On the other hand, if 'natural' is your byword for a good material, floors that are ingrained with nature – such as wood and slate, seagrass and terra cotta – come with positive, eco-friendly virtue. Their earthy palette is versatile enough for both city and country life. Raw materials and textures, such as coir and sisal, add depth.

Lesser-known materials can be cheaper and more environmentally acceptable. For example, hickory and pecan are perfect for flooring and can be less expensive than comparable grades of red and white oak. Character grades of flooring and millwork take advantage of the plentiful supply of lower-grade lumber that is always part of any timber harvesting operation. Dirt is hidden in the irregular patterns of small knots and character marks prevelant in flooring and trim made from lumber that is not clear enough for cabinet grade. Brown ash,

chestnut oak, industrial grades of cherry, black locust, red elm and soft red maple are all extremely beautiful and plentiful in their ecogolical niches. Aspen, properly dried, makes excellent paneling. Alder from the Pacific Northeast is as beautiful as cherry. Most softwood species and light color hardwood species can have blue stain that disqualifies their use as cabinet lumber. Accepting this naturally occurring discoloration can make for a beautiful floor at below market prices.

Since a floor is a large plane, its treatment influences the overall look of the room. You want it to have impact – but without trying too hard and dominating the other elements. Strong, large patterns and dark, vivid colors take your mind off the boxiness of a room and can also be used to make it look smaller. Conversely, tight patterns, light colors and plain surfaces tend to look more expansive, increasing the sense of space and tranquillity.

It's also worth taking into account accessibility to underfloor services, your home's architecture, existing

decor and furniture and how much disruption you're likely to encounter.

When renovating, plan to start at the bottom and work up. This means you need to look at the floor first. Address any signs of rot, infestation or dampness, then install a subfloor or underlayment, heat and sound insulation and adequate ventilation. Concrete and other subfloors may need rigid insulation above or below the floor so that feet won't freeze. Make sure water pipes are encased in sleeves or ducts; never run them in solid concrete floors or you risk leaks when pipes expand and contract – and subsequent major disruption. After these prosaic considerations, there is a vast range of surfaces and finishes to choose from, including beautiful hardwoods and softwoods, brilliant modern materials and ageless stone and tile.

CONNECTIONS

After deciding on the material, consider floor color and design. The floor is usually the background music to the symphony of grander collectibles and architecture in the room. Be wary of fashion's transitory images which may quickly appear dated. In large rooms, in particular, it's important to think carefully before you buy: whatever material you choose will be expensive if you have to cover a large area, so you'll want it to be able to live through changes of use and lifestyle.

Take into consideration the room's relationship to its surrounding areas. If there is a view into other spaces with different floor coverings, do you want to separate or unite the rooms? Brick and stone integrate the indoors and out, especially when an organic relationship to the patio or yard is important. Simple and monochromatic flooring that runs seamlessly from room to room conveys space, unity and pedigree, but take into consideration the different functions of various rooms: the main routes through the house, and rooms – particularly the kitchen – that see a high level of activity need to have flooring that either shrugs off dirt or is easily cleaned. Restrict carpet to rooms where self-indulgence is the order of the day.

2

3 A poured concrete floor coated with gray exterior paint shimmers when it rains; the climate of this California beach house encourages an open-door policy. By placing the mattress on the floor, an illusion of height is given in this low-ceilinged bedroom.

3

2 Sandblasted glass doors, a semicircular wall and rough plastered ceiling give the room a clean, modern look. Thin wood floorboards temper the dramatic architecture. Windows of opaque glass screen less-than-neighborly views while still letting in natural light.

4

4 Slate is used indoors and out, creating an organic relationship between house and garden. Interior built-in sofas mimic outdoor bench seating to blur the extension between the two further.

Hard flooring

1

BRICK

Though a bit out of the ordinary today, brick provides a striking floor that will outlast any other in the home. It has the added advantage of being able to work out some truly unusual patterns. Bricks come in a full range of soft orange-reds, buffs and browns. About as expensive as ceramic tile, special floor-staining bricks come prefinished with glaze to protect against staining and in reduced thickness and weight. Alternatively, if the subfloor is strong enough to take the weight, you can recycle old bricks — sold at salvage yards — which have already acquired the rich patina of age. These require special sealing if used on the floor as the brick is absorbent.
Laying Bricks can be laid in a variety of interesting patterns on a moisture proof base.
Treatment Once laid, sealed brick needs only damp mopping.

TILE

Tile resists heat and is hardwearing, easy to clean and immune to water and most household chemicals. Installation can cost as much as, or more than, the tiles themselves. By surface area, tiled floors are more expensive than linoleum or vinyl, but similar in price to hardwood flooring.

Tiles are not for the clumsy; any china dropped on the floor will probably break. They are noisy, hard on the feet, and cold — though a tile floor can be paired with underfloor radiant heating for warmth. Floor tiles must be nonslip, though water on any hard surface is always slippery — no material is skid proof. Unglazed quarry, terra cotta and cement tiles

are naturally nonslip, won't blister, burn, or discolor, though they can be slightly absorbent. Handmade, unglazed tiles, glazed tiles with an undulating, uneven surface and machinemade glazed tiles with an abrasive grit added are also suitable. Glass tiles are too slippery (even when sandblasted) and fragile for a floor, as are high-glazed tiles with smooth surfaces which mark.

Burnished terra cotta is the warmest floor tile. Handmade terra cotta tiles are of natural clay, fired in a kiln. Terra cotta never quite loses its propensity to retain heat, which makes it kind on bare feet. In about a year, terra cotta develops a rich patina which glows with a quiet fire, though walked-in grit — such as pebbles and stones — acts like sandpaper on the surface.

Ceramic tiles are crisp and smooth underfoot. Encaustic (inlaid) tiles can be remarkably beautiful, but some don't react well to pets and babies: urine is acidic and apt to stain if the encaustics are unsealed. With machinemade embossed tiles, the

2

3

4

first ones out of a particular mold are clear and crisp, while the last — many hundreds of castings later — are fuzzier and less distinct.

Quarry tiles are a dense, durable, extruded tile that are widely used. Made from unrefined high-silica clay, they have a basic appearance that suits country cottages. They are available in a similar range of colors to brick, and are slightly less durable than ceramic tiles.
Laying Tiles can be laid in a variety of patterns and with decorative borders though, especially over large areas, simple treatments usually look best. Tile needs a level, rigid base. If you have concrete screed, you can tile directly on top. If you have a wood floor, the movement of floorboards will eventually crack the bond between the adhesive, causing tiles to rear up. Cover wood floors with hardboard first or use a malleable glue that when mixed into the adhesive and brushed on a bendable floor allows movement without breaking the adhesive. If you have lovely old tile or stone floors with bad grout, you can take up the floor and reset tiles and slabs in fresh grout. Old quarry and encaustic floor tiles can be prised up from their soft mortar base, cleaned and relaid in sanded, cement-based mortar.

Grout is used to fill the gaps between the tiles. It is a mixture of Portland cement and sand and comes as a powder to be mixed with water to a quick-drying paste. New acrylic latex additives have improved grout, preventing cracking, loosening and staining. Grout on floors is bound to stain, so opt for colors that will camouflage wear. (Bear in mind that

dark grout will set up a noticeable grid pattern.) If you are using colored grouts, choose nonporous tiles so the colorants won't be absorbed. For aesthetic reasons, tight grout lines are recommended.

Tiling requires honest toil. Tiles are difficult to cut and space. Badly laid tiles may lift up and lead to water seepage.
Treatment Sealants are normally used to protect tile floors, but may darken the tile color. Resin sealants are available in a liquid form that solidifies over the floor like a heavy-duty polish, and particularly suits stone and terra cotta. Silicone sealants, similar to those used to waterproof shoes, also deepen color, usually evenly.

Unglazed tiles and quarry tiles have traditionally been sealed with penetrating oils such as linseed oil and wax to help protect them from food stains, though the treatment has to be reapplied at regular intervals. However, today's quality unglazed and quarry tiles do not require sealing. Sealants, if necessary, should

5

be applied in strict accordance with the manufacturer's instructions — sealants tend to change the color of the tile, deepening it several shades, so you should sample the effect on a spare tile before covering the whole floor. Improved production techniques for quality unglazed and quarry tiles means they can be kept clean with damp mopping with a mild detergent. For needs above and beyond this, first check the manufacturer's instructions or call your local tile dealer.

6

GRANITE

A highly durable, natural stone with visible coarse grains, granite is in increasing demand today for floors and countertops. Comparing favorably in price to marble, granite has the added advantage of being considerably less prone to staining and scratching. It is also more slip-resistant. It comes in 50 different colors, and is available now in thin tiles, as well as slabs. These tiles make laying considerably easier, and they also mean that granite can be used for flooring in upstairs rooms where slabs would be too heavy.
Laying As tile, install granite on a level, solid floor such as concrete or plywood. It can be set in mortar or dry set using an adhesive bonding agent; silicone caulking should be used as grout.
Treatment Granite is porous and should be sealed; check with your supplier to see what type of sealant is recommended. Matte finishes are skid resistant and so generally considered to be safer; however, high-sheen polished granite undeniably shows off the stone's color to best effect.

MARBLE

Marble is opulent, and expensive. The veining flatters floors and its rich color strikes the eye. It comes in slabs or tiles, including a stunning array of inlaid patterns. Marble is classified A, B, C or D based on its fragility; A and B grades are the most solid, C and D classifications are the more delicate, but also the more colorful, decorative and costly. Marble scratches and stains easily and must be sealed; unless honed,

7

etched or pummeled, making it skid-resistant, it is also slippery when wet. Choose darker colors such as green, red and brown if you want a marble floor that will hide stains.
Laying As tile, marble needs to be installed by a professional tile setter following the guidelines set by the Ceramic Tile Institute (see Useful Addresses, pages 258-67).
Treatment Polishing can prove to be labor-intensive and time-consuming, and needs frequent repeats to keep the floor looking its best. Stains in marble should be scrubbed using non-acid cleaners.

FLAGSTONE

No longer consigned just to outdoor walkways and patios, flagstone is gaining floor space inside the home as a beautiful and versatile flooring material. Named for the process of 'flagging', or slicing, stone into thin slabs, flagstone comes in many varieties and colors, in custom-cut tile and slabs. The two most common types are bluestone and slate. As a rule, flagstone costs less

8

than ceramic and quarry tiles as a basic flooring material, but is more expensive to install.

Slate is an economical, non-porous alternative to marble, and is reasonably stain resistant. It is available in smooth or rippled finishes, and hues ranging from purple and black to lush green, pale gray, red and sienna. Footprints and spills are less visible on lighter colors.
Laying Install slate on a concrete slab, screed or plywood subfloor. To ensure you have the minimum deflection in the floor and to reduce the likelihood of it bending or of joints cracking, use $^3/_4$in (2cm) plywood as a base with a $^1/_2$in (12mm) thick underlay board screwed on top.
Treatment Some flagstone is porous and can be sealed, while other less porous varieties cannot be sealed. Slate holds up well untreated or it can be sealed and waxed. It is advisable to check with your supplier as to whether or not sealing is recommended. Wipe spills clean with a damp cloth.

9

TERRAZZO

This aggregate of concrete and granular marble chippings has a beauty that lasts, requiring little upkeep. Terrazzo is tough and streamlined, fairly nonslip and available in hundreds of colors. A paganized version of marble — with a splodged or mottled effect rather than the traditional veining found in marble — it is nevertheless no cheaper to buy or install.
Laying Terrazzo can be troweled or rolled on by professionals, laid down in the form of slabs or in even more durable hydraulically pressed tiles. Terrazzo floors must be laid on a screeded subfloor, and — unless troweled — are best in panels of about 26ft (8m), with brass or zinc dividing strips. Because of its strength, it can be as thin as $^3/_8$in (9mm).
Treatment Seal as for tile. Wash clean with hot, soapy water.

MOSAICS

In addition to standard square shapes, ceramic mosaic tile also comes in a large assortment of

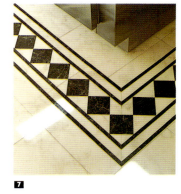

10

colorful shapes, affording many creative design possibilities. Mosaic can add glamor and romance to a room or lend it the humble charm of an old-fashioned cobblestone street. Mosaic floors are as durable and noisy as ceramic tile, and should be cared for in the same way. For easy installation, mosaics are usually sold face-mounted with paper, back-mounted with a mesh or plastic tab backing, or mesh-backed in 12in x 12in (30.48cm x 30.48cm) or 12in x 24in (30.48cm x 60.96cm).

1 Untreated brick.
2 Glazed brick laid around small encaustic tile.
3 Machinemade terra cotta tile.
4 Black-and-white ceramic tile.
5 Quarry tile.
6 Old flagstones.
7 Marble tile with border.
8 Terrazzo.
9 Slate.
10 Handmade mosaic tile laid in 'Greek key' pattern.

Synthetic flooring

CONCRETE

One of the basic building materials emerges as the simplest, most affordable flooring solution. A mixture of cement powder, sand and water, concrete is sensitive to site and climate, and it is able to take on any shape or thickness. Concrete has an austere quality in slab form, much less so as tiles, or when waxed or stained. It can be packed like clay, veined, textured with smooth glass and colored with cement pigments. Concrete forms a cold, heat- and

VINYL

Long associated with practicality, comfort underfoot, and affordability, but thought of as drab and boring due to limited style and color selections, today's top-quality vinyl is anything but drab or boring. This synthetic material is now available in a wealth of stylish colors and patterns. Today's high-end resilient vinyl flooring is durable, low maintenance, non allergenic and well suited to family life. Top-quality solid-vinyl tiles can mimic with uncanny

scratch resistant floor. Mixed with additives, it is less susceptible to chipping and cracking than the cement that is mixed in trucks and poured on sidewalks.

Laying Concrete floors are economical for new homes, additions, or when new screed is required. You can pour it on existing tile floors and reinforce apartment floors with steel rods to accommodate its solid-state style. It takes 28 days of curing to set.

Treatment Concrete can and should be sealed to be impervious to oil, food stains and water. Ask the supplier to recommend a stain best suited to the type of concrete mixture used. After the sealant dries, an application of several heavy coats of commercial paste wax followed by machine buffing will give a concrete floor a warm texture. Treating a gray concrete floor with an acid wash preserves its hard-edged character but adds a refined interior finish. Adding copper sulphate, a mineral with non-fading, saturated green color, gives a verdigris finish.

accuracy the look of granite, limestone, marble and wood but requires minimum maintenance.

High-quality 'solid' vinyl flooring is more expensive, but longer lasting than composition vinyl. Composition vinyl is a mix of thermoplastic binder, fillers and pigments. It's important to find out what the flooring is made of, and how it's manufactured. Inlaid vinyl is the best choice; it has the pattern extending throughout the wear layer. It is generally more durable than 'retrogravure' vinyl, which has the pattern printed on it. There are modified retrogravure vinyls that come labeled 'inlaid' but they aren't as durable.

Laying Some types of sheet vinyl can be laid over existing floors. Vinyl tiles are the perfect do-it-yourself materials, inexpensive and easy to install, but they may shift and come loose if laid near moist areas.

Treatment Check with the manufacturer for advice on regular maintenance. Regular sweeping and vacuuming will cut down on scratching.

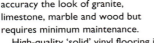

RUBBER

Rubber flooring gives a room a high-tech look. Once made from the milky sap of the rubber tree, most rubber flooring is now synthetic or manmade. Resilient, flexible and durable, it's resistant to burns and dents; built-in self-releasing wax allows some rubber flooring to self-heal most scratches and abrasions. Rubber comes in wetsuit finishes, primary and pastel colors, and in industrial studded sheets or tiles.

Laying Since undulations and dust interfere with rubber's adhesion on level floors, apply epoxy or urethane adhesive to concrete, then lay tiles. The adhesive is easy and simple to work with, making rubber tiles a do-it-yourself project.

Treatment Sweep and mop clean with neutral-pH detergents. Use a natural bristle brush to loosen dirt from crevices in pattern treads.

METALS

Though hardly conventional, aluminum, stainless and galvanized steel are original and resilient flooring materials. Aluminum and steel buffed with a sander or pressed with a diamond or chevron design reflect light in unusual patterns.

Laying Metal sheets should be welded and laminated to a level wood or particleboard base so that it doesn't sound harsh when walked on. Solder sheet seams together.

Treatment Seal with epoxy or polyurethane. An occasional rub down with a steel wool pad will keep metals from getting dull.

1 White painted and glazed concrete.
2 Vinyl.
3 Machine-pressed stainless steel.
4 Studded rubber.

Natural flooring

LINOLEUM

Mistakenly thought by many to be a thing of the past, linoleum in a variety of updated colors and patterns is still available, and in fact sought after by those who appreciate its many natural virtues. Not to be confused with vinyl flooring, linoleum is a resilient floor covering made from a combination of natural raw materials including linseed oil, pine resins, wood flour, ground cork and pigments pressed on a jute backing. Stylish, friendly to the environment

and durable, today's linoleum is also static-free, slip and burn resistant. Linoleum comes in sheets or tiles, which can be inlaid and easily spliced.
Laying Large rolls can be daunting, and if water gets underneath, linoleum will rise. Glue tiles and sheets to a clean, level plywood base or hardboard underlayment for best results; lumps and bumps of imperfect floors will show through. A straight edge, tape measure and linoleum or utility knife is all it takes to lay linoleum tiles; borders and sheets require professional tools.
Treatment Sweep, wash and wipe linoleum down with a gentle, pH-neutral detergent. A high sheen can be achieved and maintained by periodic machine waxing and buffing.

CORK

Cork flooring is one of the most resilient and durable natural floor coverings available. It comes in unfinished tiles, which work well in bathrooms where their absorbent quality is appreciated, and in pre-waxed or polyurethane-finished tiles.

Laying Cork tiles are light and cut easily with a utility knife. Tile must be stored at room temperature for at least 72 hours prior to installation to allow tile to acclimatize to its environment. The subfloor should be thoroughly cleaned, filled and primed. If laying on concrete, install a moisture proof membrane beneath the cork to prevent moisture from riding up from the slab and lifting tiles. Single wood floors of tongue-and-groove construction should be completely covered with latex fill or hardboard or plywood. Use the recommended adhesive.
Treatment Avoid abrasive alkaline or cheap cleaners. Keep cork surfaces free from grit, sand and cinders. Protect against indentation with furniture rests.

SISAL

Sisal is anti-static, relatively easy to keep clean, hardwearing and versatile. It comes latex- or cotton-backed, in sun-bleached earth tones and it can be expressively dyed. Bright sunshine may eventually fade deeper colors.

Sisal has been elevated to designer status – as a result, you pay more than for seagrass for its sophistication. Sisal can be close fitted like carpeting, or made into loose-laid mats or runners.
Laying As with all natural floor coverings, the level of wear depends on how it is fitted. Sisal is moisture sensitive. To ensure a secure fit and prevent bubbling, overcut by 1¼in (3cm) on each edge and unroll in position for at least 48 hours before laying so it can adjust to the humidity and temperature. Padding is recommended if the floor surface is at all uneven, or if more than light household traffic is anticipated. It may be necessary to lay a solid rubber padding and an additional underlay for the natural flooring.
Firmly fix edges down. Gripper rods stop the edges from fraying and flipping up and can prevent any water from seeping underneath. To join sisal edge to edge, use a latex bonding glue or a hot melt tape to give a quick, strong bond.
Treatment Vacuum and protect as carpeting. Applying a scotch guard is an option. Mop spills with absorbent paper immediately. Trim small knots with scissors, taking care not to sever a complete weft or warp yarn.

COIR

Easier to keep clean than sisal, but more expensive, coir is a stylish alternative to carpet. It is available in loose matts, area rugs, tiles and wall-to-wall strips which are stitched together. Latex backing prevents dust penetration and increases durability. Quality coir works well in heavy-traffic areas.

Laying As easy to lay and shape as carpet. For wall-to-wall, stitch lengths together and bind edges with jute tape. Padding may be required depending on the level and quality of the floor. Acclimatize coir as for sisal; coir reacts to moisture by expanding, buckling and wrinkling and shrinks when shedding moisture, which can result in open joints.
Treatment Vacuum clean and protect as carpet. Brush off any mold that may occur because of dampness or humid conditions.

SEAGRASS

Seagrass is grown in paddy fields. The hard, almost impermeable fiber is spun into tough strands and woven into practical flooring. It is soft underfoot, relatively smooth, and is more resistant to stains (and dyes) than its natural cousins.
Laying Even latex-backed seagrass needs 48 hours' breathing room to allow it to expand or shrink before it is fitted wall-to-wall. Stick down firmly with adhesives that will uplift without mess later, or use a pad. For stairs, lay seagrass with the warp (the heavy seagrass fiber) parallel to the stair tread for maximum traction and wearability. Stairs likely to be heavily used should have protective nosing on the tread. Organic, natural floor coverings wither like the plant fibers they're made from when subjected to feet scuffing against the risers.
Treatment Choose a stain-inhibiting treatment, usually a soapless chemical applied at the factory, which will put an invisible shield around each fiber. Vacuum regularly. For severe mud or dirt, use a stiff brush along the grain once it has dried, then vacuum.

RUSH

Rush is made up of hand-plaited strips sewn together to the size of the room or hall. Be careful with wheels (lift, don't push, the sofa), do not lay it on stairs and step lightly in heels. It is not backed.
Laying Normally loose laid, even when it is used as a wall-to-wall covering; padding is optional.
Treatment Periodically lift and dust underneath. Douse rush matting with water at least once a week to prevent tears, cracks and flaking.

1 Rush.
2 Linoleum.
3 Cork tile.
4 Coir.
5 Sisal.
6 Seagrass.

Wood flooring

NEW WOOD

Wood is savored for its warmth and ability to make daily life richer. Now, thanks to new penetrating sealers and advanced engineering techniques, wood is a more varied and versatile flooring material. Properly treated and cared for, it can be used to best advantage anywhere in the house – even the kitchen and bathroom. And there are new products designed for do-it-yourself installation that don't need nailing, sanding or finishing, and that are more affordable.

Both softwoods and hardwoods are used for flooring, but hardwoods have the advantage of being less likely to dent over time. The most popular choices are oak, maple, ash and pine, oak being the most common. Red oak is plentiful, finely grained, sedate. Maple, renowned for its toughness but expensive, is favored in business use and increasingly in residences, too. Exotic woods, such as teak, rose wood, iron wood and ebony, make outstanding flooring but start at roughly twice the price of oak.

Wood flooring is available in strip, plank and parquet styles. Strip flooring, the most popular type, comes in 1½ to 2¼-inch (3.8cm to 5.6cm) wide tongue-and-groove pieces cut in random lengths. Plank flooring consists of wider boards, 3in to 8in (7.6cm to 20.3cm), and is used to create the rustic look of Colonial floors. Parquet flooring, which forms repeating, mosaic patterns for a very formal look, comes in pre-assembled tiles or interlocking pieces of wood arranged in 9in to 19in (22.9cm to 48.3cm) squares. All of these styles

are available in either solid wood or laminated wood which consists of a thin veneer layer laminated to layers of wood so that it can be sanded and refinished several times. However, laminated wood is better suited to moisture prone areas such as the kitchen and lends itself to easier do-it-yourself installation.

Because wood is a natural material, it expands and contracts with changes in temperature and humidity. Proper installation allows for this slight movement.

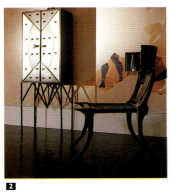

Laying It is essential that wood be allowed to acclimatize to its new surroundings prior to installation. Solid wood floors can be nailed directly over joists or level concrete. However, a subfloor of plywood or particleboard is generally used for extra strength. Especially on ground floors, a moisture retarder of either asphalt felt or building paper is laid on top of the subfloor. (With concrete, a vapor retarder must be used between the gravel fill and the slab and on top of the slab to protect the flooring against moisture, a natural enemy of wood.)

Because laminated flooring does not require a subfloor, it can be installed directly over concrete. There are some types of laminated flooring that don't require nails either, using glue or the new 'floating' method which calls for interlocking pieces to be glued together and then 'floated' atop of a foam pad laid over the subfloor.

Misjudging the location of joists and knocking nails through electric cables and water pipes is not an

uncommon error, so map out services carefully. Another mistake made by amateurs is starting in a recess or alcove on either side of a hearth or protruding wall. Since walls are rarely square, when boards come forward they will not be straight or aligned. Professionals recommend plumbing a line along the front of a fireplace or protruding wall, then working back into recesses and taking the baseboards off so that the new floor tucks neatly underneath; this also covers up any poor cuts along the edge.

Treatment All new floors that aren't laminated or presealed at the factory need a sealant to seal out dirt and moisture. New water-based finishes (urethane and/or acrylic combinations) and organic primers (with a citrus oil base) are perfect for do-it-yourself; they won't make your eyes water, are less flammable and dry in about 30 minutes. Water-based finishes also don't yellow like polyurethane. Read the entire label on finish materials before applying them, and always follow ALL of the manufacturer's safety precautions. Tung oil and wax, though nearly forgotten, can be an alternative way of finishing new floors. A waxed floor requires rewaxing, usually once a year with a small buffing machine.

Because even a small amount of moisture standing on wood can be damaging, stains and spills should be wiped up quickly. Vacuum- or sweep-clean floors weekly, and wash with a mop that has been dipped in a solution of 4 parts water to 1 part vinegar and wrung nearly dry before touching the floor. Rewaxing should be carried out about once a year. Floors sealed with polyurethane may need to be sanded and recoated every several years depending on how much foot traffic they get. If your house is excessively dry, installing a humidifier will protect your floors and furniture from developing cracks caused by dryness.

TROPICAL WOOD

Tropical woods from properly managed forestry projects are durable, exotic woods that are ecologically acceptable. Lesser known species are generally less expensive. Buying exotic timbers

from ethical plantations and forests is also a way to supply indigenous people with trade instead of aid, since projects are often run by communities, cooperatives or local groups whose aim is to minimize damage to the environment.

Chontaquiro from Peru has a ruddy red complexion and is extremely versatile. Vitex is a teak lookalike available at less than the price of ash and it won't oil spot or discolor like teak. However, no wood has teak's anti-slip characteristic, attributed to its inherent oiliness. Though pricey, kwila (a dense brown with black specks) from the Solomon Islands can be walked, chopped and splashed on. Straight-grained taun, planchonia and calophyllum from Papua New Guinea are bargains and good mahogany substitutes. Turupay, which matures from yellow to chestnut in sunlight, is so tough you need tungsten carbide-tipped blades to shape it. Kamarere is a fast-growing and strong tropical redwood from Papua New Guinea that dries and machines easily.

For elegant, dark floors, there are dense and stable newcomers in toasty shades of brown – ruddy merbau and dillenia, a striking timber that looks like rose wood. Celtis has the open, uncomplicated appearance of pine but the working properties of hardwood. It is comparable to oak in hardness, to beech in cost.

Avoid buying endangered woods and those from over-exploited rainforests. Contact the Rainforest Alliance or the Woodworkers

4

1 **Irregular-length floorboards.**
2 **Tropical hardwood.**
3 **Painted and varnished floorboards.**
4 **Polished wood strip.**
5 **Renovated old floorboards.**
6 **Parquet.**
7 **Plywood.**

Alliance for Rainforest Protection (WARP) (see Useful Addresses). These organizations keep track of suppliers and companies that produce and sell tropical hardwoods using ecologically sound techniques. Look for the 'Smart Wood' logo or seal of approval from the Rainforest Alliance on tropical wood products; a list of 'Smart Wood' companies is also available from the Rainforest Alliance. All new timbers should be kiln-dried to local moisture conditions; this is particularly important with tropical timber.

Laying and Treatment Lay and seal as native tongue-and-groove plank. Choose a species several weeks in advance of laying the floor. Timber is cut in whatever widths and thicknesses possible from felled trees and the vendor may need to accumulate the square feet required for a floor.

RECYCLED WOOD

Before polishing, staining or painting recycled boards, they must be brought back to decent condition. To strip them down to naked wood before finishing requires a lot of hard work and often entails renting expensive sanding equipment. Bare boards are noisy though durable, but can get dirty, damaged or splintery. Seal gaps between the boards with filler material to prevent drafts; test filler materials before applying since some may turn a different color when sealed or stained. Don't be tempted to insulate below ground-level boards or block up subfloor ventilation – this will lead to moisture problems. Recycled wood can either be darkened using stains

5

and sealants or lightened using special bleach systems designed for the job if you want to change the color of the floorboards.

Buying salvaged old floors is a good economy; the expense is in re-laying. Most recycled wood floorboards have been sanded and revarnished repeatedly so they are different thicknesses, which makes it tricky to re-lay them to give a smooth surface. Old strip flooring salvaged from gymnasiums and damaged structures

6

is available. Antique plank flooring from eighteenth- and nineteenth-century buildings is costlier to acquire and lay.

Laying When restoring bare boards, fill gaps with old wood where you've removed badly damaged boards. For a butt-jointed floor, ensure the fit is as tight as possible. Punch nail heads below the surface.

To preserve the lovely surface patina of old and recycled wood, lay the thickest board in the batch first. Then tack fillets to bring the remaining boards level, working from the thicker boards down to the thinnest. Alternatively, you can sand boards down to the same thickness, and at the same time remove old paint and finishes. Since even the grain of centuries-old oak will move when it is shifted from a warehouse to a centrally heated home, store old wood flooring in its new environment for at least a week before installing.

Treatment To refresh floorboards, first give them a thorough scrub with strong detergent and hot water. If the boards have been covered up by rugs or carpet, rubbing them down with sandpaper or paint remover may be all that is needed. If the boards are soiled or have a surface coating, remove damaged boards and then – working with the grain of the wood – use a natural bristle brush and stripper solution. Scrape up residue and sponge-rinse wood with water. Then rent a professional sander. Sand along the length of the boards with the grain; sanding across boards leaves ugly scratches. Empty the dust bag regularly and wear a mask. With a damp cloth, wipe down the floor, then clean with white spirit. Allow boards to dry thoroughly. Boards can be sealed, stained, limed, waxed, bleached or painted.

Stains look patchy unless applied evenly. Use a natural bristle brush, wiping the stain in with a cloth rag along the grain. Gloss or eggshell paints make attractive finishes, but are less durable than proper floor paints, which usually contain polyurethane, acrylic or epoxy resin and dry to a hard finish. Stain and paint can be applied in patterns, using stencils, cardboard squares or the floorboards as a guide for stripes.

7

Stained finishes are not enough to protect a wooden floor, however, so you need to apply a varnish or other sealant. Using a wide, natural-bristle brush, apply three coats of varnish or clear, matte, semi- or high-gloss polyurethane. For best results, let the floor dry overnight between coats and sand lightly with a very fine-grain sandpaper. Seal salvaged floors with polyurethane or water-based lacquer, or polish regularly. Spills will mark the traditional wax finish and should be mopped up straight away.

RECLAIMED WOOD

Reclaimed or remanufactured wood comes from old industrial buildings and farm buildings. The species available include: long leaf southern yellow pine; cypress; chestnut; oak; eastern white pine, also called 'pumpkin pine'; Douglas fir, and spruce. These timbers are removed from old buildings as beams and boards and put to use in a new context. They become raw material for manufacture into flooring that has many of the characteristics of new wood flooring except that the grain and color of the reclaimed wood is frequently richer and more beautiful. Reclaimed flooring costs more than new flooring, and milling can be less precise than new flooring because of the difficulty inherent in the process of remanufacture. Matching recycled flooring over a large area can be difficult, because the boards may not all have come from the same source.

Laying Installation is similar to new flooring and very much easier than recyled flooring.

Treatment Sweep and clean with a damp cloth.

Carpet

Carpet is soft, the essence of luxury, an all-but-weightless flooring with plush, pile and flat weaves meant to skim the floor. Carpet conforms to the keep-it-simple philosophy of decor. It is a cushion to sprawl out on and can be safely crawled over by even the tenderest young knees.

The style of carpeting, let alone texture and color, is perplexing. To decide where you stand, become aware of some of the broad categories of materials and construction and live with samples. Price is just one consideration. Begin by selecting a carpet dealer who is well-known in your community.

To assess quality and durability, look at the thickness or density, the weave and the material. Press your thumb firmly into the pile; the quicker it recovers, the denser and more resilient the carpet. A carpet's density is how closely knitted each individual fiber is to another, not how low or high the carpet measures. A way to test density when comparing samples of the same fiber type is to bend a sample in a fold; the less backing you can see, the

denser the carpet. Also inspect the individual yarns; the more the strands are twisted together, the higher the quality of the carpet. Ask if the yarns have been heat-set to hold the twist or check the label on the back of the carpet

Most carpet today is 'tufted' – made by a process in which hundreds of loops, or tufts, of fiber are threaded by huge sewing machines into a backing material. The loops can be all the same height ('level loop pile') or they can vary ('multi-level

2

loop pile', also referred to by retailers as 'sculpted' or 'carved' because the different heights often create a pattern). They can also be left as they are or cut to create 'cut pile', which includes velvets, plushes and saxonies. Cut pile carpets, made with today's high luster fibers which have rich highlight and shadow effects, show foot tracks more than other styles. They can also be slightly harder to clean than loop pile. Level loop pile with its smooth, level surface is very durable.

Match the carpet style and fiber with its use. Put light-use carpets with mushy plush or feathery pile in bedrooms rather than in the hall or family room. Carpet stairs and high-traffic zones with dense, tight, low-pile tufts. Professionals recommend buying extra stair carpeting; replace the odd few steps as they wear with material from the original roll.

Although it seems as if there are many more, there are essentially only five different carpet fibers: nylon, olefin, polyester, acrylic, and wool, the only natural fiber used in broadloom. For many years, the only fiber available was wool; today it is still unsurpassed in its durability – and cost. The closest of the synthetic fibers to wool is acrylic.

Confusion is understandable given the great many fibers with proprietary brand names. These are often mistaken for generic fibers, which they are not. The carpet industry produces unbranded fibers which can work well in areas where premium brand fibers (anti-stat, anti-stain) aren't vital.

There's a natural inclination to shift into neutral for large-scale, long-lasting home furnishings like carpets. While you may have a certain color preference, bear in mind that much of the soil that builds up on carpet comes from the surrounding uncarpeted areas. Darker shades of red, blue, green and brown work well where the soil is dark. Lighter colors are recommended if your soil is lighter. Before you buy, make a rough estimate of how many square yards are needed, then do some comparison shopping. Most reputable retailers provide a free measuring service to avoid the most common mistake of over-ordering.

Padding Invest in a good pad. For wall-to-wall carpet, a $\frac{1}{2}$in (12.5mm) thick pad of dense foam offers good support. A 40-ounce pad should be fine, except on stairs and for high-traffic areas where a 48-ounce pad is recommended.

Laying Installing carpet yourself is manual labor with injury potential ranging from the discomfort of cuts and bruises to those inducing a visit to the doctor. Hands and knees are most likely to be hurt. For lightweight and foam-backed carpet,

3

wear gloves and knee pads. For all other carpet, have it installed professionally. Proper installation is the difference between carpet wearing well or badly.

Treatment Stain-inhibitors are an insurance policy, not magic potions. Even though today's carpets resist stains better than they did even as recently as a few years ago, they still can stain. Carpets that have been pretreated with a clear, stain-blocking chemical at the factory make it easier to wipe up spills as they happen and before they have a chance to settle into the carpet.

Carpets should be vacuumed weekly, if not daily, to prevent dirt from imbedding at the base of the pile where it can rub and cut fibers loose. Even with regular vacuuming, carpets should still be cleaned at quarterly or semi-annual intervals. Follow manufacturer's instructions; don't use harsh chemicals, shampoos or detergent on stain-resistant carpet. Hot-water extraction cleaning is best left to the professionals.

1 Wool-and-nylon twist.
2 Pure wool with sculpted pattern.
3 Wool-and-olefin twist.
4 Pure wool.
5 Wilton carpet with a combination of cut and loop piles.
6 Loop-pile Wilton.

1

4

CARPET GLOSSARY

Acrylic Wool's synthetic twin in appearance, but at a lower price and slightly less resilient and stain resistant than wool; non-allergenic.

Axminster Like an oriental rug, fibers are woven in and out through the surface backing on an Axminster machine. This loom inserts pile tufts into the weave from above so that strands need not run along the back, enabling a multitude of colors to be used. Chosen by hotels and commercial lobbies for its durability

5

and cleanability, the surface is a cut pile, available in long and shaggy, short and smooth, stubbly or carved carpets. Yard for yard, it is comparatively more expensive than carpets made on high-speed modern tufting machines.

Berber A looped, nubbly pile carpet named after the original hand woven wool squares made by North Africa tribes. Now made by machine in natural colors. Not advisable for use on stairs.

6

Broadloom Any carpet wider than 6ft (1.8m).

Carpet tiles The selection includes loop pile, velours and tufted tiles. Tiles can be checkerboarded or used for random design patterns.

Used primarily in offices and other commercial applications, tiles don't require padding, are very flat, thin and hardwearing, but lack the bounciness of carpeting. Stained and damaged tiles can be lifted up and either easily cleaned or replaced as necessary.

Cotton Cotton carpeting is exceptionally silky and very fine. It won't wear out but does matt down. Rugs with a soft back, in which cotton yarn is used, can be tossed into a washing machine or commercially laundered.

Cut pile (Plush) Yarn filaments are cut rather than looped into the carpet.

Frieze Carpets made from tightly twisted yarns which create a dense, low-pile surface. Very rugged and hardwearing, excellent for heavy traffic areas, like stairs.

Fusion Bonded A construction process that produces a very dense cut pile, or level loop carpet fabrics in solid or Moresque colors that have a superior tuft bind.

Hand-knotted Construction process used to make Oriental and American Indian rugs whereby yarn is hand-tied into a woven backing with individual knots. High quality, and expensive.

Linen Textural, with loose-end pile, and expensive, linen carpet looks very rich and more unconventional than sisal, but still brings a natural feel to the floor. Bought for decoration rather than hard wear. Linen can be custom dyed to any color. Best with at least a ¼in (5mm) rubber pad.

Looped pile Uncut continuous loops on the surface. Performance depends on the density of construction.

Nylon The most popular of all pile fibers; non-allergenic, resistant to water-soluble stains and easy to clean. Nylon dyes easily and with a clarity of color that can't be reproduced in wool.

Advanced generation nylons cost more than regular nylon carpet but provide the latest in fiber technology with built-in static control and ability to conceal and resist soil.

Olefin (polypropylene) Inexpensive, strong and easy to clean, olefin resists moisture and mildew, but can fade. A good choice for playrooms, dens and kitchens.

Polyester Moisture and abrasion-resistant, and nonallergenic. Usually made into thick, cut-pile carpets that have a soft, rich feel; excellent color quality and retention, but can pill.

Shag Pile that is 1-2in (25-50mm) long. The side of yarn is exposed to give a shaggy look. Too dangerous for use on stairs, as heels are likely to catch in the long pile. It's often as appealing to dirt and bugs as it is to people. Susceptible to tangles and matting.

Silk Among the best weaving fibers, silk yarn is hand-loomed and machine made into fantastically expensive, exotic carpet with intricate patterns. Non-colorfast silk carpet fades in strong sunlight.

Tufted The most widely manufactured type of carpet. Instead of being woven on a loom, each individual fiber is punched into a base material, which is usually then sealed with a waterproof backing. The pile may be looped or cut.

Velvet One of three types of industrially woven carpets (others include Axminster and Wilton), velvet is normally cut-pile; available in a limitless range of colors, textures and patterns.

Wool As the only natural fiber still used in significant quantities in carpet, wool is soft, luxurious looking and unsurpassed in durability. However, wool carpets are more expensive per square foot than those made of man-made fibers and they require special cleaning, best done by professionals.

Wilton An industrial weaving technique that derives its name from the type of loom which weaves the yarn in a continuous strand. This technique permits only a few colors to be used in any one carpet. Smooth, velvety surface and top-quality construction, especially when worsted yarn is used.

CARPET WEAVES

Axminster

Wilton

Tufted

Bonded

WINDOWS

Window dressing is the balance between the outside world and your home. It is do-it-yourself light control. Curtains or drapery can obscure structural imperfections or eclipse an undesirable view. Window dressing shields us from neighbors in urban areas, shades us from the baking sun in hot climates and keeps out the chill of winter nights. But bear in mind, too, that windows are important architectural features in a room, and that you may not wish to cover them up so much as make a feature of them. Window dressing is not only about framing the view outside or coordinating the scheme with the other furnishings in your room; if the windows themselves are unusual or noteworthy, the way in which they're dressed should not detract from their intrinsic merit.

To give your windows the treatments they deserve, give some kind of nod to the architecture of your home and complement the framework of the window. Furnish windows in accordance with the room's function and with the degree of natural light. Harmonize or consciously contrast its style with the walls, floors and furnishings, but make it an integral part of your overall decorative scheme rather than a casual afterthought. Base your choice on site and context, personal need and privacy. Simply buying new curtain and drapery rods, changing hardware, picking unusual fabrics or a provocative valance may not be enough - you may decide to change the window.

As you become more comfortable selecting window treatments, you will be inspired to experiment with unusual pairings. Assembling different colors, patterns and textures works well. Opposites attract: drape lustrous brocade beside homely muslin, or sweeps of rich, thick velvet beside the crisp clean lines of tailored Roman shades. Materials can be left plain or paired with a decorative border; curtains may be simple and sculptural or patterned and pleated; valances and pelmets can be used in an understated way to draw attention to the view or they can provide decorative flourish in a room with little architectural detail. Remember, though, that less is often more. Too much clutter at a window can make a room feel oppressive and hemmed in – simple shades will often fulfil everything you need of a window dressing with a lot less fuss and for a lot less cost than fancy draperies.

1 A mullioned window frames the view outside.
2 Painting the frames of these mini-sash windows with a jolt of color draws the eye away from the room and out into the countryside beyond.

3 Light marches across this bedroom through a large, mullioned window cut into the sloping roof. Roof windows and skylights are often used to make rooms brighter and to open up small spaces.

4 Interior windows elegantly borrow light from adjoining rooms. Most exterior windows can be fitted indoors.

4

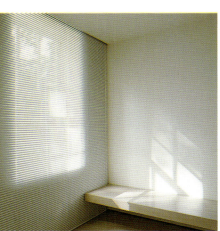

5 Venetian blinds regulate heat, reduce noise and maximize privacy without relinquishing all access to daylight. Their spare, clean lines integrate them seamlessly with the window and blend well with modern interiors.

5

Shapes

Windows let in light and air, shut out the cold and stand out as an important architectural feature. The right window makes all the difference. For buildings of considerable architectural value and for houses of little distinction the size, shape and material of windows should be consistent or in balance with the original façade so that the building is pulled into visual order. Windows need to be sympathetic to the period of your home and the architectural framework. One of the

fastest ways to devalue a house is to replace the original windows with new metal, wood or plastic renditions that clash in style.

It is important when adding windows or designing anew not to incorporate big picture windows and patio doors without any sense of composition or rhythm. Let big windows speak for themselves, to frame a fine view or make a bold focal point. But use with discretion and don't compromise the existing proportions of a room: fine examples of 1940s and 1950s architecture are being spoiled by home owners putting in wooden picture windows.

If you want to play down the size of a window, mullions can contain an expanse of glass, becoming part of the visual structure, so that large windows assume a more domestic scale. Mullions work particularly well on windows with more than 3ft (1m) of uninterrupted glass.

When existing windows are beyond repair, it pays to find replacements as close to the originals as possible. If your home needs more

light, then increasing the size of existing windows is one option. If you do not want to disturb the façade, you could add windows at the side or back or cut skylights into the roof. For a room at the top, you can take away the roof itself, leaving the party walls of a townhouse and the front parapet to the street. Light floods in but the front of the house remains the same.

Unless you are building from scratch, new windows should look as though the original home owners installed them. Match the pane sizes and proportions. Align new window heads and sills with the old. If your house is historic or has some mullioned windows, you have an obligation to continue the tradition, the more so if it contributes to the overall look of the community or street front. Don't settle for ersatz substitutes. It's better to have plain glass and a window that is well made than one with snap-in mullions that will lend your home a cartoon quality.

Windows are a longterm investment so select the best you can afford. Powder-coated steel frames are more expensive than wood, but the thinness of their profile and their flat, fine surface make them ideal for secondary glazing. A good window will be as well suited to its task 30 years from now as it is today.

For an original approach, rather than filling an interior with solid planes – walls and doors – consider using exterior windows to fill in voids. Glass blocks allow light to pass through, but they aren't entirely transparent and so work well as a screen to more private areas. Their industrial aesthetic complements modern interiors.

GLAZING

About 15 per cent of the total heat lost in homes is through windows. Double glazing windows minimizes condensation and the cold zone that you get near windows. This conceivably reduces fuel bills by cutting the heat loss from each room by half, though this saving has to be offset against the high cost of installation. As a heat insulator, the narrower the gap between the exterior window and the secondary glazing, the more effective it is.

Do-it-yourself double glazing is more cost effective than professional installation; both methods are sensible if you plan to stay put for many years. For windows of old and historic houses, be sure double glazing is not at the cost of architectural integrity and that frames are matched to those of the existing window.

WINDOW DRESSING

Like people and their clothes, what a window wears should accentuate its best attributes, provide some warmth and a degree of disguise. Windows and their wardrobe should be stylish, practical, flexible when possible, even unexpected.

Tall and narrow windows look good in just about every context. Flat Roman shades accentuate the frame, curtains with plenty of material show off their grace; only top-heavy pelmets are to be avoided. Treatments that extend beyond the sill to the floor act as a visual extension for windows that stop at chair-rail height or are centered on a

1 **Traditional sash windows.**
2 **Circular window with skylight in ceiling.**
3 **Small sash window.**
4 **Mullioned casement window.**
5 **Casement windows with arch.**
6 **Sandblasted glass.**
7 **Glazed internal window.**

wall. Making Roman shades or curtains from a translucent fabric filters light but blurs it where the window sill ends.

When windows are awkwardly low or stunted in proportion to the room, mounting bamboo shades and relaxed Roman shades on the ceiling will visually extend the apparent height of the window. Simple valances which focus the eye on the area above the window, or a cornice added to the top of the window

4

frame will give an illusion of height. With low ceilings, windows seem to hit the roof. Elegant drapes or tails and pelmets that dip to a lower point on each side will draw the eye comfortably down.

If you have a radiator under a window, keep the area of coverage to a minimum to avoid losing heat – make sure there is another heat source in relative proximity. Floor-length draperies or fabric screens work well as a means of additional heat insulation. Both can be pulled

5

back when not required. Curtains that fall in front of a radiator should not be interlined or they will block heat from the radiator entering the room when closed.

SMALL WINDOWS

Even tiny windows appear bigger if the frame is painted white. Louvered or paneled shutters broaden narrow windows. They look best when the shutters are about half the width of the window itself. Hanging dramatic

draperies on windows not large enough to accommodate them results in visual discomfort. Fabric on tiny windows minimizes them further. Shutters, tailored Roman shades and flat treatments draw less attention to the window's diminutive proportions. Recessed windows allow only a limited amount of light to permeate so leave them bare, perhaps using the sill for interesting collections of objects.

LARGE WINDOWS

For large windows, subtle and unfussy decorative treatments work best. Avoid small prints and mini-shades which create a blurred impression when spread over big expanses. If windows are broad, the flat, horizontal folds of a large Roman shade bordered with colored tape offers a tailored, tasteful solution; pull-down shades made with a metal mesh so they are semi-transparent when down also work well.

Picture windows benefit from a straightforward plain set of shutters. Textural fabrics, such as muslin and lace, diffuse light and reduce unattractive views to a soothing blur. Walls of windows are less domineering when they are united under a valance or treated to panels of sheer curtains suspended from a steel tension wire. Sandblasting some panes to an opaque finish cuts down glare and softly filters light.

Large rear windows at the back of a house can be framed within a pergola. Remember, though, that if the pergola is then planted with climbers this will cut down on the amount of light let in. At the front of the house, running trellising to the height of a picture window and planting climbing shrubs will similarly disguise and soften sheets of glass. If a window is too much of an open book for neighbors or allows in too much sunlight, louvered shutters can be inserted over one or more sections and painted to contrast with or match the window frames.

Arched and Palladian windows are a problem to dress well because of their shape and proportion. Custom-made curved shades or curtains hung high above the arch and falling to the floor look good. For arched windows, suspend drapes from the ceiling.

MISMATCHED WINDOWS

Professional decorators generally discourage using more than one type of window treatment in a room. Mismatched windows present problems of asymmetry and proportion. Rooms with small windows and French doors or dado-height windows and oversized patio doors are not uncommon but are ill-suited to uniform window dressing. Use drapes or shades made from the same fabric or color as a means of relating different windows in a room.

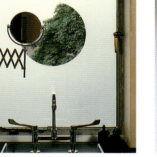

6

On the exterior, painting windows of varying shapes and proportions white makes light of the differences. Since glass appears as black or dark gray from a distance, you can paint the windows' inner framework black or gray so the glazing pattern virtually disappears.

NATURAL LIGHT

Light is a wonderful house guest; it is bright, illuminating, warm, cultivated and never stays too long in one place, casting shadows and changing in intensity through the course of the day. With sunny exposures, however, you can have such a thing as too much sun. Several treatments used in tandem – such as curtains lined with blackout over a corset of wooden venetian blinds – provide layers of control. Shade cloth comes in different colors and several degrees of opacity. Pull-down roller shades made from 50 per cent shade cloth mean nobody can see in but you can see out. Shade cloth is available from suppliers of awning fabric and makers of patio and boat covers.

Sandblasting window glass into opaque sheets or with patterns lessens the likelihood of faded fabrics. The production techniques have made available windows that moderate light – which look great when paired with bare sills and sashes – and others with electrical low-voltage charges that 'frost' at the touch of a button, diffusing light.

Another option is one developed for windshields by the automobile industry. It consists of a plastic filament centered between sheets of

7

glass. The milky white surface allows light to pass through but prevents passers-by from seeing in. Like sandblasting, this treatment obscures the view until the window is opened.

Fabrics with textural qualities, such as hessian and sheer metallics, and venetian blinds fracture the morning sun. Window treatments in 'Indian punch' colors of fuchsia and saffron, as well as bruised colors like vermilion and indigo, warm the cool blue-gray tones of shady exposures.

ORDER OF PAINTING A WINDOW

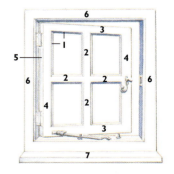

Following the grain of the wood, paint a casement window in the following order: (1) glazing putty; (2) glazing bars; (3) top and bottom rails; (4) outer uprights; (5) hinged edge; (6) frame (top, then bottom, then sides); (7) sill.

Draperies

Never be tempted to skimp on fabric. Floor-length drapes benefit from a generous mass of fabric. Choose a less expensive fabric to save money, or have just a valance on top with a sheer underneath.

1 Café clips.
2 Half-height sheers.
3 Resist-dyed cotton.
4 Roman shades behind pinch-pleated draperies.
5 Fabric tie-back.
6 Drapes on steel tension-wire track.
7 Cotton drapes bow tied to rack.
8 Cartridge-pleated cotton drapes.
9 Goblet-pleated drapes.

Any material can be fashioned into window treatments, even silk. The sun doesn't break down silk; it is the dirt that builds up on the fabric that is then broken down by the sun. If you vacuum your drapes regularly, they'll last a lot longer. Over time, sunlight, dust, and daily wear and tear lead to general fading and eventual disintegration of even the most colorfast fabrics.

Think laterally: café clips – which snap shut around fabric like clip-on earrings – a sari, an old piece of embroidery or a sheet of burlap can be attached to rods. Environmentally sound monk's cloth (no bleach, no dye) is a good finish choice and, at a low price, makes good sense. Thin cotton terry cloth towels can be French pleated and hung in a bathroom. Other materials that are meant to be worn – like the striped fabric used to line men's vests and Indian madras used for shirts – can be stitched up into a window dressing. The cloth used for sarongs falls softly when used as a window drape and turns a white room into something sensuous.

However, it often pays to invest in one good fabric rather than to dress your windows with a variety of contrasting and disparate styles. The architecture of the room should have an influence on your choice of fabric, as will the general decorative

scheme. Duck (untwilled linen used to make small sails), canvas and muslin are examples of fabrics that are able to hold a fold, and which give depth to shades and curtains. Dark fabrics on lighter window frames graphically delineate a window's sculptural silhouette.

Fabric should look wonderful all the time – both by day and night. A vibrantly dyed piece of muslin, lit from behind during the day, has all the luminescence of a stained glass window. At night, when it is time to settle down and burrow in, curtains illuminated in front by artificial light sources become opaque and blanket the room. Solid colors can range from the bold to the subtle, and will create very different effects from patterns or printed designs.

MAKING DRAPERIES

To calculate the amount of fabric you need, multiply the length of the finished drape (allowing for hems and headings) by the number of drapery widths. To determine the degree of fullness for drapes, the rule of thumb is to allow two to two and a half times the finished width for pencil and pinch pleats and three times the rod length for sheer fabrics. Unpleated drapes with a single swag need one and a half times the fullness. Don't forget to add another 1½in (4cm) for each side seam and each interlocking seam.

Use the window as a template for proportion. Accurate measuring is essential. Measure both vertical sides for curtain drops; house-settling often causes windows to become slightly distorted. If this is the case, fabric breaking on the ground will save you from having to make each curtain to a different measurement. If curtains are to be tied back, you'll need less length than if they spend most of the time hanging on a pole.

For lightweight materials and sheer fabrics, allow an extra 6-10in (150-250mm) overall for hems and heading and 10in (250mm) for heavy fabric. On patterned fabrics, order one extra pattern repeat for each curtain. If fabric isn't pre-shrunk, wash or dry clean it before the curtains are cut out and made.

LINING

A lining protects fabric from light, gives extra weight and body and conceals all the hems and raw edges. Linings also provide a professional finish to window dressing and prolong the life of your drapes. In colors, they offer an interesting view from the street, but you should first check the effect the colored lining has on the appearance of the drape material. Blackout linings (not necessarily black) totally or partially block light. They successfully make fabrics opaque, but detract from the overall beauty. Blackout linings suit bedrooms and nurseries.

INTERLINING

Usually a soft blanket layer of padding between the fabric and the lining, interlining improves heat

retention in a room, buffers noise and drafts and helps drapes hang better and look fuller by softening the folds as the drape falls. It is sold in various weights.

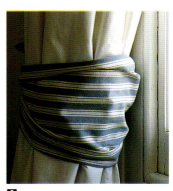

8

CHOOSING A STYLE

Traditionalists tend to view windows as opportunities to swathe and swag, trim and tassel, tail and tie. Modernists address the fact that we live in the twentieth century; since

6

we don't wear nineteenth-century clothes, our windows should be dressed in curtains that share the same simplicity, tailoring and low maintenance of current fashion.

A window shouldn't be an excuse to go overboard with chintz. When selecting curtains, consideration such as climate control, a room's architecture, and the style and proportion of the windows and their surrounds, are as important as the color, design and texture of the curtain material itself. These are the caveats in a choice that would otherwise be limitless.

The maxim is to keep curtains floor- or sill-length, unless they are hung outside the window frame as a means to disguise badly proportioned windows. Keeping it simple lets the curtain fabric or architecture of the room speak for itself. If the room lacks architectural elements, you can create them in your choice of window dressing. Curtains can be rich in a tailored, deliberate and structural way, with pelmets and valances or an undersheer. (But err on the discreet side – with each element you add, you take away some precious light.) The taller the ceiling, the more elegant curtains look. Masses of curtain tend to appear squat, over elaborate and ungainly, particularly in rooms with very low ceilings.

Colored borders provide definition to plain curtains. Curtain panels can button or zip close. Headings can be nautically knotted or bow-tied to poles. Unlined curtains with a gathered heading can be hung from a rod or pole for a country feel.

Long curtains can be used in place of cupboard doors to hide closet contents, to cordon off a vestibule and behind closed front doors for heat retention. Canopies and other bedhangings are again fashionable, though without the primary emphasis on creating a draftproof box.

HEADINGS

Fabric conveys the desired effect, but the heading defines the curtain style. A heading is the gathering or pleating at the top of a curtain. The tape

7

sewn onto the curtain back determines both the shape and size of these gathers or pleats, or the heading can be hand-stitched.

Pinch, or French, pleats are small clusters of three pleats grouped at regular intervals; they suit heavy, floor-to-ceiling curtains. Pencil pleats are tighter and run continuously across the curtain and work well with lightweight and sheer fabrics.

Gathered headings are a cross between pencil and pinch pleats, best for short, light curtains paired with a pelmet or valance.

Cartridge pleats are elaborate and rather formal, with stiff cuffs that are stuffed with interlining or rolled buckram. Smocked headings look as if they have been embroidered and must be painstakingly sewn.

CORNICES, VALANCES AND LAMBREQUINS

These are three different pieces of window furniture, separate from curtains and positioned at the top of the window over curtain headings. Cornices are generally made from wood or MDF (medium-density fiberboard) and are either painted, covered in fabric or wallpapered. Valances are made entirely from cloth. Soft, deep valances convey a mood of relaxed luxury. Lambrequins are essentially cornices with arms that reach down each side of the window. They are usually made of wood or MDF to retain their shape. All three define the window treatment and connect it with the architectural framework of a window.

POLES AND FINIALS

Poles are another visual element, available in various diameters and materials including brass, steel and wood, though driftwood can be used to great effect and economy, while steel tension wires are modern and unobtrusive. Make sure curtain rings run freely across the pole for easy opening and closing.

Finials are the decorative denouement, traditionally capping off each end of the pole. They range from the discreet to the gaudy. Wood, plaster and metal finials are available in various shapes and designs.

RODS

Curtain rods secure curtains and are normally hidden behind the curtain heading, a valance or cornice or they are disguised by swags. Rods are available in varying sizes and materials. Rods can be custom made to fit awkwardly shaped bow and bay windows so that curtains follow the exact contour of the window. For window treatments starting at ceiling height and for those using a heavy fabric, it's a good idea to use a stronger ceiling-mounted rod. Before hanging curtains, ensure that the rod is correctly and safely attached to the wall or ceiling and that it is able to take the weight of the curtains. Traverse rods come already corded, so the fabric of the curtain is handled as little as possible.

TIE-BACKS

Tie-backs help a curtain to drape or fall gracefully when drawn back, and alleviate the stress that the weight of the curtains puts on the track or pole. They're decorative restraining elements holding back curtains to make way for light from the window. A tie-back can be fashioned from almost anything, but usually consists of a doubled straight piece of fabric that is attached by rings to a hook on the window frame or wall. Bows, tassels, cord, metal chains – each serves the tie-back function well and offers a range of looks.

9

MEASURING FOR DRAPERIES

To calculate the amount of fabric you will need for drapes, first measure the width of the track ('A') – not the window – and multiply this by the number of times a heading requires. Add on the appropriate amount for seams and hems. To calculate the length, measure from the bottom of the track or curtain rings to the required point: usually the sill ('B'), about 4in (100mm) below the sill ('B'), or to the floor ('C'); then add an allowance for the heading and hem.

HEADINGS

Gathered pleats

Pencil pleats

Pinch pleats

Cartridge pleats

Smocked

Curtaining

There is relaxed, individualistic curtaining and there are traditional forms. Swags and tails are a swanky decorative arrangement of fabric hung at the top of windows, used with sewn curtains and those draped over poles. Swags are draped horizontally, tails hang on either side of the curtain.

Draping fabric over poles can be achieved simply with one fabric or by using several that harmonize or contrast. The layered look can be assembled with an eye to luxury or

1 Cotton draped to
form a cornice.
2 Muslin.
3 Complementary
sheers.
4 Cotton sari.

with ingenious economy. Fabric can be swagged, draped and looped, formally cut and sewn, or turned artfully over a pole and allowed simply to hang. Egyptian cotton voile thrown across the pole so that both ends bunch a little at floor level is quietly, but unabashedly, extravagant.

Classic romance can be achieved without excessive frills or cost. Muslin, synthetic translucent materials and medium-weight fabrics drape well. Fabrics with a contrasting lining can be wound around a pole to create an effect of bulk; the twisted section of fabric needs to be twice the pole length. Revealing part of the pole lends an air of informality. For classical beauty, drape a single length of fabric over a simple pole and allow it to hang symmetrically.

While simple curtains or draperies can soften all kinds of rooms, a layered treatment gives more control over privacy and energy savings. But excessive curtaining can look both fussy and ill considered. Stick to simple, edited-down effects for best results.

SHEERS

Whether you want a dramatic sweep of color to cut out cold winter light, or romantic swags, sheers are among the easiest window dressings to rig up. With sheers, the afternoons slip noticeably into darkness until the morning light streams in. The thinnest sheers dilute light, while patterned sheers dapple it.

Special attention to scale and line is in order even though sheers are often accompanied by frills, swags or elaborate headings. There are sheers that shine — silks, synthetic translucents, parachute silk, organdy — and those that are dull and textured — voiles, cheesecloth, gauze, muslin, batiste. When a breeze lifts the panels, or light filters through simply hung sheers, there is a gossamer effect. Sheers can also be remarkably economical. Saris of clashing colors can be clipped to tracks and poles and hung as simple, ethereal drapes. Filmy gauze takes the edge off even the most severe examples of modernism. Canvas cloth hung on tension wire and stretched in horizontal bands across a skylight creates a tent-like effect. Fine linen scrim used in theatres comes in widths of up to 13ft (4m). It is billowy and light, and can be thrown in the washing machine.

LACE

Lace comes in hundreds of off-white shades, including chalk, eggshell, ivory, gardenia, alabaster and cream, as well as colors. Lace doesn't have to look overly feminine or florid. Without spending a lot of money, you have a window treatment that can go in any direction.

Much of the lace available today is based on nineteenth- and early twentieth-century designs, including French window panels (narrower than usual to cover the width of the window only) and half-sized horizontal panels which cover the lower half of a window. Roller shades can be made out of the harder-wearing laces, such as Nottingham or Madras. Old lace can be found in antique shops and flea markets — at a price. Designs don't have to match. Windows look pretty with different patterns at each pane, particularly if they are panels.

SCREENING

Unlike curtains, screens don't crowd a window with solid material. Instead, they recreate nomadic life, giving a window constant potential for change and focusing on the contents of the room. Screens are especially good if you don't want to spend money on expensive, properly tailored draperies because you are living in rented accommodation or planning to move house.

Bracketed rods, mounted on either side of a window, can suspend layer upon layer of opalescent sheers in a pageantry of lengths and widths. Traverse rods make it simple to maximize light or to play it down.

Designers are taking high-tech materials and giving them a new twist as neutral foils for windows. Framed in steel, a sliding door of translucent, corrugated fiberglass can leave a view wide open or close off a window when privacy is required. Steel

tubular frames on wheels or commercial dress racks on wheels can shut out the world, allow slivers of light through, or be whisked away for an unobstructed view.

Sandblasted glass screens resting on the sill and reaching halfway up deflect strong sun, but still entertain nature's rays and outside views above eye level. Simpler still is to bring latticework in from the garden to obscure the view partially and to filter light, generating privacy and shade simultaneously.

Window coverings

Blinds, shades and shutters help regulate heat, reduce noise and ensure privacy. They have spare, clean lines which enable all types of window to remain uncluttered. These are the blue jeans of window treatments – immensely practical and always appropriate. Less overpowering and simpler than curtains and draperies, they are a relatively inexpensive form of window dressing. Shades work particularly well alone in contemporary homes, complementing modern architecture, furnishings and fixtures. At large windows, it usually looks better to hang two or three separate shades rather than a single shade across the whole width. This also allows you greater flexibility in controlling light and shade in the room.

ROLLER SHADES
The pull-down white roller shade is a classic. Containing just a single key piece of apparatus, roller shades can be used alone with valances or as undertreatments paired with drapes or delicate sheers. The simplicity of their operation makes them available in kit form, custom-made and ready-made in a stock range of sizes. Sill-mounted roller shades that pull up rather than down are a great urban solution, simultaneously giving privacy while letting in natural light.

Unsuitable fabrics roll unevenly; tight, flat weaves are best suited to constant unraveling. Roller shades have started moving away from the white and natural materials of most contemporary interiors, and take on very different looks when made from gold mesh or taffeta.

ROMAN SHADES
Roman shades have all the grace, strength and durability of a sail. Operating on a simple cording system, the Roman shade draws up into a series of broad, flat folds. Dowel rods, secured horizontally and concealed within pockets made from tucks in the fabric, keep the shade taut and supported. Unrolled fully they are somewhat of a letdown, resembling ordinary blinds. They look good in isolation or in combination with curtains, and are

economical on fabric. Lining Roman shades will improve the way pleats fall and keep out more light. Avoid large-scale patterns because the design will be interrupted by the horizontal pleats. Dowel rods can be made of wood (half dowels to rest flat against the fabric) or plexiglass with lightweight and sheer fabrics.

Roman shades can give a twist to the simplest of fabrics. A thin, sheer organdy Roman shade edged with linen and stretched across a window filters an ethereal light.

AUSTRIAN AND BALLOON SHADES
Austrian shades fall like curtains to end in a series of deep, ruched scallops which need a surplus of about 20in (0.5m) of fabric. Festoon blinds are flamboyantly ruched from top to bottom and gathered from side to side, differing from Austrian shades in that the fullness is distributed along their entire length. When calculating the amount of fabric, allow twice the length of the finished drop for Austrian shades.

These window treatments combine the drapery of curtains with the economy of a blind. Cords running through looped tape at the back draw up Austrian and balloon shades into a ballooned effect. When gathered and pulled, both shades suffer from the reputation of being overdressed. It's usually the excessive bows, ruffles and florals that make them too over-the-top for most rooms. Plain fabrics display the form of these shades best. They contain as much material as full-length drapes and – because of their weight – it's advisable to choose lightweight fabrics.

VENETIAN BLINDS
Venetian blinds with their trademark 2in (5cm) cloth tapes are back in style. Available in wood with a variety of finishes and aluminum in dozens of baked-on colors and patterns, the new venetians provide a more fashionable look than their thinner horizontal counterparts, the minis and micro-minis, which were not long ago the banners of suburbia. Horizontal blinds can be made to fit almost any size or shape window, from 1ft to 12ft (30.4cm to 364.8cm) wide. And old venetian blinds can be given a new lease of life with a new covering or a coat of paint.

Vertical blinds pivot open or closed, and come in a wide variety of finishes, textures and materials, including aluminum, vinyl and fabric. Motorized and remote control verticals are options. New track systems permit operable verticals on all sorts of specialty window systems, including Palladian, bay and angled windows. Vinyl vertical blinds are

less likely to twist or bow over time. With the new clear vinyl channels, you can use your own fabric or select from numerous manufacturers' choices.

NEW SHADES
More recent arrivals in shade fashions are pleated fabric and cellular shades. These shades give windows a tailored look and can be used either as single treatments or in combination with draperies. Pleated shades come in myriad colors and

fabrics, including metallized fabric for high energy efficiency. Cellular shades have a unique pleated, energy-saving construction resembling a honeycomb. Newer still are 'window shadings', a cross between a shade and a blind.

SHUTTERS
Mounted on each side of the frame, interior shutters give definition and presence to a window. Their clean appearance doesn't detract visually from the window's architecture or view. They keep out the light when you want them to while continuing to let in fresh air (if they are louvred). Shutters provide additional security and insulate against noise from outside.

Plantation shutters fold back with accordion hinges to each side of the window. Most shutters are louvered to let in fresh air and filter a little light, but some – typically in older townhouses – have solid wood panels. Old shutters can be bought cheaply, cut down and trimmed to fit your windows.

1 Sill-mounted, upwards-rolling shade.
2 Roller shades.
3 Venetian blinds.
4 Roman shades.
5 Thin wood shades.
6 Shutters.

FURNISHING

1

Furnishing a home involves translating the ideas that stir us into rooms that content us. Our homes should be as personal, eclectic and full of character as we are, reflecting our different lifestyles, preserving our memories and expressing our own brand of taste. At the same time, most people desire a sense of timelessness in design – materials that wear and weather well, furnishings that are comfortable, practical and easy on the eye.

How do you make a confident choice from the vast range of furnishings available? How do you combine different elements in a way that looks natural and instinctive rather than contrived? One of the best approaches is to allow yourself time to assimilate items into the pattern of daily living. Reconstructing a room set down to the last cushion cover stifles individuality and rules out the creative changes which keep homes alive.

It's equally important to respect what you already have. Take cues from an interesting floor, good ceiling height or fine architectural detail. Consider the quality of light and general spatial elements of each room: both of these elements can dictate or initiate color and furnishing schemes. Trying to deny a room's innate character is self-defeating. Use space, volume and history as the starting points for your decorative ideas. If your home doesn't have much in the way of architectural detail, everything has to come from the contents. If there's a strong period flavor, expressed in moldings, paneling, fireplaces and architraves, you can echo the basic framework with sympathetic furnishings, or play up the contrast in a bolder fashion.

There's always room for wit and reinterpretation. Crafting a table from builders' trestles, pulling up antique chairs to a modern, glass-topped table, juxtaposing an old rolled-arm sofa with folding metal park chairs marries old with new, the treasured with the ordinary. Interiors which lack surprise and conform to some proscribed notion of style lack any sense of vitality.

The bottom line is practicality. Visual pleasure is rapidly undermined by poor performance. Dining chairs that are too uncomfortable to sit in, upholstery which swiftly deteriorates under the onslaught of children, or tables which are too rickety to bear the weight of a cup of coffee are ultimately sources of frustration whatever the superficial merits of their appearance.

1 The uncluttered lines of glass shelving are perfect for those who believe that less is more. Glass shelves add the illusion of space and light, but their pristine surface requires regular cleaning.
2 Quilts thrown over a pair of large, slouching sofas, big, generously filled cushions and deep, pillowy armchairs create an air of charm and comfort.

2

3

3 Modern chairs and tables are often categorized by designer or decade. Lloyd Loom chairs are less likely to bruise and scar the floor than more formal dining chairs. The Philippe Starck table combines function with an original design.

4 Slip covers disguise worn upholstery and mismatched pieces of furniture, guard finishes from sunlight and dust, and instantly update and redefine a room by bringing in style at little expense.

5 Using the corridor as a space for a vast book collection creates a literary forest and a wonderful transition space between the hall and living room.

4

5

Upholstery

The price of upholstery varies according to the quality. Ideally, a piece of upholstery will last the rest of your life, just needing recovering as the fabric wears out or your taste changes. Choose hardwood frames that are jointed with screws, dowels and glue, as opposed to just glue. The best construction is called 'eight-way', which means that each spring is attached by hand with knotted twine to the eight surrounding springs and to the webbing underneath them. This attention to detail is costlier, but you'll have a more comfortable piece of furniture.

Medium-range, more affordable upholstery often consists of zigzag construction and steel frames. It is easier and less costly to construct furniture with fluid shapes, or made from a frame of tubular steel with internal straps of steel. Cheap sofas are built of sheet material or out of various densities of foam. A sofabed is a poor compromise, neither a good sofa nor a good bed.

MATERIALS

Padding is essential to a sofa's comfort. The hard frame and springs are usually covered with polyurethane foam, although polyester fiberfill, feathers and down are also used. Foam is the least expensive, but if it's entirely foam, it is probably not going to be too interesting to look at or sit in. Down is the most expensive, but assures the softest seating. Down is placed between two layers of material that are quilted to give it a smooth feel and prevent lumps. Check the sofa label for the filling content, or ask. A sofa's cushions should be firm. All-down cushions have to be fluffed after each use. Some cushions contain springs wrapped in cotton to make them more durable.

If upholstery feels soft, plump but firm, it is probably well made. Weight is a fairly accurate measure of quality; pieces that feel heavy probably have reasonable components and frames of hardwood rather than man-made boards. Steer clear if you can feel the back rail, or your legs bang against the wood edge at the front. Hard edges wear out the upholstery and are a sign of poor springs and bad crafting.

CHOOSING THE STYLE

Allow yourself to get used to the curves and dimensions of a chair or sofa. Typically, young adults want a deep-seated lounge and older adults prefer a frame chair where they feel more upright. If your family is likely to use the piece to watch television, you'll want a high enough back for relaxed viewing to rest heads and engulf occupants when seated. Smart, tailored pieces with a lot of ground clearance encourage correct posture. Upholstery with a tight back rather than loose cushions and those with a single-seat cushion tend to look neater. Sofas and chairs with a slight exaggeration of proportion – deeper, longer, more voluptuous and low to the ground – encourage sprawling. To create softness in square spaces, use large, moon-shaped or curved upholstered pieces.

REUPHOLSTERY

A piece of furniture is worth reupholstering if it's an antique, or if it simply sits comfortably and you like what you're looking at. As a

general rule, contemporary pieces merit reupholstering if restoration and renovation will cost no more than 50 per cent of the price for a replacement. For period pieces, reupholstering with traditional methods, handstitching and horsehair is generally a smart investment, even though the cost is high. Reupholstering a piece enables you to redesign it at the same time. You can tuft it or not, change the height of a skirt or cushion, box or bullnose arms and edges.

Treatment Stain-resisting treatments can be applied to upholstery fabric before tailoring. Removing stains from upholstery pieces is thereafter usually done on site by cleaning services.

SLIP COVERS

Slip covers are a stylish and practical way of dressing furniture. They can be used to disguise worn upholstery and mismatched furniture, to guard wood finishes from light and dust and to update and redefine a room. With slip covers you can self-confidently and informally bring texture, pattern and color into a room without going to the expense of changing the whole decorative scheme.

Slip covers can be used to ring the changes on a seasonal basis or to extend the life span of the fabric underneath, thereby postponing major recovering. Skirts carried to the floor and shallow kickpleats improve the figure of ungainly sofas.

Used as a flexible wardrobe, slip covers act as extra protection for your furniture. You can keep covers on all day for pets and children, then take them off at night for guests.

Treatment Though slip covers offer the precision finish of upholstery for less money, it is the saving in laundering that makes them substantially less costly. Slip covers made of a single, colorfast fabric (no linings or trims) with a simple construction that won't collapse when wet can be safely machine-washed. Laundering or dry cleaning your fabric before sewing will prevent shrinkage later on. Canvas, heavy cotton and linen should be purchased preshrunk.

MAKING SLIP COVERS

Slip covers should be tailored to fit tightly the way a suit hugs a dress form. If you are making the covers yourself, begin by cutting out a pattern of preshrunk cotton to use as a guide. This saves costly cutting mistakes, ensures a good final fit, and can double as a lining or be reused when it is time to replace the slip cover. Unless you want a translucent look, it is advisable to line lightweight fabrics with muslin, cotton or padding. Lined slip covers hang better, have more body and last longer than unlined covers. In many cases, lining the arms, backs and skirt is less expensive and time consuming than a full lining and can be an equally effective measure.

Slip covers are best kept simple, with bound or piped seams. A fitted cover free of seams and details at the hem highlights the fabric pattern and shape of the furniture. Contrasting piping lends covers a crisp look.

CHOOSING FABRIC

Before deciding on a fabric, estimate how much you'll need. The cost of slip covers and upholstery will vary dramatically according to your choice of fabric. If you want to know whether a fabric meets voluntary flammability standards, you'll need to contact the manufacturer directly.

For upholstery, you need hardy stock. 'Upholstery weight' refers to the durability of a fabric. Manufacturers are required to subject most upholstery-weight materials to a rub test, in which a sample is mechanically rubbed hundreds of times. Any good fabric supplier should be able to supply you

1 Tubular-steel and leather armchair.
2 Slip sofa cover.
3 Slip chair cover with ties.
4 Armchair upholstered in kilims.
5 Fitted sofa covers.
6 Dining chairs with drop-in seats.
7 Fitted armchair covers.
8 Bolster.

[4]

with this information. Though almost any fabric can be used, it is wise to start out with a heavy-duty neutral fabric that can easily be incorporated into different decorating schemes or adapted when you change homes. Stripes – such as gray and taupe or beige and cream – will blend with almost any decor. To avoid bland rooms, consider using bold stripes about 3in (75mm) wide. Stripes radically change the shape of upholstery. Vertical stripes lengthen squat furnishings, horizontal stripes add girth and elongate. Solid fabrics and those with an all-over pattern tend to look best kept simple. Piping and covered buttons add structure and emphasize curves.

If you intend moving the same piece of furniture from one room to another, steer towards colors such as straw, paper-bag brown, gray, beige, and neutrals with tone. White can look too fresh and harsh. Jacquards, damasks and small geometric prints are also flexible choices. They have visual interest and character, but lack the kind of strong personality that might clash with other furnishing schemes.

When choosing upholstery fabric, it is tempting to go for the darkest and busiest pattern in the hope that it won't show the dirt. It will, and this can prove a false economy since you need more fabric to ensure a good pattern match.

For longevity, choose a synthetic viscose blended with linen and cotton and weaves with a slub. Kilims make hard-wearing covers, but are thick and more labor-intensive to work – they are also flammable, a risk you should carefully consider.

Chintz and silk aren't durable upholstery materials. As the sheen comes off chintz, lending it its coveted appeal, it becomes, like silk, prone to rips.

Brushed denim, Indian cottons and vibrant cotton velvet are all comfortable, hard-wearing and possess an amazing softness and slight twill. Velvet is losing its old-fashioned connotations of stuffy clubs and airless rooms. The effect of using this simple and luxurious fabric on unusual shapes of upholstery is evocative and wickedly indulgent.

Medium-weight cotton or linen, a cotton-linen blend or a light wool that will behave well with everyday use are good for slip covers. Washable and more resistant to fading than synthetics, these natural fabrics are soft, comfortable and pliable, yet stiff and substantial enough to be a durable slip cover. The tighter the weave, the longer the cover lasts. Plaids and some floral prints can look striking and contemporary when used on sofas with fairly clean, modern lines.

[5]

TRIMMINGS

When covering a chair or sofa with a solid color, use a striped fabric for piping to provide a crisp, graphic note. Fringe can be pinned in place at the bottom of the upholstery or applied with hot glue to give a dressy, formal look and to cover the gap between the frame and the bottom of the floor. In a contemporary setting, this rich detail is a particularly nice juxtaposition. Trim can also be used to play up the lines of shapely legs.

CUSHIONS

Cushions are the easiest way to personalize and dress up a chair or sofa, thanks to a multitude of shapes, sizes and patterns. Using bursts of color and pattern in your choice of fabric for cushions can add drama and variety to the whole room, without overwhelming it in the way that curtains or upholstery in the same fabric would. Collections of cushions have a habit of moving from one chair to another, even one room to another, changing the feeling of the home.

The size and shape of cushions should be a combination of personal preference and the proportions of the room and its furniture. Square and rectangular cushions are the most popular as well as the most versatile. Ottomans range in size from that of a footstool to something big enough to sprawl across. Scatter cushions – a luxury for some, a necessity for others – encourage nodding off. Bolsters make beds more comfortable and add a touch of luxury to sofas.

[6]

Cushion covers in matched pairs or that coordinate with the curtains are fine, but to generate contrast, you could try using one bright shade of a color that has nothing in common with anything in the room. Don't overlook 'scraps' of inherited or vintage fabric which can be used as cushion panels; even very small pieces can be sewn into a patchwork. It doesn't take much in the way of braid, piping, tassels and fringe to be effective – when it comes to trimming, less is very often more.

[7]

FORMAL CHAIRS

Seat covers for dining chairs are either nailed right over the chair frame, built up over coiled springs or built onto a drop-in seat which fits snugly within the seat rail. Drop-in seats make repairing and replacing upholstery relatively easy – if doing it yourself, you should experiment first with a pattern guide cut from cotton to make sure that you get the dimensions and fit right.

There is a vast range of choice if you are looking to buy a new set of chairs for the kitchen or dining area. Mixing and matching different chairs around a table can lend an informal mood to supper time, and will also save you money – a full set of dining chairs with carvers almost always costs more than individual chairs. In addition to furniture retailers, chairs can also be commissioned from artists, or bought from local auctions and in secondhand shops. Some furniture workshops specialize in copying antique chairs with such accuracy it's hard to spot the reproduction from the original.

[8]

Light fixtures

2

1

3

1 Track lighting for halogen spots.
2 Recessed halogen spots.
3 Halogen downlights.
4 Custom-made pendant light.
5 Wall-mounted uplight.

Select your light fixtures according to the quality of light that is suited to the task and function of the room. Although lamps offer an additional and versatile form of lighting – because they're portable – they will only deliver maximum benefit if they are used to supplement the fixed lighting, which must be planned with care from the outset, if at all possible (see pages 74-9).

Artificial lighting is used to create a number of effects, and you'll require some fixtures to provide soft, relaxing, general light, others to do a specific job – a combination of decorative and effective lighting. For instance, if the dining table is primarily a place for homework and writing checks, the bright light of a halogen fixture will provide a level of illumination that allows you to concentrate without straining your eyes. But if the table is primarily used for dining, there would be no escaping the paralyzing spell of such a fixture: the ambient glow of candlelight or wall sconces would be more evocative and appropriate.

If you walk into a room and the first thing you notice is the lighting or if you find yourself squinting at the light fixtures, the room is overlit or the bulbs are not well shielded. Layer lighting for optimum effect and maximum flexibility. Overhead pendants provide general background light. Table and floor lamps are secondary light sources used to cast pools of light and illuminate reading material. Spotlights are good for task lighting or for highlighting a painting or architectural features.

In recent years there has been a rash of 'designer' lighting. But spotlighting a jumble of contrived objects or lighting a single bowl in the center of a table will only ever be as interesting as what it is illuminating. This sort of lighting can appear melodramatic and tends to make furnishings look static; it often creates too severe a distraction from the overall feel of a room. Picture lights work in areas such as a hallway, where you want to highlight family photographs or to wash the walls to display a collection of art.

When choosing wall sconces and table lamps to flank the sofa, most people choose pairs, but mismatched light fixtures offer the charm of imperfection. Taking a more individualized approach to light fixtures assumes that they can be as varied as the people who meet their gaze. However, too much witty ingenuity can be uncomfortable.

QUALITY OF LIGHT

Different lightbulbs create varying qualities of light, and this will have a direct effect on how a room looks, particularly at nighttime, changing the colors of curtain fabrics, upholstery and wall finishes.

Incandecsent bulbs are still the most commonly used, generally with screw-in or bayonet attachments. The incandecsent filament glows a warm, yellow color, its intensity dependent on the wattage. The bulbs have a shorter lifespan and are more expensive than florescent tubes, but they emit a far more flattering quality of light. They are most often used in table lamps and hanging fixtures. Some bulbs are silvered across their top to reflect light back to the fixtures, reducing glare.

Halogen bulbs provide a clear, white light that has the least perceptible effect on color. They are, in fact, a combination of halogen gas and an incandecsent filament. Standard halogen fixtures provide focused, controllable light thanks to built-in reflectors. They generate a specific wash of light or a spot of light which, because of the strength of the bulb, is often used to good effect in uplights, since the light bounces off the wall or ceiling and reflects back into the room.

Low-voltage halogen fittings were originally developed for commercial use and can be recessed or mounted on tracks in a domestic context. The main attractions of low-voltage halogen are the pristine quality of light it creates combined with the tiny scale of the fixtures themselves. But the sparkling quality that attracts consumers in off the street and into a lively retail shop can be glaring and harsh in the home. Installing these low-voltage lights in a domestic situation should be planned with care. To reduce the glare of low-voltage fixtures, set bulbs back into the fitting or use a baffle or honeycomb grille to shield the light.

Florescent bulbs have a long life, low-energy use and usually a tubular shape. They are used in boxed fixtures that diffuse light over a large area, but they cast an unpleasantly artificial green tinge. Florescent light fixtures are available in handsome, pleasing designs. They are excellent for shadowless general lighting.

New compact florescent lamps (CFLs) are thin, energy-saving $^3/_8$in (10mm) tubes folded into a cluster. They are used in place of traditional incandecsent bulbs, and last considerably longer (though they cost more). CFLs distribute light slightly less evenly than incandecsent or halogen and cannot be fitted to dimmers. Today's florescents are available in warm, flattering white light, similar in color to incandecsent.

OVERHEAD LIGHTS

Overhead lights create an illusion of greater space and provide good general lighting. However, the problem with all overhead fixtures is how to control glare. Too much overhead lighting is distracting, and banishes shadow and contrast. Fitting overhead lights to a dimmer switch greatly increases their potential, while the glare can be reduced according to the type of shade. Overhead lighting is good in halls, corridors and on staircases, where you need to be able to see where you're going; in rooms where you want to control the mood, pendant fixtures offer greater flexibility.

PENDANT LIGHTS

Pendant light fixtures hang down from the ceiling. Both the quality and quantity of the light produced depends on the type of bulbs and shades used. Choose fixtures wisely; it's not always flattering to have light coming down on the top of your head. Generally, light is more attractive when it is at average human height. Over a dining table, suspend the fixture about 27in (69.2cm) above the table so adults can stand in the room without being

4

blinded by eye-level bulbs; at mealtimes, it helps if the pendant is adjustable so that the light can be brought closer to the table to give a more intimate focus to the room.

A central light source from the ceiling is often used to form an axis, or boundary, between two prevailing outside sources of light. An overhead fixture with a dangling center bulb is often inherited. It is a mistake to try to organize all the illumination in a room from this central point. The down side of these fixtures is glare. Rather than trying to achieve illumination from one light source in a fixed position, vary the sources. Use centered pendant lights for atmosphere and general lighting.

If you have a ceiling rose, the lamp shade can provide a complementary focus. Translucent shades or a glass globe, for instance, scatter light. A crumpled paper cylinder is a clean, modern choice. An opaque shade enclosing the bulb is more attention-seeking. A metal shade, open top and bottom, gives good, general light over a table.

DOWNLIGHTS

Downlights do exactly as the name suggests. They are versatile and compact, surface mounted or recessed into the ceiling. Depending on the bulb and fixture, downlights create a range of effects from the narrow, focused beam of light from a low-voltage halogen bulb through to the broader, gentler wash of an incandecsent bulb.

Downlight fixtures can provide general, mood and task lighting. As with most types of light, their versatility is increased if they are attached to a dimmer switch, though this is not appropriate for task lighting. Modern fixtures are small and unobtrusive, great for rooms with low ceilings and those in which furniture is often moved around.

Recessed ceiling lights are completely anonymous. Recessed compact florescents are energy efficient and the quality of light is a more comfortable color than that of standard florescents. Recessed light fixtures are installed by cutting a hole in the ceiling and connecting wiring as for a simple pendant fixture. Recessed lighting cannot be used if you live in a flat or in a condo with other dwellings above. Low-voltage fixtures need a transformer, which is built into the fixture; installation of the transformer requires the services of a qualified electrician.

Track lighting allows you to position fixtures anywhere along the track, and to move them as you require. However, this versatility has to be offset against the rather lumpen appearance of many track systems. Low-energy halogen tracking is sleek and modern.

UPLIGHTS

With an uplight, the ceiling acts as a reflector. Light bounces off it and scatters in such a way that shadow and glare are totally reduced. Other advantages are that uplights are inexpensive and don't require an electrician to install them. As fixtures, uplights are less casual than either downlights or lamps. The shape of the shade or fitting — from directional cones to half-round wall dishes — will have an effect on the area illuminated and the intensity of

5

the light, though this will also, of course, be affected by the type of bulb used. You can't work in uplighting, but it provides good general background illumination. Since uplights flood a ceiling with light, they make the most of plaster moldings and ceiling cornices, but will magnify any unattractive faults. Used lower down a wall, uplights can be used to cast dramatic shadows behind plants or large freestanding decorative objects.

DIMMERS

Dimmer switches offer maximum flexibility and control of light. Turned low, they can create a romantic, soft glow; turned high, a cool bright light is achieved. As well as being wired to overhead and pendant lights, dimmers can also be wired to the electrical circuit for lamps. However, be wary of going overboard. If you are one of those people seldom likely to use a dimmer in anything except the high position and off, skip the added electrical expense.

LIGHT-BULBS

Incandescent

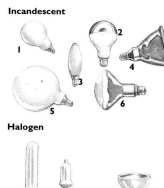

Halogen

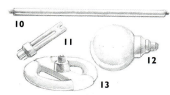

Florescent

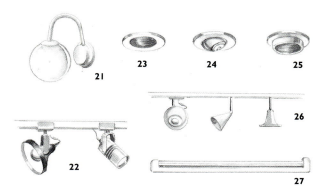

LIGHT-BULBS
(1) Standard incandecsent filament.
(2) Crown-silvered incandecsent reflector.
(3) Incandecsent candle.
(4) Parabolic aluminized reflector.
(5) Incandecsent globe.
(6) Spotlight reflector.
(7) & (8) Standard-voltage halogen.
(9) Low-voltage halogen reflector.
10. Standard florescent tube.
(11), (12) & (13) Low-energy compact florescents.

LIGHT FIXTURES
(14) Ceiling-mounted globe.
(15) Garden spotlights.
(16) Wall uplight.
(17) & (18) Pendants.
(19) Spotlight with clamp-on fitting.
(20) Picture light.
(21) Wall light.
(22) Track-mounted spotlights.
(23) Recessed downlight.
(24) 'Eyeball' downlight.
(25) Semi-recessed downlight.
(26) Low-voltage track downlights.
(27) Striplight.

LIGHT FIXTURES

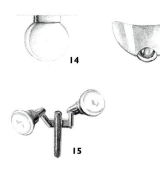

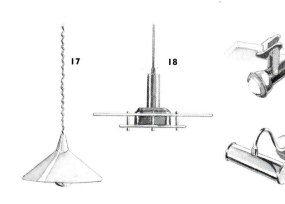

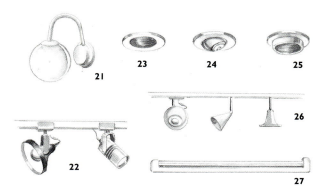

Lamps

■ **1** Anglepoise.
■ **2** Sconce with candle bulb.
■ **3** Clamp-on desk lamp.
■ **4** Paper-shaded table lamp.
■ **5** Table lamp with halogen bulb.

■ **2**

Table and floor lamps are used either for task lighting or for local illumination. Consider the function of the lamp and its shape, color and impact on a room. Does the lamp have to be very powerful, pushing light up toward the ceiling, or do you want something soft and warm for low, ambient background light? Other criteria to consider include the quality of light (and so choice of bulb), maintenance, how long you want the lamp to last and how much energy it uses.

Floor lamps can be used for general light or to light up corners of rooms; table lamps shed localized light for reading, sewing and other close work – as long as they have an appropriate shade. Many modern floor lamps, particularly those using halogen bulbs, have adjustable heads, so that they can be used for general uplighting but, when necessary, the head can be swiveled around to point downward and provide task lighting for reading by. The traditional standard lamp remains an invaluable piece in the lighting

LAMPS
(1) & (2) Table lamps.
(3) & (4) Desk lamps.
(5) Standard lamp.
(6) Pole-mounted spotlights.
(7) & (8) Floor uplights.

equation, though their siting should be carefully considered to avoid trailing wires and awkward paths through a room.

Table lamps often function as a decorative focus of the room, though this shouldn't necessarily equate with lamp shades coordinated with the soft furnishings. Over the century, the design of table lamps has changed dramatically, though the major styles all still have their advocates: from the Art Nouveau look of a Tiffany (or reproduction) lamp through plastic

■ **3**

lamps of the '50s and '60s to the sculptural pieces of Philippe Starck and numerous Italian designers. If the choice seems overwhelming, you can soon narrow it down by considering the context in which you'll place the lamp – what looks cool and modern in a study or home office may appear harsh and confrontational in the bedroom or living room.

It generally makes practical sense to distinguish between table lamps and desk lamps. The former are primarily decorative 'tools' providing general ambient light, whereas the latter offer specific task lighting. The design history of the desk lamp is a lesson in the dictate that 'form follows function', epitomized by the classic cantilevered Anglepoise. Modern updates of the Anglepoise take advantage of the sharper light made available by halogen bulbs.

If you want lamps to add a subtle but rich warmth, those with bases of textural porcelain and terra cotta make good choices. The shape, size and color of bases for table lamps offer many choices: color will largely

be determined by the scheme of a room; shape and size should reflect the proportions of the room and the location of the lamp in it. Clear- and colored-glass bases sparkle and refract the light that pours down from the bulb. Small lights, such as candle lamps on a mantel and lamps tucked into bookcases, instil mystery and charm. Commercial studio lamps and pharmacy-style floor lamps are practical and barely make their presence known.

LAMPSHADES
The shade acts as a form of control. It either allows light through, in which case it acts as a diffuser, or it is opaque and allows light out through the top and in a distinct pool below. Lampshades need to look good whether the light is on or off. A shade colors the quality of light. When lit from behind, a shade shouldn't appear too textured or take on a garish tone.

Hold a swatch of your chosen lampshade material a few inches in front of a bare, lit bulb to gain a fairly accurate idea of the effect it will have on the light. Look for fabrics or materials with 'give' in them so that they can be stretched around the frame. Anything that isn't too stiff, thick or bulky is suitable. Fine-textured linen, thin cotton and silk are good choices.

Lining a shade with gold warms up the light and gives it a rich glow. A pale-blue lining slightly cools the color of the light; a pink or peach lining warms it. Lining the inside of a shade with flesh-colored silk gives the room a flattering peachy glow, which works well in a bedroom.

■ **4**

Well-suited lamps and shades are comparable in style, shape, size and type of hardware fixtures, all subject to personal taste. A rough principle is that the bottom diameter of the shade should be equal to the height of the lamp base. This varies according to the shape of the lamp. If a lamp base tapers or is tall and skinny with a bulbous bottom, alter the shade to suit. The look of the room as a whole is almost more important than the lamp base when choosing a shade.

■ **5**

Generally, the more formal the lamp, the richer the shade material should be. Brass can take card shades as well as silk. Silk and fine linen are good choices for ormolu and porcelain bases. Textural materials such as parchment, raffia, pierced metal and Indian cotton work well with simple and modern lamp bases.

Shades usually follow the geometry and shape of the lamp base. Rounded lamps are best suited to rounded shades, oval lamps to oval shades, square or rectangular lamps to paneled shades. A shade must also be wide enough to allow the bulb at least 1in (25mm) of space all around; 2-3in (50–75mm) for bulbs of 100 watts and above. In principle, a lampshade should be long enough to cover the electrical fixtures and stop just above the lamp base when viewed at eye-level; lower for lamps made from Chinese vases whose long skinny necks demand greater coverage. Narrow, tapered shades work nicely as candle shades, since candles or flame-shaped bulbs fit easily inside.

Rugs

There is a lot of snobbery associated with buying rugs and it is not always justified. Antique kilims and specially commissioned designs can cost a fortune, but perfectly acceptable – and cheaper – alternatives can still deliver the desired effect. As a rule, rugs bought to coordinate with the decor work less well than rugs treated as a piece of art on the floor.

A rug can be as nonchalant as a white T-shirt, used simply for warmth underfoot, a place where sleepy cats curl up and friends sprawl. Rugs can be used in combination with other flooring materials, or as one large cloak for the floor. Runners take the chill off a flagstone floor and highlight the foot of a staircase or make a hallway more welcoming. A rug can assume a central role in your design motif without overwhelming the room. Sunroom and basement floors, susceptible to moisture, benefit from rugs which can be taken up and aired from time to time. Another point in their favor is that you can take rugs with you when you move.

Natural floorcoverings – such as sisal and jute – and carpets sometimes look better if they are loose laid, made up into mats and runners. Linen and cotton pile are almost unaffordable fitted wall-to-wall but become more attainable scaled down.

Rugs represent amazingly good value for money. The cost of a hand-knitted, hand-sheared, hand-dyed carpet that will provide a lifetime of pleasure can approach the price of a designer suit or a new car. If you can't afford the perfect kilim or Oriental now, consider taking inexpensive coir and binding it yourself. Rather than settling for a reproduction with less integrity than an antique, choose from the wide range of modern possibilities, not the least of which are contemporary rugs that are an artisan's free expression.

If the rug is going to be laid over bare floorboards you should include a layer of underlay for protection. It's important that a rug should lie flat on the floor, not only so that it looks good, but to prevent people tripping. Lightweight rugs and any rugs placed on a slippery floor surface should be lightly secured in place.

TYPES OF RUGS

Bokhara or Turkoman These rugs have small, repeating geometric designs and are normally fine quality. The elephant foot and octagonal 'gul' motifs tend to look best in smaller sizes that make the most of the intricate pattern. Not the hardest wearing, they are recommended more for decorative use than high-traffic areas. Woven in areas of Turkmenistan, Uzbekistan, Kazakhstan, Afghanistan and Pakistan, the Russian examples tend to generate the most interest in investment circles.

Caucasian With their distinctive bright colors, stylized childlike figures and elaborately decorated borders, Caucasian carpets are appealing and simple. They work well in both traditional and contemporary settings and are flexible enough for new or old homes. The simplicity of their patterns makes them easy to work with, although they are only available as scatter rugs: it is rare to find an example over 6x9ft (2×3m). The opening up of eastern Europe has made available some exciting Caucasian kilims.

Dhurry This is the Indian word for flatweave (the Persian word is kilim). Inexpensive, reversible, casual and easy to live with, dhurries are available in a wide range of sizes and colors, as well as in a stonewashed finish. Made of handwoven cotton, they are not advisable as heat-insulators in winter. Although made of cotton and therefore washable, strong colors are likely to run if put through a washing machine; gentle handwashing should minimize the risk of the rug shrinking.

Flokati Made in Greece, these are heavy, shaggy wool rugs in white or off-white with very long pile. The shag tends to matt down.

Kilim This is a tapestry rug woven from fairly harsh, thick wool. The artistry is high compared to the price and there is a fantastic variety of designs. The best pieces are often in long, narrow strips rather than room sizes. As a flatweave they are arguably not as practical as some other rugs and have a tendency to pucker up. They are made by

nomadic peoples in Turkey, Iran, Iraq, Russia, China, Pakistan, India and Morocco. Kilims were originally intended as a pliable warm carpet that could be placed on a sandy desert floor and easily packed on a camel or horse. Kilim designs represent different tribes and regions. Kurdish versions are brighter, sometimes mixed with embroidery, and generally cheaper. Turkish kilims feature Mediterranean colors of gold, orange and turquoise. Iranian kilims are grounded in burgundy, rust, heavy blues and heavy greens.

Oriental Thick and rich, high in art content, often in multi-colored patterns or featuring representational designs. The typical color range includes black, soft yellow, pastel pink, peach, apricot and blue. Originally hand-woven in China, Oriental carpets are now made in Romania, Iran and India as well. They represent good value as labor costs remain low. The most expensive rugs are woven from silk, cheaper ones from wool.

Persian The main advantage with Persian rugs is that the older they get the better they look. These are high-quality carpets of knotted wool, and are not deemed to be at their best for some 30 to 40 years. There is a wide variety available, some of fine wool and others coarser. Usually rectangular in shape or made up into long runners, they come in rich colors with stylized motifs. Deep red and blue are the most popular ground colors.

Rag With a lineage back to the seventeenth century, rag rugs are pieces of fabric looped or stitched together using odds and ends. They can also be custom-made from cloth that matches the curtains or upholstery. Rag rugs wear well. Their popularity recalls Scandinavian and German folk art.

Rya High-pile rugs from Denmark and Finland with a 1960s shag effect, these are now coming back into fashion. They are available in strong colors which matt together in contemporary, abstract designs and quite often in less conventional shapes such as circles and ovals.

Serape Coarsely woven Mexican and south-west American tribal blankets, these are coarsely woven flatweaves with fringed ends. Old serapes with Navaho Indian designs are expensive and highly collectible.

Turkish The Turks have turned back the clock on the Industrial Revolution and are going back to the old ways of handspinning wool and using vegetable dyes. These are incredibly good value for hand-made rugs. Each region has its own distinct look, although religious motifs can often be discerned in the design.

1 Dhurry.
2 Kilim.
3 Persian.
4 Kilim.
5 Contemporary.

Propping art on a shelf or table also discourages objects from becoming too precious and is much less staid than permanent hanging. This frees you to buy something without the worry of where it will go. If you are hesitant about drilling holes in the wall, you can run picture rails above a mantel or along a blank wall, add a ledge, or use traditional picture molding and hang your paintings from picture hooks.

In a bland space it pays to be decisive and organize a graphic focal point. You can design your own by mixing different shapes, sizes and styles of artwork. The conventional

choosing a green painting for a green room. Whether you have one painting or a large collection, let the room grow around it. Though buying art can be an investment, it should be bought for pleasure. There's nothing wrong with living with a bare wall for a while at first. When in doubt, a mirror might provide the necessary magic. Mirrors liberate small rooms by opening up and lightening tight spaces. An interesting touch is to hang a group of mirrors in frames

ornate. A frameless mount consists of two plates – one of glass, the other a backing board – and plastic clips at the top and bottom. It is a frame designed simply to allow what is inside to be the focus.

Antique frames can artfully hang on a wall empty, or be made into mirrors. Shop at flea markets and auction houses for frames with character and replace missing border details with modeling clay and gesso. Make sure that what you place within the frame is appropriate: a humble watercolor bought on holiday will look pretentious and lose its charm hung in an elaborate frame.

crafts shops.

Shelving

Shelves fulfill two functions — they can provide a concentrated form of

Finishing touches

As life becomes more complex, we tend to demand greater simplicity at home. Finishing a room does not imply that you need to fill it with clutter, to weigh it down with frills and bows. Quietly comfortable, simple interiors soothe us and serve our needs far more than thematic set-decorating and pre-digested packages of style. Instead of agonizing over a room's contents, focus on finding a few well-chosen items that reflect your personal style and the way you live.

It helps to think of finishing touches in a broader context than just the living room. The odds and ends of everyday life offer opportunities for simple self-expression. Lining up a row of bathroom towels in bright tones of saffron yellow, navy or fuchsia makes an artful statement. The undulating lines of a ribbed-glass bowl and the symmetry of milk pitchers ranged in ascending size on a kitchen shelf have a simplicity and subtle beauty that is easy to appreciate. Pots and pans hanging close to the oven, a glass-fronted dresser packed with plates and dishes or a row of gleaming kitchen accoutrements combine aesthetic appeal with practicality.

In the living room, displays are often most effective if they take their cue from an interest or hobby. A battered microscope from your childhood, a brass music stand or an old dressmaker's mannequin can form the basis for a display. Often, the more idiosyncratic the combination of items, the better. The kiss of death is to display items

which you believe will accord you a certain status. Display doesn't mean showing off; it means sharing your true enthusiasms and passions.

Discretion is the necessary counterpart to display. This entails taking account of those ordinary but essential elements — such as wastepaper baskets, light switches and door furniture — to ensure that unlovely or poorly designed details don't strike a jarring note.

COLLECTING
Home is a natural haven for collections. There's something organic and faintly cranky about the true collection, which both defies logic and ignores market value. Most natural born collectors can't help themselves and go on acquiring the objects of their desire long after they have run out of houseroom. Teapots, antique telephones, mechanical toys, salt and pepper shakers and many more ephemeral artefacts have all inspired grand collecting passions. For most of us, collecting never quite reaches such heights of obsession. But everyone has an acquisitive streak, and displays of favorite things give life and humor to everyday surroundings. Weathered wood, shells and beach stones trawled from the sea shore, fragments of broken patterned pottery unearthed in the back yard, postcards, packaging and family photos serve no earthly purpose at all, but may be treasured for the memory of a perfect holiday, the thrill of discovery or the simple attraction of color, graphics or form. There are no rules for this instinctive impulse, only pure personal pleasure, but you can heighten what you display by contriving groups that have some sort of an element in common, whether it's color, shape or provenance.

OCCASIONAL TABLES
In the 1920s the occasional table became part of domestic life. A low table was the hard surface next to the divan to park a cocktail glass and cigarette case. The 'coffee table' made its debut in a 1939 American furniture catalogue which pictured it as a knee-height table set out with an after-dinner coffee pot. Though sneered at by some, for most of us

the occasional table is an indispensable accessory in the living room. You want to be able to shed light on its surface with reading and table lamps and be able to put a glass down without thinking. In this respect, the height and dimensions are important points to consider. You don't want occasional tables to block important traffic routes through a room, nor do you want them to involve you in awkward maneuvers when you reach out for your cup of coffee.

One large coffee table can overly dominate a room. Scattering several small tables more or less in front of a sofa is as appealingly functional but less overbearing. Foot stools, as long as they are not over-upholstered, can make useful substitute occasional tables. Wicker tables recall more exotic climes. A straw-colored tabletop provides a neutral background on which to display lamps and objects to great effect. If you're looking for something a little

different from the central coffee table, antique trunks and blanket boxes can be put into service, and at the same time provide you with an additional source of storage.

SCREENS
A screen allows you to dispense with doors but still defines the boundaries of space. Screens can be covered in fabric, wallpaper, postcards, greeting cards, or sketches, padded with one luxurious piece of material or pieced together patchwork fashion from scraps of fabric, and trimmed with tapes, gingham or rope.

You can use a screen to close off a section, hide things behind, create a sleeping alcove or eating area. A screen can be pieces of MDF or particleboard hinged together, fabric stretched over padded panels, or wallpaper glued to plywood boards. Frames of glass and glass windows hinged together form a barrier that you can see beyond. Brass mesh and aluminum screens likewise divide off rooms. In lieu of closet doors, hemstitched linen curtains or sandblasted glass screen panels make sensible partitions.

HANDLES AND CATCHES
Novel door pulls, handles and hinges are easy upgrades. They are a fast and affordable way to bring change to even the humblest surface. Hardware can counteract the negative characteristics and age of a house, door or piece of furniture.

Traditionally a cupboard had a crystal knob, a door to a dining or living room had a bronze or brass knob, and front doors a lever or big pull. Hardware made from inexpensive resin and cast aluminum or from bits of nature furnish dull and tired doors and cupboards with spirit and renewed vigour.

An old chest of drawers can be spruced up with with a new set of pulls or handles that are simply attached with the turn of a screw. Choices include bronze stars and flowers, twigs gathered on a camping trip and seashells. You can match the door handle with the function of a room — open the bathroom door with a fish or scallop, a door to a child's room with plastic dinosaurs. Pulls need not match; designers often

1 Vase of flowers.
2 Bathroom accessories.
3 A themed display.
4 Occasional tables.
5 Folding screen.
6 Door catch and hinges.
7 Door knocker.

4

6

7

5

mount complementary but not identical hardware on bureau drawers and upper and lower closets, an attention to detail that lifts a room without making a dramatic statement.

As a rule, it is advisable to relate door hardware to the shell of the space rather than the furnishings. Silent unseen catches and bare doors that spring open at a touch are modern. Nothing jars or intrudes in the open space, not even handles.

Old door accessories don't cost more than new, you just need to have the determination to find them. Shop in salvage yards and flea markets for old hammered and hand-forged wrought-iron and brasswork hinges, eighteenth-century strap hinges and rat-tail hinges.

The way a door knob opens is important. Hinges should enable a door to swing nicely and operate soundlessly; door pulls and handles should be tactile and easy to turn. If a wood door pull twists, it is inadequately fixed and will probably snap off. Wood hardware should be both glued and screwed in place. Bolt-fix ceramic knobs from the back. Good porcelain knobs should have a plastic or rubber washer separating the porcelain collar from the pull; two pieces of porcelain rubbing against each other will set up high stress and the back plate will eventually crack.

If left matt, brass must be polished or moisture in the air and on your hands will tarnish it. Handles and pulls of solid brass are undentable.

Hollow brass hardware rings less true and if one handle bangs into another from doors opening back to back, they are liable to bruise.

Stainless steel and iron hardware is trouble-free. Black iron tends to be made in foundries and stainless steel in engineering factories. The most appropriate door handles from the perspective of multi-generational design have generous oversize grips that are easy for the arthritic and older children to grasp.

FLOWERS

Flowers are the quintessential finishing touch, at home in every location. They bring color, life and the invigorating dimension of scent to a room, reflecting the changing seasons and providing a potent reminder of the natural world. If you have a garden, potted plants and cut flowers are a way of merging outdoors with in; if you live in a city, flowers offer a breath of country air.

You can pick up a dominant color in a decorative scheme by choosing flowers in the same shade, or inject a note of bold contrast. In spare, minimal rooms, the sculptural forms of contorted twigs and branches have a Zen-like quality. Formal florist's arrangements always look stiff and contrived; a generous mass of simple garden flowers in a plain vase has a natural appeal which is hard to better.

Keeping your home supplied with fresh flowers need not involve horrendous expense. Flowers which are currently in season tend to be cheaper than more exotic specimens or those brought on early in hot house conditions. If you have a

garden, you can grow flowers specifically for cutting and bringing indoors, and supplement the blooms with foliage, twigs, blossom or berries. In winter months, when there are few flowers, seasonal arrangements of evergreen, seedpods, dried leaves and bright berries more than compensate.

There are endless variations for the creative. Single blooms in test-tube containers, bright flowerheads floating in a low glass dish as a table centerpiece, cherful flowers spilling

out of an old watering can make witty displays that owe as much to the choice of container as the selection of flowers. You can also arrange flowers in old jars filled with water and conceal the jars inside containers – such as baskets – which aren't strictly waterproof.

As with any decorative arrangement, size and massing create impact. A number of small vases of flowers dotted around the room have a fraction of the interest provided by one sumptuous display in a key location.

As the lure of the sunroom testifies, houseplants also look best grouped together, which tends to make practical sense, since there are generally only a number of places in the home which provide the right growing conditions. Pots of herbs ranged on a sunny windowsill make an indoor kitchen garden; ferns thrive in steamy bathroom atmospheres. Indulge in several specimens of your favorite variety for maximum impact; a scattering of different species lacks coherence.

Over the last **30** years the incredible popularity of do-it-yourself as a disparate set of craft skills practised in millions of homes has also created a worrying trend to alter, remodel and 'improve' just for the sake of it, or to hone newly acquired talents. No matter how non-materialistic you believe yourself to be, a house or an apartment is a working machine. Like a car, it needs regular maintenance and fuel, but if it is going well, leave it alone. If you don't, you can easily upset the fine balance which often exists between working order and breakdown. You'll also create problems which tend to have punitively expensive remedies, reflecting the professionals' dislike for sorting out an amateur's badly finished work.

A roof-top whirlpool tub, a loft addition, yes, of course you can do them yourself, and very well too. But not before fixing the leak in the roof or, more importantly, taking precautions against it leaking in the first place. Almost everything in this section is achievable, and achievable without breaking your neck, your budget or creating such domestic chaos that even the cat leaves home.

However, nothing is for nothing. Time, even your own do-it-yourself time, is money which might be better spent. Usually, the only commodity you have to offer is time, but this is a judgment only you can honestly make. So don't fall into the easy trap of starting off with the enthusiasm to do everything yourself unless you're quite sure you have the necessary skills. Most importantly, ensure you really want to do the work. That way you'll become interested, involved and enjoy the experience. If you approach a project with fear and loathing, it's doomed before you even start.

Making your home both a place that reflects your own sense of style and one in which potentially hazardous situations are minimized is largely a matter of common sense. Here, the brake at the foot of the ladder secures it firmly to the floor.

1

1 **Many accidents in the home involve children in kitchens. By keeping countertops as clear of clutter as possible, you will be able to prepare food more efficiently while minimizing the chances of accidents.**
2 **Stairways are a potential hazard, particularly for the young, old and infirm. Make sure halls and staircases are well lit, and that there is a banister or safety rail along the stairs to hold on to.**

2

Planning and maintaining a schedule for a job is difficult; unexpected problems occur, and these cause depressing delays. Installing a new window frame, for example, can reveal dry rot which has to be totally eradicated before the original project can proceed. So you'll have to live with a large hole in the wall covered with a piece of plastic sheeting until that's done. But, more positively, you will have diagnosed, investigated and cured a serious fault which might have been plastered over in the past. As a general rule, don't start anything on a Saturday that you cannot finish by early on Sunday night. For on Monday morning, another life awaits.

Be organized, make work lists, prioritize jobs and order materials in time. If you like to write things down, keep a daily diary of work, note peculiar lessons learnt, problems encountered, mistakes made or shortcuts discovered. All this information could be valuable in the future. In the rush of things, it's simple to forget which bare wood has been primed, and which has been undercoated. Both look similar, so you could waste time doing the job again to be sure. If you feel you're confronting the impossible, be convinced that there is almost always an easier way of doing things if you sit down with a cup of coffee and spend a pleasant half hour or so thinking about the problem in hand.

Take care of yourself and make time to be safe. Dress properly, in overalls or whatever is comfortable and practical. Jeans, open-neck shirts and sneakers may look fetching in the ads but they're scant protection in a dusty and potentially dangerous situation.

Wear work gloves and goggles whenever you can; use masks and earmuffs in dusty and noisy situations even if they seem inconvenient, or even irrelevant.

You may feel too embarrassed to wear a hardhat in your own home until a piece of wood, a length of pipe, or lump of masonry falls on your head. If you see a rusty nail poking out of a wall,

stop and take it out at once. Read up on basic first aid and know where the first-aid box is kept.

Safety precautions are mainly a matter of common sense, but there are a few which apply to most do-it-yourself jobs. Don't work with tools or climb ladders when you're tired. Make sure anything you're working on is absolutely secure. Never overreach when you're up a ladder – climb down and move it along.

Carefully read all instructions for tools, chemicals and so on well before you use them, and file for future reference. Lock up all tools and chemicals well out of the reach of children.

You can't do anything well without good tools. Doing it yourself should save you enough money to be able to afford to buy the best tool dedicated for a particular task, whether it's cutting, smoothing, or drilling. Renting tools is expensive and time consuming unless you're certain you'll never need one like it again, or the purchase price is more than you can afford.

Avoid becoming a collector of gadgets. Outside the mail-order catalogs there is no such thing as the all-purpose tool. The accuracy of a power tool that is dedicated to a specific job can help compensate for lack of skill. But remember that all tools, even the innocent screwdriver, are potentially dangerous if they are abused or misused. Read and understand the instructions and practise using the tool in a relaxed but alert manner.

Few aphorisms are more profound than 'Measure twice times, cut once'. Accurate measuring and marking out is vital otherwise things just won't fit. The retractable pocket measuring tape can take measurements up to about 16ft (5m) and it can be locked at any dimension. Try and get hold of one with a tape as wide as $\frac{5}{8}$in (16mm) which makes it rigid over long lengths. (Consider the advantages of this when there is no one else available to hold the other end tight against a wall for you.)

4

3

3 A purpose-built tool shed offers ideal storage space for woodworking equipment, garden furniture, lawn-mowers and the like.
4 If you are an enthusiastic handyman it makes sense to take good care of your tools. A tool cupboard provides dedicated space for each item, encouraging you to put equipment back after use, and ensuring that pieces do not become damaged or prematurely worn because of carelessness. Make sure the tool cupboard has a lock on it, and that it is out of the reach of children.
5 The attractions of an open fire have to be offset against the potential hazards. A fire guard prevents burning fuel falling from the fire onto the floor, while the adjacent cubby hole here allows coals or logs to be stored discreetly nearby.

A good 24in (60cm) carpenter's level is also a vital purchase; it will ensure that things are properly horizontal or vertical. So too is the versatile, all-steel combination square. This provides a 90° angle, a 45° angle (for miters) and a lockable sliding blade of up to 12in (30cm) which is invaluable as a depth gauge for marking out and accurately repeating or transferring measurements. Get one with the measurement markings clearly etched into the blade. On cheap squares they're lightly printed and quickly rub off.

There always seems to be a mass of things to buy, even before you begin a project. You can't have everything in stock, but you will always need a good supply of one of the most basic components – screws. These are most economically bought in boxes of 100 or 200 from mail-order distributors who generally give a discount for large orders. Going out and buying screws as you need them is both expensive and time consuming.

Much home remodeling involves lifting heavy things; a bag of cement will seem rooted to the ground. Keep your back straight and use your knees to power the lifting. If you are unfit and overweight, don't even attempt to do it!

Take extreme care with demolition work; do not tamper with structural things such as chimneys breasts, tie beams or trusses – call in professionals.

5

Home safety

FIRE SAFETY

Fires don't just happen to other people. Carelessness with matches, deep fryers, open fires and discarded cigarettes all contribute to fatal infernos.

- Many fires happen at night. If you smell smoke, you may have only a few seconds to escape.
- Forget about valuables, wake everyone, and if you quickly establish where the fire is, close the door to that area. Keep all doors shut – they inhibit the spread of fire through the rest of the building.
- Get out fast and get neighbors to call the fire service.
- If the stairs are blocked, go to a bedroom, close the door and seal around it with bedding or clothes. Only then open the window and call for help.
- Jump out of an upper-floor window only as a last resort, and reduce the drop by lowering yourself feet first from the sill.
- Security keys for window locks should be stored close to a window, but not on the frame itself.
- Practise an emergency fire-drill but, above all, try not to panic.
- Remember how to deal with particular fires. Fires in deep fryers and frying pans erupt without warning. Never throw water on them or use a fire extinguisher. Don't attempt to move the pan. If you can reach the cooktop controls, turn them off. Cover the pan with its lid, a damp towel or chopping board. Better still, always have a fire blanket ready in the kitchen. Leave it over the pan for at least 30 minutes, or the fire could reignite.
- Smoke and fumes from blazing polyurethane foam-filled furniture kill, and although the manufacture and sale of untreated foam filling is now prohibited, any older furniture should be treated with a special flame-retardant spray, which offers some protection. If the furniture does catch fire, get out of the room, close the door and dial 911.

- Only use an extinguisher on electrical fixtures or appliances after unplugging them, or switching off power at the fuse-box. Never use water on televisions or computers.
- Cut off power and cover electrical appliances with a fire blanket or damp coat or blanket.
- Remember that, even in a smoke-filled room, the 2-3in (50-75mm) of space above the floor will be clear.
- Flank cooking areas with a noncombustible countertop material.

PREVENTION

- Install smoke alarms in rooms where there is a fire hazard – except for bathrooms and kitchens where steam from hot water or smoke from cooking may trigger them off accidentally. Even a small house should have a minimum of two alarms – one at the bottom of the stairs, the other on the landing. It is important to test smoke alarms regularly and replace the batteries every year.
- If you have secondary glazing, or security grills, ensure that all windows will open in an emergency.
- A fire blanket for the kitchen is a necessity; most other domestic extinguishers, because of their size, can only deal with small fires. As there are different types for different fires, it would be unfeasible to invest in them all unless you live some way from a fire station; make sure you know how to use them and have them checked and serviced regularly.
- Water extinguishers are only effective on common materials such as wood or cloth, and must not be used on flaming liquids or on electrical fires. Foam and dry-powder extinguishers are for liquids like fats, oils and spirits and are very messy.
- Carbon dioxide, BCF or Halon extinguishers deal with electrical fires. They need to be used with great care as they smother fires with gases which are toxic or an asphyxiant.

- Don't store combustible materials such as paints in the house, never leave deep fryers unattended or dry clothes in front of an open fire or electric heater. You'll also be safer, and healthier, if you stop smoking.

GAS SAFETY

- Even a small gas leak can produce a large amount of highly inflammable vapor which could cause a fire or explosion. If you smell gas in the home, turn off the mains gas tap near the meter, open all doors and windows, turn off all naked lights and electric fires. Do not operate any other switches and do not smoke.
- If you cannot detect an obvious cause, such as extinguished pilot-lights on the central-heating boiler or cooktop controls left on but unlit, call the gas board.
- LPG – liquefied petroleum gas – is in popular use. Accidents happen when it leaks from cylinders or cartridges when they are being changed or connected to appliances. This must be done in the open air. Never smoke or have a naked flame near an LPG cylinder that is being changed. Check all hoses and connections regularly; leaks can be detected by applying a soapy water solution around the suspect area. It will bubble around any gas leak. Store spare cylinders upright, outside the house but locked away securely.
- Only buy appliances that are approved by the gas regulating body.
- All installations and, vitally, regular annual servicing should be carried out by the local gas utility company.
- The servicing should also include safety checks on ventilation, which means having efficient trickle ventilators above windows and a ventilation brick in an outside wall. Only appliances such as gas boilers with balanced flues, which take their air supply from the outside, are exempt from this strict safety rule.

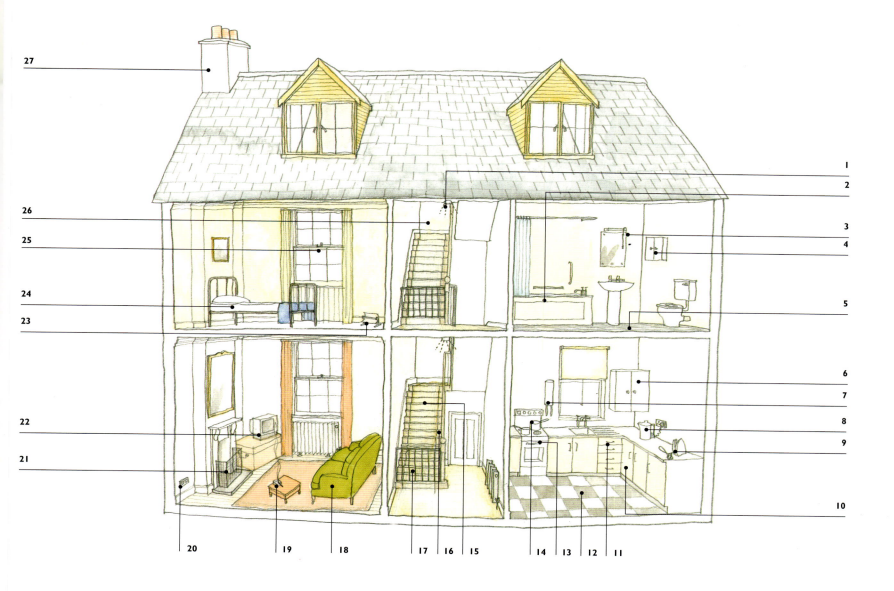

27

26
25

24
23

22
21

20   19   18   17 16 15   14 13 12 11

1
2

3
4

5

6
7
8
9

10

1 Fit at least one smoke alarm on each floor: they will give you vital minutes to escape, are cheap, and are easy to install. Check the batteries routinely, and change them annually.
2 The bathtub should have a nonslip base. Additional hand grips are a good idea.
3 Pull-cord light switches are essential in the bathroom. Electrical equipment in the bathroom is potentially very dangerous.

4 Keep medicines out of children's reach. Fit a secure lock on the bathroom cabinet.
5 Fit a non-slip flooring material.
6 Store household cleaners out of the reach of children.
7 Keep a fire blanket near the stove and burners.
8 Never let electrical cords trail across a sink or stove top.
9 Turn off the iron immediately after use, and put it somewhere safe to cool down.

10 Fit safety catches on low-level cabinets that contain potentially dangerous equipment.
11 Keep sharp knives in a drawer or knife rack, out of the reach of children.
12 Wipe up any spills straight away.
13 Ideally, keep small children away from the cooking area.
14 Always keep saucepan handles pointing inwards; and never leave frying pans or deep fryers unattended.

15 Keep the stairs clear of mess and in good condition.
16 Make sure there is a firmly fixed banister or safety rail.
17 If you have young children, fit safety gates at both the top and bottom of the staircase.
18 Fabrics and furnishings should be fire-resistant; make sure they are retreated after washing.
19 Extinguish cigarettes properly; better still, stop smoking.

20 Fit safety covers over low-level outlets if you have small children, and never overload individual outlets.
21 All fires and heaters should have a safety guard; check open fires are safe before leaving the house or going to bed.
22 Switch off electrical appliances after use; safer still, unplug them from the mains supply, particularly at night or before going on vacation.

23 Portable fires and heaters should be kept away from furniture, bedding and curtains; never dry clothes near or over them, and switch them off and unplug from the mains before going out or going to bed.
24 If you have an electric blanket, follow the manufacturer's instructions precisely.
25 Fit safety catches or locks on windows, but make sure they can be opened quickly in an emergency.

26 Stairs should be well lit; artificial lighting on staircases should be operable from both upstairs and downstairs with two-way switches.
27 If you have an open fire, keep the chimney regularly swept.

ELECTRICAL SAFETY

Have your system professionally checked over at least every five years; systems that have been in place for 20–25 years will probably need replacing. Many people are put off electrical work because they imagine it to be a complicated and potentially dangerous business. It is relatively straightforward; much of the work involves lifting floorboards and carefully routing wiring. It's perfectly safe, interesting and productive as long as you are careful and thoroughly understand what to do. However, in some countries – such as Australia – it is illegal for anyone except a qualified electrician to undertake electrical work.

- Always switch off at the mains before starting work and never, under any circumstances, assume that any wire or electrical part which you are about to work on is dead.
- If you feel you are getting out of your depth, stop straight away and call in a qualified electrician.
- Never make temporary repairs. Always have the installation tested before connecting it if you haven't got proper test equipment yourself.
- Provided you test and re-test every bit of wiring and every component before working on it, you'll be safe.
- Simple tests on fixed house wiring are easy with an electrical tester. You can, for example, check that a new circuit or circuit extension is wired up correctly. But testers are no substitute for a proper inspection and test carried out by an electrical contractor. For instance, you would not be able to prove that an installation has an adequate earth, nor that the modern residual current safety devices are operating correctly.
- There are several good mains testers available. They all come with clear instructions and have two properly insulated probes, a needle indicator and/or lights, as well as an AC setting; they are capable of handling voltage up to 240V. The best are called multimeters which can be used for continuity and mains voltage testing. Don't confuse these with a test screwdriver which has a neon light inside the handle. Even so, test the tester before starting work. Touch it on a fitting you know to be live.
- Few householders have any idea how healthy their electrical installation is and consequently are unaware of trouble until it happens. Fuses blow for a reason. It's conceivable that this could be old age, but more likely that there is a fault in the circuit which the fuse protects. So don't, as many people do, just mend the fuse, or switch the miniature circuit-breaker back on and hope for the best.
- All electrical appliances should be used in strict accordance with the manufacturer's instructions. Never overload individual outlets, and make sure that power tools are properly insulated with heavy-duty waterproof cables. Pay particular attention to the use of electrical appliances in the bathroom, where there is greatest risk of an electric shock.

CHECKING THE SYSTEM

You can run a simple check of your electrical system. Start at the consumer unit or, in older installations, the fuse-box. Turn off the power at the main switch, and with a flashlight make sure the unit is securely mounted on its fire-resistant board and that the casing is undamaged. Look at the cables running in and out of it. The sheathing should go right into the unit. If you find rubber, or even older lead-sheathed cables, they should be replaced as soon as possible.

With the power still off, open up the unit and look for any cracks or signs of overheating. Remove any of the older, rewirable fuses, one by one, and look out for signs of damage or charring. Check rewirable fuses for wire of the right rating – simply compare this with new fuse wire – and ensure that the wire is securely held by the terminal screws but is slightly slack in the holder; taut wire burns out earlier.

A dangerously out-of-date wiring system will include separate fuse-boxes for individual circuits, rewirable circuit fuses, rubber-sheathed cable, socket outlets with round holes, light switches mounted on wooden blocks, no earth continuity tester on lighting circuits and no protection against current leaking to earth. If your system has any or all of these features, it is time your house was completely rewired, and you should call in a licensed electrician.

DEALING WITH ELECTRIC SHOCK

As long as you treat it with due sense and respect, electricity is relatively safe. Modern appliances are stringently monitored and are properly earthed, but shocks do occur, particularly when the hazardous combination of electricity and water is present. Electricity and water make dangerous partners. To ensure electrical safety – especially in rooms such as the kitchen and bathroom – you should take the precaution of installing a ground fault circuit interruptor (GFCI). GFCIs do not erradicate all possibility of an electric shock, but they will prevent it being fatal.

- If someone gets an electric shock, turn off the current by removing the plug or switching it off at the consumer unit. If you can't do this, don't touch the person – the current may pass through to you. Instead pull the victim free with a dry towel, rope or something similar. If you can, knock them free of the electrical source with a piece of wood; as a last resort use their loose clothing to pull them free.
- People who have fallen badly may have sustained other injuries; wrap them in a blanket or coat to keep them warm and seek medical advice.
- Electrical burns should be treated similarly to other burns. Reduce the heat of the injury under cold running water and seek medical advice.

FLOODS

The most serious flooding occurs when a water main bursts or a river bursts its banks. On a domestic level, however, flooding is far more commonly the result of human oversight or mechanical error – an overflowing bathtub, defective overflow pipe or a leaking washing machine or dishwasher. You can take precautions if you live somewhere where natural flooding is a known hazard. Common sense and regular maintenance will help guard your home from small-scale flooding.

- If you live in an area at risk from flooding, be prepared with strong, plastic shopping bags filled with sand or soil. These can be placed outside doors and against ventilation bricks at the bottom of the house walls. If you do have a sudden flood, the doors may quickly become too swollen to open and you may have to smash open a window to gain access.

- Flood water is often contaminated with sewage, so – once water levels have subsided – floors and walls will need scrubbing with a strong antiseptic solution.

- Turn gas and electricity supplies off and, when the flood has subsided, remove as much furniture as you can, lift carpets and other floor coverings and mop up. If the flooding has been severe, remove some of the floorboards so that the under-floor area can be pumped out using an electric submersible pump when it is safe to use power supplies.

- In less drastic flood situations, bail out and mop up as much water as possible. 'Wet and Dry' vacuum cleaners will help to dry out soaking carpets, and a dehumidifier can be hired to dry out a room. These are also invaluable for removing heavy condensation and speeding up the curing of plaster before decorating. Be careful not to use dehumidifiers too enthusiastically, however, as they could also cause severe cracking.

SAFETY FOR CHILDREN

Most parents have horror stories of near-tragedies involving children in the home. But how do you childproof a house or apartment? It's not easy second-guessing a two-year-old who can crawl or clamber into the most dangerous places and with devilish dexterity open an upstairs window and climb out on to the ledge. It sometimes happens, so it's best to be prepared.

Some of the danger zones are pretty obvious; stairs and bedroom windows seem to share a fatal attraction to young children, as do medicine cabinets and the kitchen cabinet where you store the household detergents.

- If you have a baby or toddler, it is vital to buy secure safety gates for the stairs – shop around for the type that can be opened, by adults, with one hand.

- Think about how many pieces of glass you have at child-height, not just French windows, but pieces of furniture such as glass-fronted bookcases. Shattered glass can, and does, kill and glass window- and door-panes should either be replaced with safe laminated glass or covered with special film.

- Make sure toys are age-appropriate, and throw out any that get broken. Beware of small, detachable parts that babies and small children might choke on, and ensure rattles are big enough not to become lodged in a baby's throat.

- Never put anything a child can climb onto near a window and decorate large and low panes with stickers to reemphasize their existence.

- If you're going to use painted second-hand furniture in a nursery or child's bedroom, it is safest to strip it completely and repaint it: if paint was applied before 1978, there's a chance it contains lead. Use a test kit to be sure, or contact your local health department. Paints and varnishes labeled 'non-toxic' must not contain any heavy metals.

- If you do buy second-hand items like cradles, make sure they conform to current safety standards, particularly with regard to details such as the spacing of the bars.

- When your child moves into a 'grown-up' bed, fit a safety rail on the side; the better versions form a tubular framework and have a soft mesh infill. You'll certainly need one of these if you intend putting children in bunk-beds.

- Before decorating a child's room consider whether there are enough suitably placed electrical outlets. Make sure that every outlet has a safety cover and that there is absolutely no need for trailing flexes.

- Fit guards that totally enclose heaters in a child's room, or that have a thermostatically controlled valve fitted so that you can modify the heater's temperature to a safe level.

- A three-year-old has enough strength to pull a packed bookcase over, so secure any free-standing furniture firmly to the wall.

- Fit proper safety catches to all the windows – buy locks which allow the window to open slightly for ventilation. However, make sure that all windows can be quickly unlocked in an emergency.

- The kitchen is potentially the most dangerous room in the house – even half a cupful of hot water can cause scalds. Keep all electrical appliances at the back of the countertop. You can lessen the risk of pans being overturned by habitually cooking on the back burners, well out of the reach of inquisitive children.

- Kitchen cabinets and drawers and refrigerators/freezers can be locked with a number of simple and inexpensive devices, but it's worth buying a door-slam protector to prevent tiny fingers being crushed.

- Keep sharp knives out of reach in a knife-rack out of sight or in a drawer fitted with a safety catch.

Emergency plumbing

Pipes burst when the water inside them drops below 32°F (0°C) and expands, splitting the casing. You may not know about it until the pipe thaws and the flow is re-established. If, during a cold spell, water fails to flow from a faucet or won't drain away, then freezing seems the most likely explanation.

An occupied and heated house stands little chance of suffering a burst, as long as the pipes in vulnerable places, such as under the ground-floor floorboards and in the loft, are well insulated. This is most easily done by encasing them in foamed plastic tubes. In some areas of the country prone to deep freezes – you know who you are – turning the heat off or too low if you go away can be risky. A timer on your boiler is the most reliable way to keep heat circulating.

It might be worth installing a pipe-heating system specifically geared to prevent freezing – these are usually in the form of low-wattage electrical cable wrapped around the pipes and connected to a 13-amp electrical outlet.

If you leave a house empty for a long time in winter, the only safe measure is to drain down all water lines. After first switching off the boiler, turn off the main valve on the rising main and run off the water from all hot and cold taps. If there is a drainage valve on the rising main, drain what water is left in the pipe from that point. Drain the hot-water cylinder and flush all toilets. Don't forget to re-fill the system before lighting the boiler.

The minimum you will need to undertake an emergency repair to the plumbing is a slip coupling and leak sealant, a pair of pliers, a monkey wrench, a sink plunger, penetrating oil, a junior hacksaw, a length of hosepipe with a jubilee-clip fastener (for draining), shallow containers to catch leaks in inaccessible places and a flashlight with leakproof alkaline batteries.

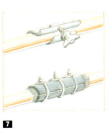

7 If a leak occurs in a pipe, you can make a temporary repair using a clamp-type repair kit (above); or improvize using a piece of hose-pipe reinforced with wire and insulating tape (below).

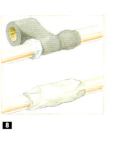

8 Where a leak occurs at a joint, you can use two-part repair tape (above): wind the first tape around the pipe; cover this with the second tape; make a third covering with the first. Alternatively, pack putty around the leak (below).

ACTION IN AN EMERGENCY

Despite the best precautions, bursts and leaks happen. Once you've mopped up the flood as best you can, get to work repairing the damage (or containing the leak until a plumber arrives). A semi-permanent repair can be made quite easily by using sealants for small leaks and clamps and couplings for bursts.

Some epoxies are two-part; you mix the contents of two tubes then apply the mixture to a clean and dry pipe. They set very hard in a day, but you can shorten this time by blowing hot air on it. Some kits also recommend you reinforce the repair with special self-adhesive PVC tapes, just to be sure.

Clamps wrap around the pipe to encase a leaking section. They are generally made of rubber-cushioned gaskets enclosed in a stainless steel casing. They are tightened on to the burst section with a wing nut or hexagon nut. The coupling repair is by far the most permanent, although it is a bit more complicated. Cut out the burst section and replace it with a 'slip' coupling which can be slid on to one pipe and back up on to the other.

Re-filling water pipes often creates air bubbles. These will be indicated by knocking or an erratic flow from the faucet, often accompanied by hissing

9 If the toilet is blocked, try plunging the bowl using an old mop with a plastic bag tied around the head. Move the mop up and down to try and dislodge the blockage. This can be messy but is surprisingly effective.
10 If the toilet remains blocked, use drain-clearing rods to clear the pipes, working from the nearest inspection chamber. You may have to call in a specialist drain cleaner for this.

1 A gate valve controls the water flow in some low-pressure pipes. When the metal gate (wheel) is open, the water flow is unrestricted; turn the gate to cut off water.
2 The mains stop cock is linked to the rising main and controls water flow. Turn the handle clockwise to cut off the water.
3 Replace the washer on a dripping faucet: turn off the water supply, then turn the faucet on; remove the cover (it may pull off or be fixed with a screw) and unscrew the head gear (the large nut above the jumper unit, 'A'); remove the jumper unit and replace the washer ('B'); grease the joints and threads and reassemble.

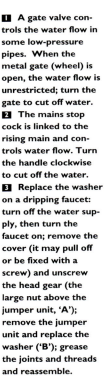

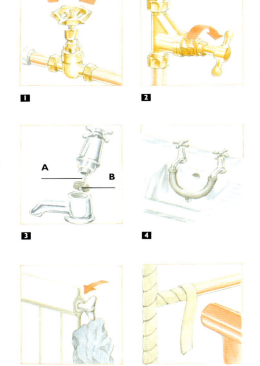

4 To clear an air lock in a faucet, connect one end of a hosepipe to the affected faucet and the other end to a faucet supplied from the rising main. Turn the faucets on full: water pressure should drive out the air lock.
5 To clear an air lock in a radiator you need to bleed (or vent) it: get a square-ended bleed key and insert it into the air-bleed valve at the end of the radiator; turn key counter-clockwise; hold a cloth under the valve to catch any water, then retighten the valve once the air is cleared.
6 Frozen pipes can be thawed using a hair dryer: undo the lagging and blow warm air over the whole pipe to disperse the ice plug as soon as it starts to melt.

11

12

13

14

15

11 A rubber plunger may be all you need to unblock a sink. Hold a damp cloth tightly over the overflow, and plunge up and down over the plughole.

12 If the above fails, you can try probing the waste trap in the pipe below the sink with a piece of wire hooked down through the plughole (not shown). Should this fail, you will need to access the waste trap more directly. If the waste trap is old and made of lead, place a bucket underneath it and undo the drain plug using a wrench. Lead piping is very easily damaged, so you should hold it steady while you work with a piece of wood.

13 With newer piping made of plastic, you can simply unscrew the nuts to disconnect the trap. This can be messy, so wear rubber gloves and overalls.

14 If the blockage is within the waste pipe, flexible drain-clearing wire may be enough to dislodge the block. Place a bucket or other container beneath the pipe to catch the debris.

15 If the outside drain is blocked, use a small trowel or a stick to break up sediment in the trap, and then remove it (wear a pair of strong rubber gloves). Finally, flush the drain clean with water from a hosepipe.

and spluttering. Air locks can be unblocked by running a length of hose from a faucet that is supplied from the rising main to the affected faucet and securing each end. Turn on the faucet from the rising main and then the other faucet. The pressure of the water should force the air bubble out.

The most common problem with faucets is a small, constant drip. No matter how hard you turn the handle, the drip won't stop. In this case, you need to dismantle the faucet assembly and replace the washer at the bottom of the stem. If the faucet leaks around the base of the stem and the stem wobbles, the stem is probably worn and needs replacing. Many hardware stores sell special stem-replacement kits, but the problem with these is that the diameters of the faulty stem and replacement stem don't match. If you know which manufacturer made your faucet, you may be able to order a replacement stem through them. However, colors, styles and dimensions change from year to year, so you still might not be able to find the correct parts – it's then a case of installing an entirely new faucet.

Toilets come in a range of colors and designs, but the most significant feature is the amount of water they use to flush. There is now a Federal mandate controlling this: siphon jets are by far the most efficient, followed by siphon whirlpools; last and least effective is the simple flushdown. If you experience problems when flushing the tank, it may be because you need to replace the flush valve (see steps 18 and 19). This is a relatively straightforward procedure, and something you can do yourself. Replacing the actual toilet is a more ambitious task, best left to a plumber. When buying a replacement toilet, you need to be sure that toilet will fit the allotted space: it sounds obvious, but you need enough clearance between the seat and tank and the wall in relation to the drain. A leaking toilet may indicate a break in the soil line.

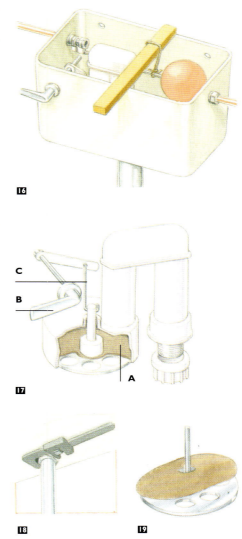

16

17

18

19

16 To make repairs to the toilet tank, you first need to empty it of water. Remove the cover of the tank and tie the arm of the float to a piece of wood resting across the top. This will stop the water flow. Now flush the toilet and mop up any remaining water in the tank.

17 If the toilet needs repeated attempts before the tank flushes, you need to replace the flush valve ('A') in the siphon assembly. First, empty the tank (see step 16). Then follow the procedure outlined below.

18 Use an adjustable wrench to undo the pipe nut immediately underneath the tank, and also the nut holding the siphon assembly in place inside the tank (not shown).

19 Disconnect the flushing handle ('B') from the metal link ('C') attached to the flush valve ('A', see step 17). Lift the siphon assembly up, replace the flap valve with a new one, then reassemble the siphon and refill the tank.

Simple roof repairs

Leaking roofs and gutters are a constant source of trouble. There is nothing very difficult about repairing them, though it is potentially dangerous work. Safe access is of paramount importance, even for the smallest repairs. It is imperative to have tower scaffolding professionally erected for anything more complicated than the routine cleaning of gutters. Tower scaffolding will give you confidence to complete most repairs. If you can't arrange a safe way of getting on and off the roof, don't even think about trying.

You'll certainly need to rent a roof ladder with a ridge hook. This is slid up the roof on its wheels, and flipped over so that the hook secures on the peak of the roof. You only need a few basic tools, a soft pair of shoes and a calm, preferably overcast, day.

You probably won't have much idea about the size and type of roofing materials you will need until you get up

1

2

1 A roof ladder runs up the tiles on wheels.
2 When the wheels reach the ridge, turn the ladder over so that the hook engages over the ridge.

3

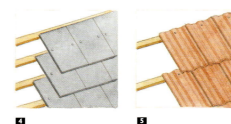

4

5

3 Plain tiles overlap one another to give a double thickness. Nibs at the top of each tile hook over horizontal tiling battens which are nailed to the rafters.
4 Slate tiles are fixed using two nails in each slate to attach it to the tiling battens. To keep the covering waterproof, slates should be staggered to overlap the previous row.
5 Interlocking roof tiles are laid in a single layer. Like plain tiles, they have nibs and are nailed to tiling battens.

there. Make sure you know where to get replacements and that they definitely have what you want in stock – not simply listed on a computer.

Most roofs that have them suffer from cracked tiles or slates at some time. If you think you have a leaking roof, the site of the damage probably won't be obvious from inside the house unless you climb into the loft when it's raining. You can then use a flashlight to trace the drip back to its point of entry, which may be some distance from where it drops onto the loft floor. Binoculars will also come in handy for making an external inspection of the roof.

Leaks can happen at abutments, typically at an extension, or around a chimney stack where weak mortar cracks or breaks away. These problems can be inexpensively cured, in the short term at least, by bitumen-backed self-adhesive flashing strip. Professionally installed lead flashings last longer, but are much more costly and difficult to fix. Don't try to repair cracked slate or tile – replace them. However, a mastic sealant can be used as an emergency stop gap. Roof tiles laid atop a decking material such as asphalt or rubber on buildings constructed around the turn of the century, are usually hooked together by means of interlocking grooves along their sides. You may also discover wire clips holding some types of tiles, or they may be individually nailed, but a little wiggling about will easily free any tile.

If you have the kind of plain tiles that are usually piggy-backed one on top of each other, use wooden wedges to lift the tiles in the row above the damaged one and slide a brick-layer's trowel underneath the broken tile. You'll see how simply it is fixed when you remove the broken one, and replacement is similarly straightforward. Support the new tile on the trowel and slide it into place until the nibs hook in place.

6 Replacing a broken roof tile is relatively straightforward. Fit wedges to lift the tiles in the row above, then remove the broken tile: you may be able to do this by hand, but it will probably be easier to use a trowel.
7 Slide the replacement tile in place, and hook the nib over the tiling batten. However, you will not be able to nail the tile in place. Remove the wedges from the row above, taking care not to damage adjacent tiles.

6

7

8

9

8 Hip tiles are fixed to the eaves of a sloping roof. A hip hook (metal bracket) at the end should be screwed to the hip rafter before the hip tiles are put in place: this will help prevent dislodged tiles sliding off the roof.
9 Damaged ridge tiles (which seal the peak of the roof) and hip tiles are easily replaced by bedding a replacement tile on new mortar. Leave a gap below the tile as shown to allow air to circulate freely.

Ridge tiles are used to waterproof the peak of the roof, while hip tiles seal the external corners where two roofs join. These can often work loose in high winds because the mortar they're fixed with is merely a fill-in material and has no real strength.

Ridge tiles should be carefully pried up and away (they are not difficult to crack), given a thorough soaking in a bucket of water and then bedded down again on a cement mortar (one part cement to four sharp sand). You will need to clean off the old mortar first, and seal all the ends and edges of the replacement tile, but keep the underside of it clean and open to enable air to circulate and prevent the roof timber below from rotting.

Alternatively, hardware stores sell clips which will give ridge and hip tiles a stronger hold on the roof. End hips are kept in place with anchors which are screwed directly into the rafter. If the mortar between hip or ridge tiles is only slightly cracked, use a caulking gun to inject a non-setting mastic.

Slate has to be replaced differently. Elderly slate roofs suffer from 'nail sickness' – the copper nails fixing them rot, allowing the slate to slide down and away. If the slate is damaged and loose, it will simply pull out. If it's firmly

10

11

12

10 To replace a damaged slate you will need a specialist slaters' ripper. Slide this underneath the broken slate and move it to one side until you feel one of the fixing nails. Pull the rip down so the barb on the end pulls out or cuts through the nail. Repeat for the nail on the other side. With both nails removed, pull out the damaged slate.
11 Next, nail a strip of lead about 8in (200mm) long and 1in (25mm) wide to the roof timbers in the position shown, using galvanized nails.
12 Slide the replacement slate in place, and fold the bottom of the lead strip so that it holds the lower edge of the slate, doubling it back to keep it firm.

fixed, you'll need to rent a sword-like weapon called a ripper which is slid underneath the damaged slate, moved sideways over the nail and then pulled down to sever the nail. If you do have occasion to re-nail tiles, copper or aluminum nails should be used. Never use galvanized, or anything else.

Slate is replaced using lead strips about 8in (20cm) long and 1in (25mm) wide, the top part of which is nailed to a piece of wood. The new slate is then pushed into place and the bottom of the lead strip is folded up to hold it. It is a simple repair, but can easily come undone if, for example, a heavy load of melting snow slips down the roof, unfolding the lead strip.

Heat waves play havoc with a roof, continually expanding and contracting its timbers and tiles, cracking cement flashings around the chimney and, on flat roofs, shifting the felt coverings and blistering them. The first sign of trouble is likely to be a damp patch appearing on the ceiling. Most flat roofs are built up from a three-layer felt construction laid on a sub-base and bonded to each other using a bitumen-based adhesive. Unlike tile or slate roofs, which are built of several separate parts that are designed to move independently of each other, roofing felt relies on its elasticity to expand and contract in response to changes in the atmosphere.

Flat roofs should be inspected at least once a year. Their maintenance involves very little time or trouble: just the common sense removal of debris; careful inspection of the points where the felt covering reaches the side of a chimney stack, surrounds on central-heating flues or vent stacks or the edge of a dormer window; and clearing the gutters of gravel and debris before they block downpipes.

Keep an eye out for patches where gravel is missing; it is in these areas that you are likely to find cracks, blisters and bubbles. Deal with a crack by first scraping away any embedded gravel

13

14

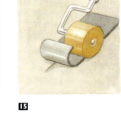

15

16

17

18

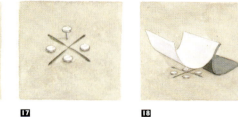

19

20

19 Lead flashing seals the join where a roof meets a wall. Fine cracks can be repaired using a generous layer of bituminous mastic to fill the crack and make it waterproof.
20 You can replace flashing with a self-adhesive strip. Clean and prepare the surface, then press a strip of flashing to the roof and wall. Fit a second strip to overlap the first.

around it. Use a hot-air stripper gun to dry out the area and soften the felt; don't use a gas blowtorch.

When the area is dry, brush it clean, reapply the hot-air gun to melt the felt further and press the felt down with a wooden wallpaper seam roller. Finally, coat it with flashing strip primer, and then roll down a strip of self-adhesive flashing tape along the crack. Should you find that the crack is particularly wide, fill it first with bituminous mastic before covering it with flashing tape. If you find a crack in flashing tape where it is covering a join in a building (for example, where an extension roof meets a wall) then it can be sealed using bituminous grout.

Blisters and bubbles are caused by rainwater seeping between the layers of felt, and then being 'boiled' by the sun. Repair them in the same way as you would a crack, except that an X-shape should first be made in the blister, so you can fold the edges back while you dry the felt underneath. The flaps should then be sealed with a cold bitumen compound before being pressed and rolled back into place. Complete the repair by sticking a patch of self-adhesive flashing over it. Make sure you cover all repairs with a good layer of gravel, to provide further protection.

13 Minor splits to flat roofs are easily repaired. First, clean the area around the split, then dry out and soften the asphalt roof covering using either a blowtorch or a hot-air stripper.
14 Next, apply a coat of flashing tape primer to the damaged area.
15 Cut a piece of self-adhesive flashing tape so that it will generously cover the split, then press this in place, sealing it using a wallpaper seam roller to bed the patch firmly.
16 Blisters are repaired in a similar way to splits. Dry out and soften the area around the blister; then, using a sharp knife, make two cuts in a cross shape across the blister. Apply a generous coat of bituminous mastic.
17 Press the flaps back down onto the layer of mastic, and fix them in place using galvanized clout nails. Brush flashing tape primer over the repair to seal and waterproof it.
18 Peel the backing paper off a piece of self-adhesive flashing tape and press it over the repair. Ensure the flashing tape is firmly sealed using a wallpaper seam roller.

Damp and rot

RISING DAMP

If it is left unchecked, rising damp can, in a couple of months, lead to wet rot, which is bad enough, or dry rot, which is catastrophic. It will transform your desirable house into something even brokers couldn't describe as less than a 'handyman's special' – in other words, gut rehab. If you find *merulius lacrymans*, dry rot fungi, sprouting in the cellar, there's a sporting chance you can cure it. Otherwise, call in an expert.

In areas of the U.S. prone to moisture from rain or snow, houses will probably have a damp-proof course (dpc). Rising damp will show up in a number of ways, commonly blistering paintwork, peeling wallpaper and crumbling plaster.

There are several remedies, all rather tedious and time consuming, so first check that the damp isn't caused by broken or clogged drainpipes or gutters, damaged stucco, porous or damaged flashing, plumbing leaks, faults in the drainage, or broken windowsills. All these can have the same effect as rising damp, as can garden soil banking up against an outside wall, effectively bridging the damp-proof course.

Some damp is caused by poor ventilation underneath the floorboards. This can be cured by fitting a bigger masonry grill. It is worth renting a battery-powered hydrometer, which has two prongs for prodding gently into plaster and lights that indicate damp; these meters have to be carefully calibrated.

The most effective remedy is also the most difficult – installing a new dpc. Cut out a row of bricks – 3ft (1m) at a time – and insert impervious engineering bricks in mortar mixed with a water-proofing compound. The dpc should be about 6in (15cm) off the ground. It is tempting just to fix the spot where damp occurs, but it's far better to replace the whole wall.

Alternatively, rent an angle grinder and cut out a horizontal mortar course between the bricks, again 3ft (1m) at a time. You then insert a new purpose-made membrane strip into the gap and seal it with mortar. The easiest do-it-yourself solution is to inject a water-repellent silicone – a chemical dpc – which acts as a barrier throughout the thickness of the wall. You can rent the complete unit: an electric pump with half a dozen nozzles.

The efficiency of this method depends on how well the fluid permeates the wall. It involves drilling $\frac{3}{4}$in (2cm) diameter holes 4–6in (10–15cm) apart, preferably from inside the house, although it's easier and less disruptive to work outside. However, if your area is prone to freeze-thaw cycles, this is not as effective as replacement of the dpc.

The floors and walls of basements and cellars are below the normal line of a dpc and are therefore particularly prone to damp if the damp-proof membrane protecting them has failed – but there may be an obvious, easily fixed fault such as a broken drainpipe.

The traditional method of coating or 'parging' the walls with a four-coat sand and cement mixture containing a damp-proof compound is still the most reliable, but difficult work for an amateur. Floors are more easily treated by a damp-proof compound covered with a sand and cement screed. But if they are really wet, the only solution is to dig up the floor and re-lay it over a thick, damp-proof plastic membrane – not for weekend carpenters.

ROT

Houses are incredibly resilient things. They can take a considerable beating from the most unskilled hands, yet will capitulate quickly in the face of a rot attack, especially if this gets into the structural timbers of the floor or roof. Don't think that you're safe because you've bought a brand new home. Bad practices in the construction trade, when wood is left in the open air for months on end before being used, means that some houses can actually have dry rot built into them.

If you do discover dry or wet rot in your house, you can be assured of one thing: the damage is likely to be far worse than it looks. It is vital to take some immediate, fundamental steps toward a cure, but first identify what sort of decay it is. Rot happens when the wood soaks up more than 20 per cent of its mass and remains wet for a considerable time – months rather than weeks.

The misleadingly named dry rot, far worse because it spreads very quickly, relies on damp to breed in places like roof voids, bathrooms and kitchens. Its effect on timber is to produce a rusty red spore dust on the surface, while the body of the wood will shrink, splitting into cubical patterns, and cracks will appear along the grain of the timber. Brittle gray strands by which the rot spreads can often be the first sign of attack, or there could be cottonwool-like patches on the timber. In the worst possible form of attack, a soft pancake-like growth develops.

Wet rot is found in damp places like cellars and roofs and exterior doors and window frames. The wood is darkened, with severe cracking along the grain.

The treatment for dry rot amounts to drastic surgery. Rotted wood must be cut out allowing a safety margin of at least 3ft (1m) each side of the damaged portion, and replaced with sound wood which has been soaked in a dry rot killing liquid. This liquid should also be liberally sprayed on to surrounding timber. The best method of fixing the replacement timber is by bolting pairs of steel connector plates on to it and the existing sound timber. Remove and burn the infected timber as soon as possible.

Infected plaster must also be removed, allowing a 3ft (1m) safety margin. Scrub the walls with a wire brush, and sterilize them with a masonry dry-rot killer. The treatment of wet rot is similarly messy and tedious. In both cases it is vital to discover the source of the dampness that caused the rot, and cure that first.

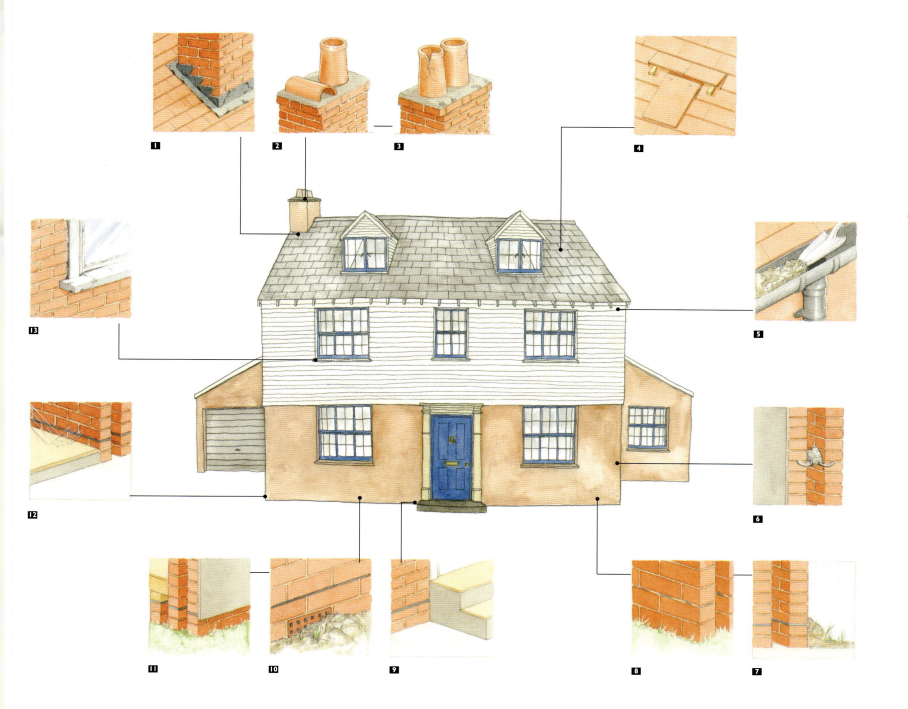

1 Make sure that lead flashing around the chimney is not loose or damaged. You can undertake simple repairs yourself (see page 247).
2 Rain falling down the chimney can cause damp if a fireplace has been blocked up without ventilation. Vent the chimney with an air-brick and fit a capping pot or a half-round ridge tile in mortar at the top.
3 Replace loose, cracked or broken chimney pots.

4 Replace missing, loose or damaged roof tiles (see pages 246-7).
5 Clear gutters of waste and debris, working away from the drain outlet. If the drain becomes blocked, use drain-clearing rods to remove the debris, working from the top.
6 Ensure debris does not become stuck in cavity walls.
7 One common cause of rising damp is soil piled up above the dpc. Ensure the dpc is not blocked.

8 House settlement can fracture your dpc. Have a new dpc professionally installed.
9 Concrete steps built above and across the dpc will allow damp to rise into the walls, and will also rot the door and its frame.
10 Air-bricks provide essential ventilation: keep them clear and make sure they do not become clogged.
11 Make sure that rendering to the exterior of the house is not extended below the level of the dpc.

12 A path built alongside the wall of the house should fall clear of the dpc; further, it should be low enough to ensure that, during spells of heavy rain, water does not splash up on to the wall above the dpc, as this can lead to damp.
13 Keep window frames and door frames in good order. Fill any cracks and gaps you find. Keep drip grooves clear under the window-sills and replace crumbling putty.

Insulation and subsidence

INSULATION

When it gets cold, fuel bills rise – sometimes unnecessarily. Then, when the summer comes, we expend further energy to power the air-conditioning unit. If you house is properly insulated, you can control the flow of unwanted heat in and out of your home. Houses built before World War 2 generally weren't built with any insulation between inner walls and ceilings, and will certainly benefit hugely from it; those built since then usually have been insulated so the savings – though considerable – will be proportionaly less.

Insulating the loft is not difficult work, but it is dusty and irritating. Wear some eye protection, a dust mask and rubber gloves. Remember that once it has been insulated, your roof space will probably be one of the coldest places in your entire house.

All pipes in the loft can be easily lagged using lengths of foam-molded tubes designed to fit around them. An economical black-light heater can also be installed in the loft. The heater, which can be run from a junction box into an electrical outlet, can be safely left on throughout the winter months. It simply takes the chill out of the air; its heat is otherwise imperceptible.

If you use your loft for storage, you should lay the insulation between the joists and board over them. If you can see the underside of your roof tiles, staple heavy-duty plastic sheet to the underside of the rafters, keeping the ventilation of the eaves clear.

SUBSIDENCE

Cracks that suddenly appear in ceilings and walls can strike terror in the bravest home-owner. Don't panic, but don't ignore them either. Although it is very rare for a property to become so badly damaged by subsidence, or settlement, that it is on the point of collapse, cracks give due warning that something has to be done. This might not be anything more drastic than redecoration.

Subsidence happens when the earth supporting a building's foundation dries out and starts collapsing. Clay soils are particularly prone to this. Subsidence shows up after an especially long, hot summer, but trees planted too close to a house are more often blamed as a serious contributory factor to drought because they have sucked moisture out of the ground. Willow, poplar and oak are particularly thirsty.

If you have a mature tree near your house, don't fell it just to prevent cracks. Doing so could cause 'ground heave', created by the swelling of clay as water returns and the water table rises. It can affect even very deep foundations, lifting them and cracking walls below ground level, and those below floor and sill levels.

Tree roots can extend a great distance. As a rough guide, if the distance between tree and house is less than the height of the tree, then the tree is likely to be the cause of the cracking problem.

There are no hard and fast rules with trees, but remember that they play an important part in stabilizing the water-level, so if the tree was there before the house, particularly if it is fully mature, leave it alone beyond pruning it back. In the early spring fill in any cracks in the walls you suspect it has caused. They shouldn't reopen.

If the tree has been planted more recently, it is probably best to remove it altogether. You may see cracks appear in the walls afterwards, and these should be filled in the following spring.

Ground shrinks vertically and horizontally, but as the house itself shelters the ground beneath it, that part remains fairly stable. Beyond the house the ground tends to shrink down and away from the house, resulting in diagonal cracks at doors and windows.

If, after heavy winter rain, the ground is getting waterlogged and the cracks in your house show signs of closing up again, this indicates that they are typically caused by clay shrinkage.

Some degrees of subsidence can be caused by overloading the foundations, which could occur after alterations to the property. Although houses usually impose a fairly even load all around their strip foundations, sometimes – typically when a large hole is made in a wall to install a patio door or bay window – the lintel carrying the load of the building exerts too much pressure on the piers at each end of the gap and the foundations settle further down into the ground. Clay ground, in particular, exaggerates this effect.

Inadequate foundations to porches or sunroom additions can lead to cracks occurring at the point where the extension joins with the main wall of the house; these cracks will also tend to close up during spells of wet weather.

Problems often occur where houses are built over the site of a former ditch or pond, or on landfill. On these 'soft' sites special attention should have been given to the types of foundation used at the time of construction, but if large cracks appear in steady progression you should ask your local building department whether there are any maps of the plot on which your house is built; if there are, look to see if they show reclaimed ground.

Subsidence caused by soft ground will almost always call for some form of underpinning. The foundations may need to be widened rather than deepened in order to spread the load, or some form of piling may have to be undertaken. If it is necessary to deepen the foundations, this is carried out close to the wall, so it may have to be done by hand – and at some expense.

Inside the house, it is common for cracks to appear at the junction of the ceiling and wall. This is the weakest point of the structure and the cracks open due to normal seasonal movement. Filling the cracks with plaster filler is only a short-term cure: the permanent solution is to fit coving, which will permanently conceal the problem.

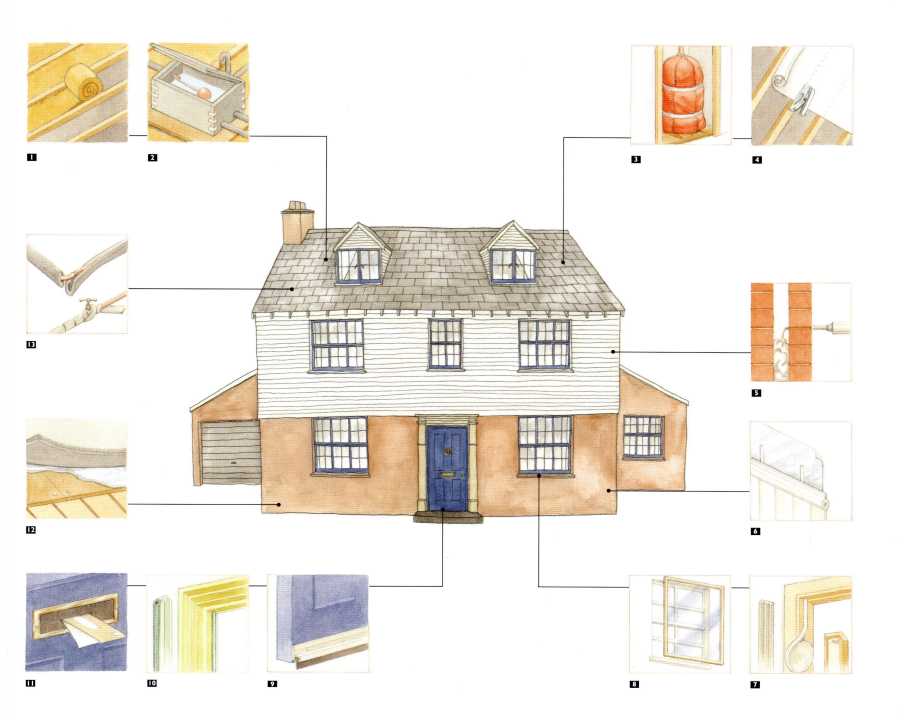

1 Fit insulation blanket between the joists in the loft. If the loft is already insulated, check that it is adequate: the blanket should be at least 6in (150mm) thick.

2 Your storage tank should be insulated with insulation blanket, polystyrene sheets or a purpose-made jacket. Leave cut-outs for the pipes, and fit a lid. However, the tank should not be insulated underneath.

3 The hot water cylinder should be lagged with a jacket at least 3in (75mm) thick.

4 Line the roof with building paper or plastic sheeting stapled below the rafters.

5 Cavity-wall insulation can reduce heat loss. It is injected through exterior walls and should be carried out by professionals.

6 Specially coated foil paper can be stuck behind radiators to reflect heat back into the room.

7 Insulate windows using brush seals for sash windows, and V-shaped plastic strips or self-adhesive PVC foam strips on casement windows.

8 Secondary glazing is expensive but may be worthwhile as a form of insulation, particularly at windows you seldom open. It also makes windows more difficult to use as a point of entry for intruders.

9 Fix a threshold draft excluder to the inside of the front door at the bottom.

10 Fix rigid brush or tubular strips around the door frame.

11 Fix a brush-type draft excluder to the letterdrop, or fix a secondary flap on the inside of the door.

12 Fill gaps between floorboards with wood strips or filler. Cover the floorboards with particleboard and foil-faced reflective foam underlay beneath carpets. You can incorporate additional insulation beneath the floorboards using loft-insulation blanket or polystyrene boards.

13 Lag hot-water pipes with special preformed molded foam insulation, which is split along its length. For more complicated pipework use pipe lagging which is taped or tied in place.

Home security

Domestic break-ins these days are an all-too-common occurrence, and it's easy to become paranoid about home security as result, turning your home into a high-security fortress. Different homes require different security arrangements. If you live in the countryside and your home is some distance from your neighbors, your priorities in terms of how to protect your property will be different from those of someone who lives in a busy city. But while no amount of precautions will protect you against the truly determined burglar, there are a number of simple, common sense measures you can adopt.

Never leave money or valuables lying around, and don't carry keys in a pocket or purse that also contains your address or a means of identification. Similarly, it may seem to make life easier if you hide a spare key under the doormat, hidden in a flowerpot or hanging inside the mailbox, but thieves will look in all the usual places; it's far better to leave a spare set of keys with a trustworthy friend or neighbor.

Your household goods insurance policy can never recover the sentimental value that may be attached to a stolen piece of jewelry, for example, but you should make sure that it allows you to replace goods at their real cost. Keep an inventory, and note the serial numbers of electrical goods, etc. The policy may also stipulate certain security requirements: make sure you conform to these, or your claim may not be paid.

SECURING YOUR HOME

- For very little expense you can make every window difficult – though not impossible – to use as the means of entry favored by two out of three burglars. Ground floor and basement rear windows are the most vulnerable. Window locks do work, but don't hang the keys from the window frame.

1 Make sure that the exterior of your house is adequately lit. Fit a detector light, which automatically switches on when someone approaches. Models are also available that automatically switch on when dusk falls and switch off at dawn.
2 Doors to any outside buildings such as a garden shed should be securely padlocked. If you have been using a ladder and need to leave it out, keep it locked to something secure, away from the house.

- Whether you live in a house or an apartment, the softwood framed front door found in most homes is the first and fairly poor line of defense. Paneled doors with inset glass panels should be protected with simple

3 If you have patio doors at the back of the house, fit purpose-made locks at the top and bottom. Keep the key out of sight, but close at hand so that you can get out easily in an emergency.
4 If you have French windows, fit bolts to the top and bottom of both leaves, as well as a five-pin mortise lock half way down.

5 A viewer enables you to identify the caller before opening the door.
6 Hinge bolts help to reinforce the frame on the hinged side of the door, reducing the chance of the door 'giving' under force.
7 A mail holder across the letterdrop makes it more difficult for someone to tamper with the locks by sticking a hand in through the slot.
8 Rim-mounted cylinder deadlocks lock automatically from the outside, but can be opened without a key from inside.
9 A door chain allows you to check a caller's identification.
10 Five-pin mortise deadlocks can only be opened with a key, making entry difficult.

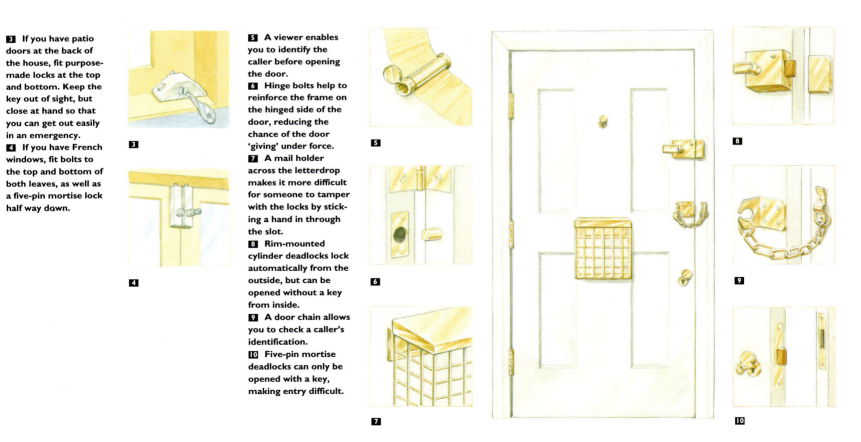

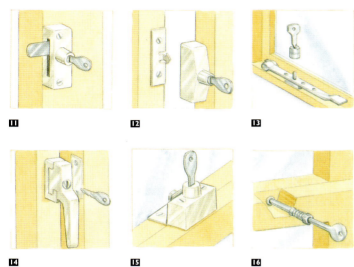

11

12

13

14

15

16

You should fit locks on all windows that can be opened, but especially on all downstairs windows and those on upper levels that are easily accessible. A wide range of locks is now available.
For casement windows:
11 A pivot lock prevents inward-opening windows being forced.
12 A snap lock is fitted to the surface of the window surround and the frame.
13 A stay lock bolts the stay to the frame when the window is closed.
14 A surface-mounted lockable handle.
For sash windows:
15 A sash bolt fits most wooden frames. The bolt in the top unit locks into a plate fitted to the bottom frame.
16 A dual screw is recessed into the frames, locking them together when closed.

wrought iron grills, and thin plywood panels must be reinforced with stronger outer panels. The most effective door is made of hardwood or has a solid hardwood core not less than 1¾in (45mm) thick.
• Replace a two-pin lock with a five-pin mortise deadlock. Remember that cutting the hole for a mortise lock weakens the door at the point where it should be strongest. This can be overcome by reinforcing the wood in the lock area with a metal plate.
• With the exception of the front door, all doors need to be reinforced with strong, preferably key-operated bolts fitted at the top and bottom. Hinge bolts on all doors, which would prevent them being jimmied out of the frame, are a sensible extra. There is little point in fixing strong locks if the door frame isn't in good condition. If it is weak, the frame and door can be levered out in a matter of seconds.
• If you still feel your home is vulnerable, then consider installing a burglar alarm. Although you can always find a licensed locksmith in the Yellow Pages, it won't hurt to contact your police department. They may have a program that offers advice both specific to your home and generic in terms of locks and alarm systems.

You'll save money and rental charges by fitting an alarm system yourself, but buy with care. Some systems use cheap, unreliable components. Don't buy a dummy box – thieves can spot a fake.

Surface-mounted door contacts may be easy to fit but they don't rate as highly as the type that are hidden in the edge of the door. Pick a system with four-core, double-pole cable rather than the twin-wire frequently offered.

Some systems have the facility for adding on devices like movement detectors, but the significant factor is that a system should be tamper proof, so that any criminal interference with the circuit sounds the alarm.

Door contacts can be effectively backed up by passive infrared (PIR) sensors which react to rapid changes in temperature caused by an intruder's body heat. They can be very effective in switching on outside security lights, but they have to be positioned with some care to avoid dazzling innocent visitors.

The best sensors for inside a house are dual units which incorporate PIR and ultrasonic or microwaves. Both elements have to be activated to trigger an alarm system. Most such systems, called central-station alarms, are linked to a monitoring company or directly to the local police precinct.

19

20

19 Burglar alarms are expensive but effective. You may want to consider buying one if you otherwise feel unsafe, or if you have been burglarized on a number of occasions.
20 Automatic time switches allow you to program lights to turn on and off at different times if you are going to be out.

17

18

17 Exterior side doors and rear doors should be fitted with lockable bolts at both the top and bottom.
18 A five-pin mortise deadlock offers an near-impregnable line of security.

The control panel, which supplies the power, monitors the system and triggers the alarm, is connected to the mains supply via a fused spur. It contains a standby battery which will take over in the event of power failure. It is always fitted on the main exit/entry route, but should be kept well out of sight of anyone who might happen to peer through the letterdrop.
• Plug-in time switches that can be programmed to go on and off at random within a pre-chosen timescale are far preferable to the ones that light up at precisely the same time each evening. Always make sure that you leave your curtains half drawn in rooms fitted with these switches.
• Before going on vacation – having first cancelled the paper, mail and any other regular deliveries, and arranged some reliable neighborhood watch – deposit your valuables at the bank. Items such as portable televisions and video recorders can be hidden in the loft; most burglars will seldom take the time and trouble to look there. They usually won't bother looking under carpets either, so a good idea is to remove a section of floorboard, place a box containing your precious things there and screw the floorboard down again.

Multi-generational design

Multigenerational, or universal, design approaches the design and layout of a home with the idea of finding solutions that work regardless of age or disability. Over the years, we have learnt to steer clear of labeling somebody a 'disabled person': impairments such as loss of sight or lack of mobility are often compensated for by an increase in other faculties. Design that caters for the special needs of the elderly or the physically impaired often used to underline the disparity between them and the rest of the population; current thinking, however, recognizes that design which seeks to increase ability rather than handicap the less able works well for everyone.

Designing homes for people with physical disabilities is a complex matter which is difficult, if not impossible, to resolve simply by means of a universal checklist: the needs of a young, fit adult paraplegic in a wheelchair will be quite different from those of a frail, elderly person. Each disability is different, and the needs of individuals – and the solutions – are necessarily a matter of detailed consultation at the planning stage. It is important that the demands, requirements and suggestions of the individual are addressed towards the aim of improving their independence; the fact that homes so redesigned will perform more efficiently for all users is not only fortuitous, but a positive aim.

Bathrooms and kitchens are important areas in any house, and should be designed with particular care. Specialist doctors, occupational therapists and registered charities may have valuable advice on general requirements.

Converting a kitchen to meet the criteria of universal design is probably the greatest challenge, not least because, in a family context, children no more fit into a kitchen designed for mobile adults than do wheelchair users. However, many of the fashionable design elements in modern kitchens allow for some flexibility of appliances and their layout. The separation and

Designing a kitchen for use by people with varying degrees of mobility requires careful planning. The layout shown here incorporates a number of features that can aid the less mobile, incorporating plenty of under-counter leg room so that people can comfortably sit and work. In a small kitchen such as this, storage is a problem, and the wallmounted units would not be accessible to a wheelchair user: you need to check the limits of a person's reach upward, downward and across.

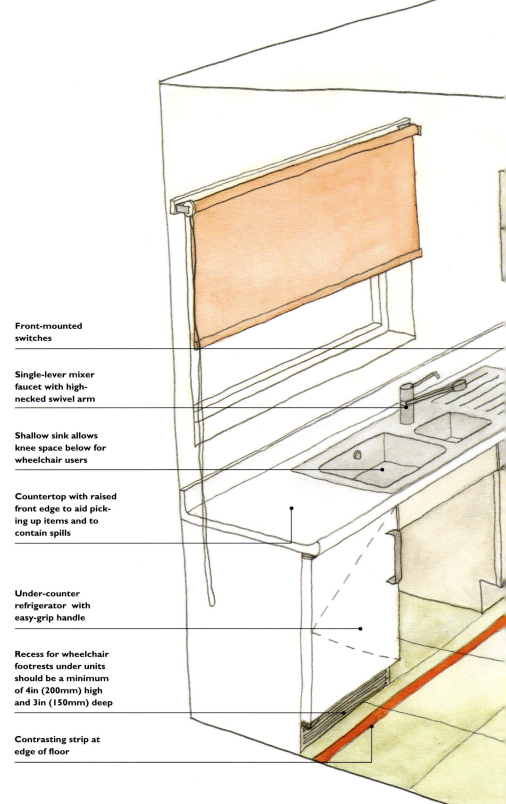

Front-mounted switches

Single-lever mixer faucet with high-necked swivel arm

Shallow sink allows knee space below for wheelchair users

Countertop with raised front edge to aid picking up items and to contain spills

Under-counter refrigerator with easy-grip handle

Recess for wheelchair footrests under units should be a minimum of 4in (200mm) high and 3in (150mm) deep

Contrasting strip at edge of floor

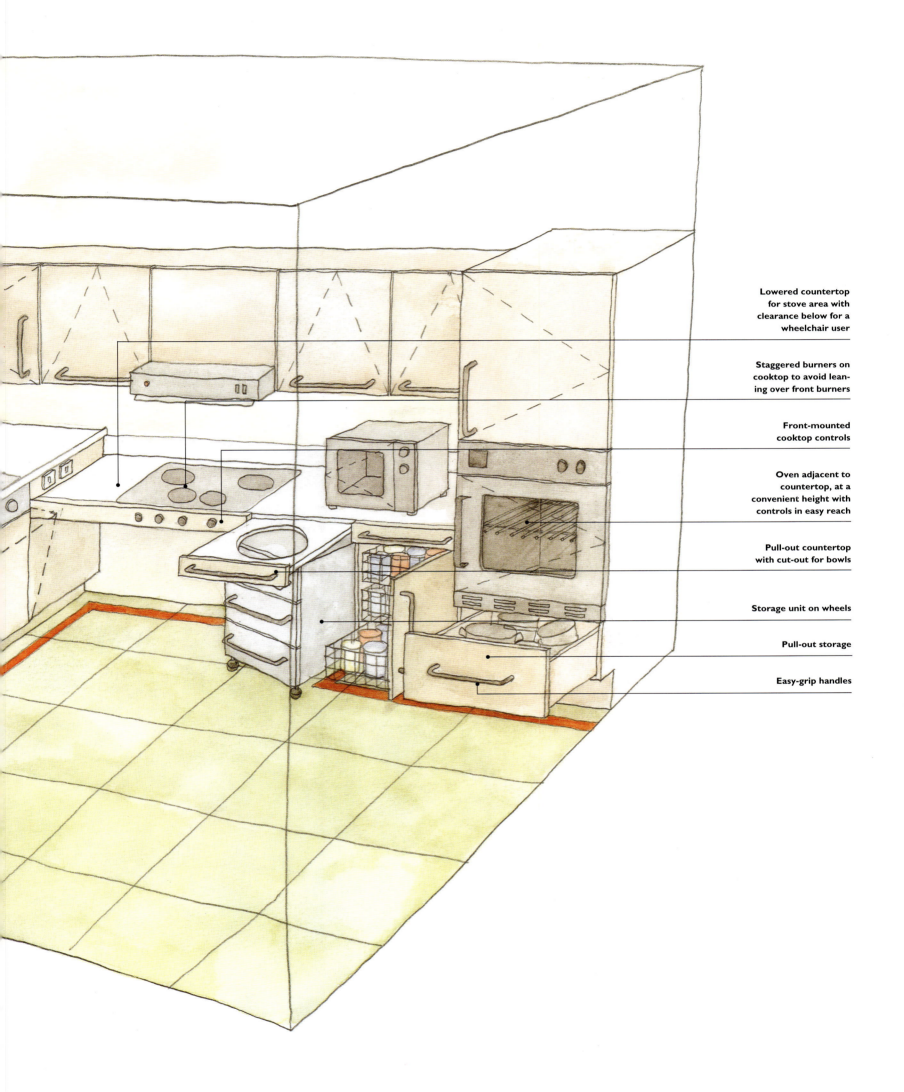

Lowered countertop for stove area with clearance below for a wheelchair user

Staggered burners on cooktop to avoid leaning over front burners

Front-mounted cooktop controls

Oven adjacent to countertop, at a convenient height with controls in easy reach

Pull-out countertop with cut-out for bowls

Storage unit on wheels

Pull-out storage

Easy-grip handles

1 A bathtub seat should be adjustable to fit most tubs. It locks in position close to the hand grips to make getting into and out of the tub a much easier process for the elderly and infirm.
2 A hinged, fold-down shower seat and grab rail allow people with a range of disabilities to take a shower on their own. Both the seat and grab rail should be positioned with care, preferably in consultation with the person for whom its use is intended.

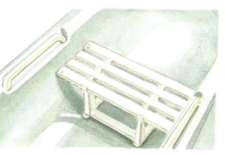

1

2

The U- or L-shaped kitchen layout is the most convenient for disabled users, particularly those confined to wheelchairs which don't readily move sideways. Such a configuration enables a number of tasks to be carried out from approximately the same spot provided there is enough space to position a wheelchair beneath lower work surfaces. Accessories such as pull-out boards, some with holes cut out for bowls, and cabinets with slide-out shelves that hold heavy appliances ready for use are available from commercial kitchen companies as part of their range. Slightly raised nosings on the leading edge of countertops make it easier to pick up things and contain spills.

It is essential that all kitchen fittings should be sturdy, as a person with reduced mobility may grab them for support. Drawers should obviously open smoothly, and their design should include stays to prevent them being inadvertently pulled out completely.

Electrical outlets could be extended to double switches on the front of, or directly underneath, the countertop nosing for easy access. The front edge of the countertop should be rounded over to minimize potential injury.

Suitable ceramic tiles or flagstones provide a firm, level and slip-resistant floor surface which is easy to clean. However, unless the tiles are exactly flush, they may cause people to trip and limit the mobility of wheelchair users; and anything breakable will shatter if dropped. Sealed cork tiles or washable carpet tiles are viable alternatives.

BATHROOMS

Bathrooms require careful planning and, for wheelchair users in particular, need to be a generous size. If your home is on more than one level, there should be provision for a toilet, at least, on every floor. A shower may seem like a good alternative to a bathtub, allowing many disabled people to bathe independently. A seat and grab rails are safer,

3

3 You can buy special faucets that can be operated by the elderly and arthritic. You can also convert existing faucets with lever covers. Both solutions enable users to turn the faucet on and off with greater ease.
4 A grab rail can be fitted at the foot of the stairs for support. Well designed versions are available in left- and right-handed models; these are not interchangeable and should be bought according to which side of the stairs the banister is positioned.
5 Plugs with large, easy-grip handles allow elderly and arthritic people to operate electrical appliances much more easily.

4

5

juxtaposition of the cooktop and oven is essential: splitting these appliances should enable them to be placed at heights which make cooking easier and safer, although the presence of young children would obviously have to be taken into consideration.

Cooktops can be installed side by side in pairs so there is no need to reach over a front burner to a pot cooking behind. Controls mounted on the edge of the countertop, in front of the cooktop, are easier to reach and operate safely. Ovens with drop-down or side-hung doors can be installed at any height. Both appliances should be close to a generous area of countertop.

less intrusive and cheaper modifications to make to a shower enclosure or bathtub compared to hoists over a tub.

Shower areas can also be designed to incorporate a toilet and sink, with carefully sited drop-down rails and pull switches. Such an integrated unit would also solve problems by containing water supplies and other plumbing services within it, while at the same time keeping the rest of the bathroom dry.

Access to showers should provide few difficulties for the ambulatory disabled, but there could be problems for wheelchair users. Careful placement could provide a shower over the bathtub.

If a progressive disability makes the provision of overhead hoist tracks imperative in the future, careful in-line planning of the layout of the fittings, together with the strengthening of the ceiling joists, could save disruption and expense. Although bathtubs can be lowered into the floor, this is a complicated, and therefore expensive, option.

Nonslip tiles are a necessary and obvious floor covering, providing their surface does not make cleaning difficult.

Whether bathroom doors open in or out depends on the available space, but sliding or concertina doors could be an alternative. Whatever the type of door, provision should be made for opening it – both from inside and outside the bathroom – in an emergency.

AIDING MOBILITY

Although most public places now provide dedicated and designed parking facilities for the disabled, it is just as important that a person should be able to park as conveniently outside their own home. Private parking courts should be clearly identified for disabled drivers or passengers only, as close to the home as possible and wide enough to allow car doors to be fully opened while someone transfers to a wheelchair. The car-parking area should be smooth and kerbs between it and the house should be dropped for wheelchairs.

Wheelchair users need ramps outside their home; a gradient of 1:15 would be considered normal, and 1:12 the maximum. Portable or semipermanent ramps made of wood are a possible alternative, as long as they have a slip-resistant finish.

Some ambulant disabled prefer steps to ramps. The going, or tread, should be no less than 11in (28cm) and the riser a maximum of 6in (15cm). Handrails made of a 'warm', non-slip material such as hardwood or plastic-coated steel are essential and should be colored to be more easily distinguishable.

Sheltered entrance areas, in the form of porches or canopies, provide protection for people who may take a long time to open a door and enter a house.

Doors for wheelchair users should have a minimum opening of 31in (80cm). Doors should be of solid construction for security and to provide fixing for pulls and fixtures, although laminated glass extending low enough for a wheelchair user to be seen and to see in and out may be preferred.

Door locks are important, both in terms of easy operation by disabled people and in an emergency when helpers may need to gain access.

While the selection of surface materials and finishes is important to all disabled people, they are vital to people with sight and hearing impairments. Hard surfaces reverberate more than soft, and this can confuse people with impaired hearing. Glossy walls and floors reflect light which can hamper people with poor sight.

Wheelchairs move more easily on firmly fixed floors, which should be of a shallow, dense pile if carpeted. The joins between different flooring materials should be carefully executed so as not to hamper the wheels, or trip ambulant disabled, or those with poor sight.

Lightly textured walls and floors provide important information of their whereabouts to people with little or no sight, but boldly patterned flooring can confuse people with impaired sight. Floor surfaces should be slip resistant, particularly in an area where they may become wet, such as just inside a front door, in the kitchen or bathroom.

Although good lighting is essential for everyone, the partially sighted require greater levels (up to three times as much) to achieve a satisfactory level of illumination. Perhaps the main criterion is that lighting should be controllable and adjustable to meet individual needs. Passive infrared sensors could activate booster lighting, but keeping windows, shades and lamps clean will also maximize the amount of available light, both natural and artificial.

Lights should be positioned so as not to cause glare, reflection or confusing patches of light and dark. Uplights fixed above 6ft (2m) deliver a good level of comfortable, glare-free illumination.

Components in fluorescent lighting can cause a loud hum in hearing aids, and the background noise from heating and air conditioning units can similarly be distracting and tiring. Radiators and other heating units should be recessed wherever possible to avoid sharp angles.

If windows aren't carefully considered, they will introduce problems of glare and loss of privacy as well as difficulty with controls and cleaning. Their sheer size is not necessarily an asset and should be secondary to that of their position. Smaller windows are easier to open and clean, and a combination of, say, a large window to give overall light to a room, and a small window to provide a view for a bed-bound person may be the formula arrived at. Tolerances of heat and cold and other discomforts are often very fine with disabled people.

Bad positioning of windows can create glare from too much sunshine for a person confined to bed, or too much reflected light from light-colored paving for the wheelchair occupant. Adequate, variable and easy-to-operate ventilation without opening the main window should be incorporated in the plan.

Useful addresses

The aim of this resources section is to furnish you with a starting point by listing major supliers and manufacturers. Many of the larger companies listed here have toll-free information lines and supply catalogs on request (some free, others for a small fee). The addresses listed here give the headquarters or main showroom of a company if there is more than one address throughout North America — but from them you should be able to get a contact address for the nearest distributor, showroom or stockist in your area.

You can supplement the information here by talking to local retailers and shopping around for the most competitive prices and best deals. Additionally, many magazines on interior design and decorating carry 'product literature' coupons, where you can send off for up-to-date catalogs and information. These magazines are also a good place to start if you are looking to use the services of an interior designer or architect.

ADVICE

Association of Home Appliance Manufacturers
20 North Wacket Drive
Chicago
IL 60606
Publishes buying guides for appliances

American Institute of Architects
1735 New York Avenue N.W.
Washington
D C 20006

American Society of Home Inspectors
85 West Algonquin Road
Suite 360
Arlington Heights
IL 60005
Provides a list of 1,250 accredited members

American Society of Interior Designers (ASID)
608 Massachusetts Avenue, NE
Washington
DC 20002

American Society of Landscape Architects
4401 Connecticut Avenue, NW
Fifth Floor
Washington
DC 20008

The Carpet and Rug Institute
P.O. Box 2048
Dalton
GA 30722
Supplies information on buying rugs and carpets

Ceramic Tile Institute of America
12061 Jefferson Boulevard
Culver City
CA 90230-6219
Supplies guidelines for installing marble, ceramic and other kinds of tile flooring

Conservation and Renewable Energy Inquiry and Referral Service (CAREIRS)
P.O. Box 3048
Merrifield
VA 22116
Supplies non-technical information on how to select energy-efficient appliances, fans and ventilation systems and on other energy-conservation topics realted to the home

Gas Appliance Manufacturers' Association
1901 North Moore Street
Suite 1100
Arlington
VA 22209
Publishes consumer directory of certified efficiency ratings for residential heating and water-heating systems

Granite Industries of Vermont
Barre
VT 05641
Brochures on granite appllications and installation

The Green Consumer Letter
1526 Connecticut Avenue N.W.
Washington
DC 20036
Information on environmental products

Hardwood Manufacturers Association
400 Penn Center Bld
Suite 530
Pittsburgh
AP 15235
Information on choosing and maintaining hardwood floors; free, detailed guide to sofa construction

The Hydronics Institute
35 Russo Place
P.O. Box 218
Berkeley Heights
NJ 07922
Provides pamphlets on hot-water heating, radiant heating and related topics

Juvenile Products Manufacturers Association
2 Greentree Center
Suite 225
P.O. Box 955
Marlton
NJ 08053
Provides up-to-date information on safety standards of products designed for children

Log Knowledge
P.O. Box 1025
LaPorte
CO 80535
Independent assessment of log-house companies

National Association of Home Inspectors
5775 Wayzata Boulevard
Suite 860
Minneapolis
MN 55416
Provides a list of 1,100 accredited members

National Association of Plumbing, Heating and Cooling Contractors
P.O. Box 6808
Falls Church
VA 22040
Answers consumer inquiries about plumbing, heating and cooling

National Ground Water Association
6375 Riverside Drive
Dublin
OH 43017

National Kitchen and Bath
Association
687 Willow Grove Street
Hackettstown
NJ 07840-9988
*Publishes an annual directory of
certified kitchen and bath designers*

National Oak Flooring
Manufacturers' Association
22 North Front Street
660 Falls Building
Memphis
TN 38103
*Information on buying, installing
and finishing oak floors*

Rainforest Alliance
65 Bleecker Street
New York
NY 10012-2420
*Identifies and certifies companies
that produce and sell tropical
hardwoods harvested using
ecologically sound techniques*

Rainforest Relief
P.O. Box 281
Red Bank
NY 07701
*Supplies information on
alternatives to tropical timber*

Tile Council of America
P.O. Box 2222
Princeton
NJ 08543-2222
*Provides free brochures on
decorating with ceramic tile*

The Timber Source
P.O. Box 426
431 Pine Street
Burlington
VT 05402 - 0426
*Provides information on where to
buy North American woods —
from Douglas fir and maple
plywood to birch and cherry —
from sustainably managed forests*

Upholstered Furniture Action
Council
P.O. Box 2436
High Point
NC 27261
*Information about upholstered
furniture and flammability
standards*

U.S. Consumer Product Safety
Commission
Washington
DC 20207
*Publishes fact sheets on home
appliances*

Woodworkers Alliance for
Rainforest Protection (WARP)
P.O. Box 133
Coos Bay
Oregon 97420
*Maintains list of retail 'good wood'
suppliers — those who sell some
wood from a well-managed or
recycled source*

ARCHITECTS & DESIGNERS

Anderson/Schwartz Architects
40 Hudson Street
New York
NY 10013

Kiss & Zwigard
3rd Floor
60 Warren Street
New York
NY 10007

Richard Lavenstein
Bond Street Design
33 Bond Street
New York
NY 10012

Brian Murphy
1422 Second Street
Santa Monica
CA 90401

Randolph-Tomb
IOOA
10 Heron Street
San Francisco
CA 94103

Walz Designs
141 Fifth Avenue
New York
NY 10010

Deborah Weintraub, A.I.A.
1540 North Sierra Bonita
Los Angeles
CA 90046

Wilkinson & Hartman
330 Sir Francis Drake Boulevard
San Anselmo
CA 94960

Vincent Wolf
333 West 39th Street
New York
NY 10018

ECO-FRIENDLY

Childesign
17 East 70th Street
New York
NY 10021
*Environmental consultants
specializing in childcare*

Conservation and Renewable
Energy Inquiry and Referral
Service (CAREIRS)
see Advice

Felissimo
10 West 56th Street
New York
NY 10022

Fred Segal for a Better Ecology
420 Broadway
Santa Monica
CA 90401

Livos Plantchemistry
614 Agua Fria Street
Santa Fe
NM 87501

Real Goods
966 Mazzoni Street
Ukiah
CA 95482
Mail-order catalog available

Seventh Generation
Colchester
VT 05446
Mail-order catalog available

Terre Verde Trading
120 Wooster Street
New York
NY 10012

Water Quality Association
4151 Naperville Road
Lisle
IL 60532

FABRIC

Ainsworth Noah & Associates
351 Peachtree Hills Avenue
Suite 518
Atlanta
GA 30305

B&J Fabrics
263 West 40th Street
New York
NY 10018

Bennison Fabrics
76 Greene Street
New York
NY 10012

Bergamo Fabrics
979 Third Avenue
Floor 17
New York
NY 10022

Clarence House
211 East 58th Street
New York
NY 10022

Jane Churchill
Cowan & Tout
D&D Building
979 Third Avenue
New York
NY 10022

**Cohama Riverdale Decorative
Fabrics**
A division of United Merchants &
Manufacturing, Inc.
980 Sixth Avenue
New York
NY 10018

Collier Campbell
907 Broadway
New York
NY 10010

Covington Fabrics
267 Fifth Avenue
New York
NY 10016

Craig Fabrics
979 Third Avenue
New York
NY 10022

Design West, Inc.
1855 Griffin Road
Suite A474
Dania
FL 33004

Designer Fabric Outlet
1360 Queen Street West
Toronto
Ontario M6K 1L7

Designers Choice
119 Merchandise Mart
Chicago
IL 60654

Dressew
337 West Hastings Street
Vancouver
British Columbia V6B 1H6

Habert Associates
170 Bedford Road
Toronto
Ontario M5R 2K9

JAB Fabrics
31-11 Thomson Avenue
Long Island City
NY 11101

Kravet Fabrics
225 Central Avenue South
Bethpage
NY 11714

Lace Country
21 West 38th Street
New York
NY 10018

Ralph Lauren Home Collection
1185 Sixth Avenue
New York
NY 10036

Manuel Canovas
D&D Building
979 Third Avenue
New York
NY 10022

Mitchel Fabrics
637 Main Street
Winnipeg
Manitoba R3B 1E3

Osborne & Little
65 Commerce Road
Stamford
CT 06902

Paper White
769 Center Boulevard
Fairfax
CA 94804

Paron Fabrics
239 West 39th Street
New York
NY 10018

Quadrille
979 Third Avenue
New York
NY 10022

Randolph & Hein, Inc.
Pacific Design Center
Suite 310
8687 Melrose Avenue
Los Angeles
CA 90069
and
Galleria Design Center
Suite 101
101 Henry Adams Street
San Francisco
CA 94103

Dan River Inc.
111 West 40th Street
New York
NY 10018

J. Robert Scott
8737 Melrose Avenue
Los Angeles
CA 90069

Schecter Martin
1 Design Center Place
Suite 111
Boston
MA 02210

Silk Surplus
235 East 58th Street
New York
NY 10022

Trebor Textiles
251 West 39th Street
New York
NY 10018

Eileen West
33 Grant Avenue
San Francisco
CA 94108

FLOORING

Albro Sisal
8807 Beverley Boulevard
Los Angeles
CA 90048
Natural floorcoverings

American Marazzi Tile
359 Clay Road
Sunnyvale
TX 75182

American Olean Tile
1000 Cannon Avenue
Lansdale
PA 19446-0271
Olean

American Tile
24 Cummings Park
Wilburn
MA 01801

Armstrong World Industries
P.O. Box 3001
Lancaster
PA 17604
Vinyl

Armstrong Vinyl Flooring
P.O. Box 3001
Lancaster
PA 17604
Vinyl

Bruce Hardwood Floors
16803 Dallas Parkway
Dallas
TX 75248
Wood

Ceramic Stiles
51 West 19th Street
New York
NY 1011
Tile

Country Floors
15 East 16th Street
New York
NY 10003
and:
8735 Melrose Avenue
Los Angeles
CA 90069
Ceramic tile, terra cotta and stone

Couristan, Inc.
2 Executive Drive
Fort Lee
NJ 07024
Carpet

Decorative Wood Floors
8687 Melrose Avenue
B680
West Hollywood
CA 90069
Wood

Dodge-Regupol, Inc.
P.O. Box 989
715 Fountain Avenue
Lancaster
PA 17608-0989
Cork tile

Eco Timber International
P.O. Box 882461
San Francisco
CA 94188
Wood

Empire Block
1805 2nd Street
Santa Fe
NM 87501
Brick, pavers, stone

Entrée Libre
110 Wooster Street
New York
NY 10012
Rugs

Florida Tile Industries, Inc.
Lakeland
FL 33802
Tile

Forbo Industries, Inc.
Humboldt Industrial Park
Maplewood Drive
P.O. Box 667
Hazleton
PA 18201
Linoleum

**Hoechst Celanese Textile
Fibers Group**
1211 Avenue of the Americas
New York
NY 10036
Carpet

Italian Tile Center
*A division of the Italian Tile
Commission*
499 Park Avenue
New York
NY 10022
Tile

Johnsonite
A division of Duramex, Inc.
16910 Munn Road
Chagrin Falls
OH 44023
Rubber and vinyl

Kentucky Wood Floors
P.O. Box 33276
Louisville
KY 40213
Wood

Laufen International
4942 East 66th Street North
Tulsa
OK 74156
Tile

Michaelian & Kohlberg
10 East 12th Street
New York
NY 10010
Rugs

Milliken & Co.
201 Industrial Lane
La Grange
GA 30240
Carpet

Missoni Roubini, Inc.
443 Park Avenue South
Second Floor
New York
NY 10016
Contemporary rugs

Monarch Tile, Inc.
834 Rickwood Road
Florence
AL 35631

Paris Ceramics
31 East Elm Street
Greenwich
CT 06830
Mosaics

Plaza Carpet
819 North La Cienega Boulevard
Los Angeles
CA 90069

Plaza Hardwood, Inc.
5 Enebro Court
Santa Fe
NM 87505
Biodiversity hardwood

Ruchstuhl USA Ltd
Larsen Carpet
41 East 11th Street
New York
NY 10003-4685
*Natural-fiber, including coir, sisal
and wool*

The Rug Barn
P.O. Box 1187
Abbeville
South Carolina 29620

S&S Mills
2650 Lakeland Road, S.E.
Dalton
GA 30721
Carpet

Ann Sacks Tile & Stone
115 Steward Street
Seattle
WA 98101

Sheoga Hardwood Flooring and Paneling, Inc.
13851 Station Road
Burton
OH 44201
Wood

Stark Carpet
979 Third Avenue
New York
NY 10022

Summitville Tile
P.O. Box 73
Summitville
OH 43962
Ceramic tile

Tiles de Santa Fe, Inc.
P.O. Box 3767
Santa Fe
NM 87501
Handmade tile

Barbara Zinkel
333 Pilgrim
Birmingham
MI 48009
Rugs

FURNITURE AND FURNISHINGS

ABC Carpet & Home
888 Broadway
New York
NY 10003

Ad Hoc
410 West Broadway
New York
NY 10012

Arango
7519 Dadeland Mall
Miami
FL 33156

Artemide, Inc.
150 East 58th Street
New York
NY 10155

At Home Furnishings
3811 Porter Street N.W.
Washington
DC 20016

Atelier International
595 Madison Avenue
New York
NY 10022

B&B Italia
150 East 58th Street
New York
NY 10155

Baker, Knapp & Tubs
1661 Monroe Avenue N.W.
Grand Rapids
MI 49505

Blumenthal, Inc.
979 Third Avenue
New York
NY 10022

Current
815 East Thomas Street
Seattle
WA 98102

Dakota Jackson
306 East 61st Street
New York
NY 10021

Dialogica
484 Broome Street
New York
NY 10013

Domestic Furniture
7385 Beverly Boulevard
Los Angeles
CA 90036

Domus
1214 Perimeter Mall
4400 Ashford-Dunwoody Road
Atlanta
GA 30346

Elements
738 North Wells Street
Chicago
IL 60610

Expressions Custom Furniture
P.O. Box 6018
Metairie
LA 70009

Fern I. Tchur
350 Old Stockbridge Road
Lenox
MA 01240

Fifty/50
793 Broadway
New York
NY 10003

Forma + Design
1 Selleck Street
Norwalk
CT 06855

The Galleria
2384 East Sunrise Boulevard
Fort Lauderdale
FL 33304

Home Depot
449 Roberts Court Road
Kennesaw
GA 30144

ICF, Inc.
305 East 63rd Street
New York
NY 10021

J.S.D. Studio
243 Elizabeth Street
New York
NY 10012

Knoll International
105 Wooster Street
New York
NY 10012

Robert Kuo
8686 Melrose Avenue
Los Angeles
CA 90069

Ligne Roset
200 Lexington Avenue
New York
NY 10016

McGuire
151 Vermont Street
San Francisco
CA 94103

Miya Shoji
107 West 17th Street
New York
NY 10011

Modern Age
795 Broadway
New York
NY 10003

Modern Living
8125 Melrose Avenue
Los Angeles
CA 90046

Mohr & Mcpherson
290 Concord Avenue
Cambridge
MA 02138

Ted Muehling Store
47 Greene Street
New York
NY 10013

Pace Collection
986 Madison Avenue
New York
NY 10021

Palazzetti
515 Madison Avenue
New York
NY 10022

Pottery Barn
100 North Point Street
San Francisco
CA 94133

Saporitti Italia
U.S. Agent, Campaniello Imports
225 East 57th Street
NY 10155

Shabby Chic
1013 Montana Avenue
Santa Monica
CA 90403

Shaker Workshops
P.O. Box 1028
Concord
MA 01742

Shakers Cottage
23730 Bothell Highway South
East
Suite B
Bothell
WA 98021

L. & J.G. Stickley
1 Stickley Drive
P.O. Box 480
Manlius
NY 13104

Taos Furniture
232 Galisteo Street
P.O. Box 2624
Santa Fe
NM 87504

U.S.E.D.
17 Perry Street
New York
NY 10021

Wicker Works
267 Eighth Street
San Francisco
CA 94103

Frederic Williams
200 Lexington Avenue
611
New York
NY 10016

LIGHTING

Able Studio
54 West 21st Street
Suite 705
New York
NY 10010

Ballard Designs
1670 DeFoor Avenue
Atlanta
GA 30318

Broan Manufacturing Corp.
P.O. Box 140
Hartford
WI 53027

Digecon Plastics International
3050 Copter Road
Pensacola
FL 32514

Donovan Design
Niedermaier 900
120 Wooster Street
New York
NY 10012
and
900 North Michigan Avenue
Chicago
IL 60611

Fabby Lighting
450 South La Brea Avenue
Los Angeles
CA 90036

IKEA U.S., Inc.
Plymouth Commons
Plymouth Meeting
PA 19426

Intermatic Malibu
Intermatic Plaza
Spring Grove
IL 60081

Just Bulbs
938 Broadway
New York
NY 10010

Just Shades
21 Spring Street
New York
NY 10012

Leviton
59 Little Neck Parkway
Little Neck
NY 11362

Lightolier
100 Lighting Way
Secaucus
NJ 07096

Luminaire
301 West Superior
Chicago
IL 60610

Thomas Industries
P.O. Box 769
Hopkinsville
KY 42241

Unique Lampshades
247 East 77th Street
New York
NY 10021

Willow Green Co.
P.O. Box 16096
Ludlow
KY 41016

PAINT

Accent Paints
300 East Main Street
Lake Zurich
IL 60047

Ashley House Wallcoverings, Inc.
1838 West Broadway
Vancouver
British Columbia V6J 1Y9

Coast Decorating Centre
4464 Main Street
Vancouver
British Columbia V5V 3R3

Crown Berger
Bentley Brothers
2709 Southpark Road
Louiseville
KT 40219

Livos Plantchemistry
614 Agua Fria Street
Santa Fe
N 87501
Natural paints and stains

Glidden Paint Co.
925 Euclid Avenue
Cleveland
OH 44115

Benjamin Moore & Co.
51 Chestnut Ridge Road
Montvale
NJ 07645

The Old Fashioned Milk Paint Company
P.O. Box 222
436 Main Street
Groton
MA 01450

Plaid Paints
1649 International Boulevard
Norcross
GA 30091

Pratt & Lambert
Box 22
75 Tonawanda Street
Buffalo
NY 14240

Rust-Oleum
11 Hawthorn Parkway
Vernon Hills
IL 60061

Sherwin-Williams Co.
101 Prospect Avenue
10 Midland Building
Cleveland
OH 44115

The Stulb Company
P.O. Box 597
Allentown
PA 18105

Walls Alive
1328 17th Avenue S.W.
Calgary
Alberta T2T 0C3

Western Paint and Wallcovering Co.
521 Hargrave Street
Winnipeg
Manitoba R3A 0Y1

SAFETY

First Alert
Pittway Corporation
780 McLure Road
Aurora
IL 60504

Perfectly Safe
7245 Whipple Avenue N.W.
North Canton
OH 44720

Safety by Design
P.O. Box 4312
Great Neck
NY 11023

Safety 1st
210 Boylston Street
Chestnut Hill
MA 02167

UNIVERSAL DESIGN

Advanced Living Systems
428 North Lamar Boulevard
Oxford
MI 38655

Barrier-free Design Centre
150 Eglinton Avenue East
Suite 400
Toronto
Ontario M4 1E8

Barrier-free Environments, Inc.
P.O. Box 30634
Raleigh
NC 27622

Center for Accessible Housing
North Carolina State University
School of Design
P.O. Box 8613
Raleigh
NC 27695

Good Grips
230 Fifth Avenue
New York

National Rehabilitation Information Center (NARIC)
8455 Colesville Road
Silver Spring
MD 20910

Resource Center for Accessible Living
Architectural Modification
Consultation
602 Albany Avenue
Kingston
NY 12401

VENTILATION

Air Changes Marketing
1297 Industrial Road
Cambridge
Ontario N2H 4T8
Canada

American Aldes Ventialtion Corp.
4537 Northgate Court
Sarasota
FL 34234

Boss Aire
2901 S.E. Fourth Street
Minneapolis
MN 55413

Conservation Energy Systems
2525 Wentz Avenue
South Saskatoon
Saskatchewan S7K 2K9
Canada

Des Champs Laboratories
E-Z Vent
P.O. Box 220
Natural Bridge Station
VA 24579

Honeywell, Inc.
P.O. Box 524
Minneapolis
MN 55440

Kooltronic Inc
P.O. Box 300
Hopewell
NJ 08525

York International Corp.
P.O. Box 1592
York
PA 17405

WALLCOVERINGS

Acme Brick P.O. Box 425
Fort Worth
TX 76101
Glass brick

Agnes Bourne
2 Henry Adams Street
220
San Francisco
CA 94103
Wallpaper

Armstrong World Industries
P.O. Box 3001
Lancaster
PA 17604
Moldings

Aronson Carpet and Tiles
135 West 17th Street
New York
NY 10011

Boren Clay Products
P.O. Box 368
Pleasant Garden
NC 27313
Brick

Bradbury & Bradbury Art Wallpapers
P.O. Box 155
Benicia
CA 94510

C&A Wallcoverings
23745 Mercantile Road
Cleveland
OH 44122

Dryvit Systems, Inc.
P.O. Box 1014
West Warwick
RI 02893
Stucco

Eisenhart Wallcoverings Co.
P.O. Box 464
Hanover
PA 17331
Wallpaper and borders

F. Shumacher & Co.
79 Madison Avenue
New York
NY 10016
Wallpaper

G.B. Systems
P.O. Box 2307
Englewood
CO 80150
Glass brick

Glashaus Inc.
415 West Golf Road
Arlington Heights
IL 60005
Glass brick

Glass Blocks Unlimited, Inc.
126 East 16th Stret
Costa Mesa
CA 92627
Glass brick

Hosek Manufacturing Company, Inc.
4877 National Western Drive
Denver
CO 80216
Moldings

Pittsburgh Corning
800 Presque Isle Drive
Pittsburgh
PA 15239
Glass brick

Stroheim & Romann
31-11 Thomson Avenue
Long Island City
NY 11101

York Wallcovering and Fabric
750 Linden Avenue
York
PA 17404

Waverly
79 Madison Avenue
New York
NY 10016
Wallpaper

Index